From the Classroom:
Grounded Activities for Language Learning

MILES TURNBULL, JILL SINCLAIR BELL, SHARON LAPKIN

EDITORS

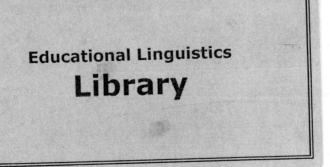

Copyright © *Canadian Modern Language Review/La Revue canadienne des langues vivantes*

Edited by
MILES TURNBULL, JILL SINCLAIR BELL, SHARON LAPKIN

Illustrations by
DWAYNE ELLIOTT/ORIGINALS

Printed in Canada by the University of Toronto Press Incorporated
ISBN: 0-9691796-9-3

Table of Contents

Preface

When we took on the editorship of the *Canadian Modern Language Review* in 1995, we made a commitment that pieces appearing in the classroom issues section, 'A Touch of Class,' would offer teachers theoretically grounded suggestions for implementing new approaches and techniques. We are pleased to have the opportunity to present *From the Classroom: Grounded Activities for Language Learning*, featuring a selection of pieces that appeared between 1995 and 2002.

From the Classroom: Grounded Activities for Language Learning is a resource book of activities for a wide range of language programs. Core and immersion French, English as a Second Language (ESL) for children and adults, heritage and international languages, academic, workplace, and vocational programs, are just some of the situations that teachers in Canada face daily. No language activity can cross such boundaries without adaptation at some level and a careful consideration of context. For these reasons, we believe that it is important for the theoretical rationale behind classroom ideas to be explicitly presented to enable teachers to decide whether an activity is suitable for a particular teaching situation.

We have therefore aimed to help teachers identify activities appropriate for use in their programs and to help them adapt others. To this end, we have identified the key objectives for each suggested activity, and provided adaptations that make the activities suitable for a wide range of programs. We trust that practising teachers will find that these suggestions expand their inventory of useful classroom activities.

We would like to express our gratitude to the contributing authors and to the Board of Directors of the *Canadian Modern Language Review/La Revue canadienne des langues vivantes* for permission to reprint the 'Touch of Class' articles contained here. We are grateful to Joyce Scane for her help in the preparation of this manuscript, to Michelle Pon for her ongoing support, to Nicole Keating for her translation expertise, and to Anne Marie Corrigan, Audrey Greenwood and the team at University of Toronto Press. The production of this book has been made possible by a grant from Canadian Heritage.

Miles Turnbull, Jill Sinclair Bell, Sharon Lapkin

August, 2002

Préface

Quand nous avons accepté de devenir rédacteurs de *La Revue canadienne des langues vivantes* en 1995, nous nous sommes engagés à ce que les articles publiés dans la section consacrée aux questions touchant à la salle de classe, « A Touch of ... Class! », offriraient aux enseignants des suggestions comportant un fondement théorique pour la mise en pratique de nouvelles approches et techniques. Nous sommes heureux d'avoir l'occasion de présenter *From the Classroom : Grounded Activities for Language Learning* offrant une sélection d'articles publiés entre 1995 et 2002.

From the Classroom : Grounded Activities for Language Learning est un manuel d'activités se prêtant à une large variété de programmes de langues. Le français de base et l'immersion française, l'anglais langue seconde (ALS) pour les enfants et les adultes, les langues ancestrales et internationales, les programmes universitaires, sur les lieux de travail et de formation professionnelle, représentent seulement quelques unes des situations auxquelles les enseignants doivent faire face quotidiennement au Canada. Aucune activité langagière ne peut passer d'une situation à une autre sans une adaptation éventuelle et un examen soigneux du contexte. Pour cet ensemble de raisons, nous pensons qu'il est important que le raisonnement théorique sous-tendant les idées utilisées en classe soit présenté de façon explicite afin de permettre aux enseignants de décider si une activité convient dans une certaine situation d'enseignement.

Nous avons donc tenté d'aider les enseignants à identifier les activités appropriées à leurs programmes et à en adapter d'autres. Dans ce but, nous avons identifié les objectifs principaux pour chacune des activités suggérées, et offert des adaptations afin que ces activités puissent servir pour une large variété de programmes. Nous espérons que les enseignants en exercice trouveront que ces suggestions élargissent leur répertoire d'activités utiles.

Nous aimerions exprimer notre gratitude envers les auteurs collaborateurs ainsi qu'au Conseil d'administration de *La Revue canadienne des langues vivantes* de nous avoir accordé la permission de réimprimer les articles de « A Touch of ... Class! » figurant ici. Notre reconnaissance va à Joyce Scane pour son aide dans la préparation de ce manuscrit, et à Michelle Pon pour son appui soutenu. Nous remercions également Nicole Keating d'avoir traduit cette introduction et Anne Marie Corrigan, Audrey Greenwood et l'equipe des Presses de l'université de Toronto. Ajoutons enfin que la réalisation de ce livre a été rendue possible grâce à une subvention du département de Patrimoine canadien.

Miles Turnbull, Jill Sinclair Bell, Sharon Lapkin

août, 2002

Note

* Nous tenons à préciser que, par souci de concision et de clarté, le masculin (générique) désigne aussi bien les femmes que les hommes dans cette introduction.

Getting started: A conceptual framework for second language classroom activities

Miles Turnbull, Jill Sinclair Bell, Sharon Lapkin

Introduction

As teachers, we all want to identify interesting and engaging activities that will allow us to provide rich language experiences for the students in our classes. Because no two classes are alike, activities that work well for one class may not be suitable for the class down the hall, much less for the one across the country. Student proficiency level, age, needs, interests, and linguistic background must be taken into account. Imposed curriculum or examination pressures may also shape our choice of activities. Our own experience as teachers, and our comfort level in the target language, may also affect activity selection, as may access to target language speakers, and target language texts or electronic resources.

Teachers facing such complex situations need quick ways to recognize the value of suggested activities, and a way to assess the roles of these activities in a balanced curriculum that addresses all aspects of language development. A particular activity might work well to help learners develop their communicative listening skills, but if it is not balanced with activities that address other language needs it soon becomes inadequate. In most programs, a balanced curriculum is multidimensional. It involves developing learners' fluency and accuracy in both productive (speaking and writing) and receptive (listening and reading) skills. In addition, students need guidance to use language in culturally appropriate ways, and they need strategies to enable them to function independently when the support of the classroom is withdrawn. Clearly some programs, such as those in English for Academic Purposes, require a special focus on specific uses of language, and balance here must be understood within that context. Learners also bring particular strengths and weaknesses to a program that the teacher needs to address. A balanced curriculum for students who already have strong reading and writing skills might imply a heavy focus on oral work. Efforts to identify and address these needs characterize teachers' curriculum planning cycles as they continually assess and adjust the balance of activities in their classrooms to ensure that the different components of a communicative language program are developed.

To help teachers assess the nature and relevance of the activities in our collection to their long-term goals, we have developed the following conceptual and organizational framework. It provides a way of situating each activity in terms of its major focus. This framework was the product of our discussions as we worked our way through the activities compiled in this collection; we tried to ensure that our framework was sufficiently comprehensive to accommodate the wide variety of activities included, and sufficiently practical to allow us to classify the activities visually in an accessible and useful way.

1

	Speaking	Writing	Listening	Reading	Language & Learning Awareness
Communicative & Experiential					
Language					
Culture					

Understanding our framework: The vertical axis

As many teachers will recognize, the categories on the vertical axis are drawn from the work of H.H. Stern. Stern (1983, 1992) developed a multidimensional approach to the second language curriculum that included the three components listed in the left-hand column: communicative and experiential, language, and culture. [1]

The communicative and experiential component

Most of us recognize the overriding importance of teaching language for communication. Our students need to know how to order a meal in a restaurant, listen to a taped message on the phone, read a news item and understand the main points, or write a letter of application for a job. Such uses of language fall squarely into the communicative domain. To be considered experiential (see e.g., Allen, 1983; Luckmann, 1996), they should involve authentic language used in real-life contexts. A student who accesses a web site to find the train schedule for the upcoming class visit to the zoo is reading information for an authentic purpose: to plan a real-life class excursion. Such an activity is both communicative and experiential. If the train schedule activity remains classroom-based, the true experiential dimension is lost, although valuable communicative practice remains because of the reading component.

We recognize that ESL teachers in English Canada have many opportunities to provide experiential activities for their students, whereas the situation is very different for those who do not teach within a target language community. Such teachers cannot easily organize field trips into target language settings, for example. Where educators have no easy access to the target language environment, they can strive to incorporate a quasi-experiential dimension in their classrooms by invoking potential real-life contexts and using authentic materials, including virtual resources available on the World Wide Web.

The language component

The language component of a balanced curriculum (see e.g., Hébert, 1990; Williams, 1995) is perhaps the most familiar to all of us because it focuses on language forms and functions as objects of study. Constructing grammatical sentences from smaller 'building blocks' is certainly part of the language syllabus. But any language system is also more complex, going well beyond grammar, vocabulary, and pronunciation to include language functions: how to express opinions, make requests, make demands politely, express emotion, and so on. Analyzing how language varies to take into account the specific social context, including the relative formality of particular situations, is also part of the study of any second language.

The culture component

The culture component (see e.g., Atkinson, 1999; Byram, 1997; LeBlanc, Courtel, & Trescases, 1990; Seelye, 1986) aims to develop cultural awareness, broadly defined. The multicultural character of Canadian society provides fertile ground for exploring ethnicity and the social and cultural values of many different groups. A study of the literature, music, or art of the target language group can inform and capture students' interests and these aspects of culture are usually integrated into the curriculum. It is equally important to examine the culturally appropriate uses of language and develop sociolinguistic competence. Using language in a culturally appropriate way requires an understanding of how people interact in the target culture. For example, we can make a request that is grammatical, but still give offence to a listener if we have not phrased that request in a sufficiently polite manner, given the sex, age, and status of the conversation partner. Knowledge of the target culture involves issues such as knowing whether it is appropriate to ask questions relating to age or income level, understanding patterns of silence, or knowing how close to stand to the person with whom one is speaking.

Understanding our framework: The horizontal axis

Moving to the horizontal axis of our conceptual framework, again we sought to do justice to the complexity of what it means to use a second language. Many curriculum and assessment documents (e.g., Ontario Ministry of Education, 1998; Johansson, 2000) rely on breaking language development down into the traditional skill areas, but while useful, this approach still presents problems. Where, for example, does vocabulary fit into the traditional skill areas of listening, speaking, reading, and writing? Clearly, vocabulary knowledge is involved in both the productive and receptive language skills. Knowing how to organize an oral or written text (see e.g., Canale & Swain, 1980; Canale, 1983) is relevant to listening (predicting what items of information will be provided in sequence), speaking (planning what we want to say), reading (using clues such as logical connectors in the text to aid comprehension), or writing (learning how to organize text as native-speaking writers would).

Though we recognized the dangers of over-simplification in our organizational framework, we found that the four skill areas provided a way of categorizing the activities in this collection that is practical and familiar to teachers. Thus, across the top of our framework, these skills are listed: first the productive skills of speaking and writing, next the receptive skills of listening and reading.

The final heading on the horizontal axis is 'Language and Learning Awareness.' This category encompasses Stern's general language education syllabus (see also Hébert, 1990) and includes language learning strategies (e.g., Oxford, 1990), communication strategies (Chamot & O'Malley, 1992), and metalinguistic awareness (Little, 1997; van Lier, 1996), among others. Language learning strategies, for example, might include writing grammatical rules or lists of vocabulary items in a notebook for future reference. Communication strategies include techniques such as circumlocution to get around the lack of knowledge of a vocabulary item, paraphrasing, calling on body language, and the like. Metalinguistic awareness involves understanding how language works and is put together. It includes, for example, learning script conventions, studying rules of word formation, or analyzing typical word-order patterns in sentences.

Understanding our conceptual framework: Some examples

To illustrate how we approached the categorization of the activities in this book, we offer the following examples to illustrate each cell of our framework.

	Speaking	Writing	Listening	Reading	Language & Learning Awareness
Communicative & Experiential	Asking for information from a travel agent for a projected trip	Writing a letter to the editor of a newspaper about a topic of personal interest	Listening to a sports broadcast to find out the latest baseball standings	Reading instructions for installing some software that the student wants to use	Calling on prior knowledge to use a bank machine abroad
Language	Practising requests using the imperative	Transforming a written text in present tense to past tense	Listening for specific lexical items in a radio newscast	Reading a text and underlining prepositions	Classifying words into categories (e.g., parts of speech, semantic themes) in a notebook

Culture	Role-plays designed to reflect specific cultural situations	Writing an invitation in a culturally appropriate way	Identifying the probable age and status of participants in selected radio interviews	Reading a text on attitudes to gender roles in the target culture	Discussing cultural stereotypes in TV programs

There is a wide range of possible activities that might be placed in each cell. Many activities incorporate elements of more than one cell. We therefore had to make decisions about their principal and subsidiary foci, which are indicated by solid and hollow bullets respectively in the appropriate cells.

Let's consider an example in detail. The teacher identifies a particular situation and asks students to work in groups of two or three, to take roles, and to act out the situation as they imagine it. Students might, for instance, be asked to imagine ordering food in a cafe. At its simplest level, this is clearly a speaking activity. The focus of the language being produced is to express meaning or communicate, so we would put a solid bullet in the cell for Communicative & Experiential/Speaking. The students also have to be able to listen to each other and respond, so the activity also includes some listening practice. However, if they have been given any chance to prepare the material, the students will probably have a good idea of what is going to be said well in advance, so the listening role is less challenging and the focus therefore less strong. We indicate this subsidiary focus by using a hollow bullet, as shown in the chart below.

	Speaking	Writing	Listening	Reading	Language & Learning Awareness
Communicative & Experiential	●		○		
Language					
Culture					

Teachers, of course, rarely assign a role-play in quite such a simple manner. They may ask students to work in groups to prepare their scripts, thus adding a strong writing focus to the task. They may introduce a target language menu from which the students must order, thus introducing an element of reading. They may ask individuals to prepare their remarks alone, so that the waiter does not know which item will be ordered, and must therefore listen more carefully. These variations would increase the range of skills being practised, but would nonetheless continue to be classified as communicative and experiential tasks, as they all focus on conveying and understanding meaning.

The teacher may feel, however, that the activity would be more useful to the particular class if it were more tightly focused. Perhaps she has been teaching modals such as 'can/ could/ would' and she wants the students to practise their use during the role-play. She might provide pre-set request phrases incorporating modals that the students practise in advance of the role-play. To increase the opportunities for modal use, she might instruct the waiter to say that whatever is initially ordered is not available, or she might require customers to order three or more things. Now the activity clearly has its strongest focus on the correct use of the language, so it would be coded as follows:

	Speaking	Writing	Listening	Reading	Language & Learning Awareness
Communicative & Experiential	○		○		
Language	●				
Culture					

Another teacher might feel that it was important for his students to feel confident in restaurants in the target culture, be able to predict the likely sequence of events, and able to order with the appropriate degree of courtesy. He might therefore provide a simple schema to be followed with a set of phrases to be incorporated into the dialogue. Here there would be a cultural element to the activity and we would see solid bullets in the cell for Culture/Speaking (using culturally appropriate language) and Culture/Language & Learning Awareness (under-standing the patterns of behaviour in the restaurant), as below:

	Speaking	Writing	Listening	Reading	Language & Learning Awareness
Communicative & Experiential					
Language	○				
Culture	●				●

Deciding on the principal focus of any activity is not always as clear-cut as we might like. In attempting to chart the activities presented in this book, we have enjoyed some interesting discussions as we worked to agree on exactly where to place a bullet. Many of the best activities seem to involve the students in a range of tasks so that one could conceivably place a bullet in virtually every cell in the chart. However, this would not be of much help to teachers in their efforts to achieve a balanced curriculum. We have therefore bulleted only those areas that seem to us to represent the main thrust of the activity as conceived by the writer.

Factors influencing activity selection

As well as coding the activities for their principal and subsidiary language learning foci, we have also indicated other factors that may help teachers select or identify activities suitable for their classroom situation. For each activity, we have indicated the grade levels for which we feel it is most suited. For more mature learners, we have distinguished between academic and non-academic study, using the term 'post-secondary' to refer to college and university programs, and 'adult' to refer to community classes.

Many activities require both a degree of maturity and a certain proficiency level for successful completion. For example, while an activity might be within the cognitive range of a student in Grades 4 to 6, it might also require a higher level of language proficiency than would likely be found in students outside of an immersion program. In such cases, we have indicated the appropriate program after the grade level designation.

It is, of course, impossible for us to know the specifics of the situation that a teacher faces, so we cannot offer definitive suggestions for the most successful ways to adapt the activities that follow for a particular classroom. We therefore encourage teachers to think about the needs and interests of their students, bearing in mind such issues as native language, degree of heterogeneity in the classroom, student purposes for learning, and so on.

In addition, classes take place within particular contexts of both time and place. Activities suitable in the early part of the year may seem irrelevant when examinations are looming, and a fascinating task based on baseball scores might look stale once the World Series is decided for the year. The physical facilities also influence our choices. Activities may prove too noisy for certain locations or require access to electronic resources not easily available. Teachers need to be aware of the conscious choices they make, and ensure that the activities they select are indeed appropriate and realistic for their learners and themselves. This may require considerable adaptation of published material.

Tailoring activities to suit specific groups of students

There is a common temptation to dismiss a classroom idea because it was not created for the context in which one teaches. But why? Is there any real reason why one cannot take a great idea that worked well in a Grade 8 core French class, for example, change it and make it work equally well in an adult community-based ESL class, or in a university Spanish class?

To accommodate the many differences among classes (students' ages, interests and needs, linguistic and cultural diversity, previous experiences, learning styles, skill levels, timing, etc.), we have proposed two adaptations for each activity in our collection. We hope that, after working with our organizational framework and considering the ideas we propose, our readers will understand how they can use the framework and the activities to fill in the gaps while striving to achieve a balanced, multidimensional curriculum in their classrooms. Below, we propose a four-step process for teachers to consider when they think about the balance of their curriculum and ways to adapt an activity for use with a particular group of students.

Thinking about the balance of your curriculum and classroom activities: Four simple steps

Step 1: The search for a suitable activity has to start with the students, the curriculum, and your program's goals rather than with a particular activity. Think about the goals of your program and your students' progress and abilities in the target language.

- Do you need an activity to help your students reach a particular goal?
- Is your curriculum missing a particular component (e.g., culture)?
- Are your students having trouble with a certain skill or task?
- Are there short-term or long-term goals that you would like or need to address?

If the answer to any of these questions is YES, you need to find an activity to meet your needs. You could create your own activity, or you could adapt or tailor someone else's activity for your students. Before selecting an activity, however, you must consider the questions in Step 2.

Step 2: Part of the process of selecting a classroom activity involves asking the following questions: Are there specific features of your class and school that you cannot change? How do these influence your activity choice?

- How many students do you have? How frequently do you meet your students?

8

- What type of learners do you have? How old are they? What about their cognitive development?
- How much time do you have? What is your workload? Are there any physical constraints to consider? Do you share a class with another teacher? Do you have access to computers?
- What type of budget do you have?

Step 3: Selection of an initial activity: With steps one and two in mind, a possible activity is chosen for adaptation. As far as possible, it should match the required criteria to minimise the number of adaptations required. A colleague may suggest an activity to consider. The chosen activity might also be a result of brainstorming or of your scanning activities in this book.

Step 4: Fine-tuning the chosen activity: Once you have chosen an activity that helps fill a gap in your curriculum, and after considering factors over which you have little or no control, you may need to fine-tune the chosen activity according to your particular group of students.

- Do you need to adapt the activity to make it more or less linguistically challenging for your students?
- Do you need to adapt the activity to suit your students' interests or cognitive development?
- Do you want to adapt the linguistic focus of the activity? Do you need to focus more on fluency or accuracy with your students?
- Is the activity culturally sensitive to the make-up of your class? Could you adapt it to become more suitable?
- Do you have students with learning difficulties for whom you need to adapt the activity?
- Could you adapt the activity to respond to your students' multiple intelligences?

Our adaptations

To create our adaptations, we brainstormed activities that we have used in the range of classroom contexts in which we have taught and explored the value of these activities in other second language and foreign language settings. First, we 'coded' each activity using our organizational framework described above in the section, 'Understanding our conceptual framework: Some examples' (p. 4); we also thought about other teaching contexts and the factors that influence how an activity plays out in real classrooms. As we brainstormed, we sought to extend each activity by changing or adding to its principal or subsidiary foci; we also tried to think of ways to adapt the activity to make it useful with different types of learners in different programs. The following examples of text summaries and information gap activities and their accompanying adaptations will help to make these processes clear.

> ## Example 1: Text summaries
>
> This text summary activity was originally designed for and used in a Grade 12 core French class. It could be used as a warm-up, as a change of pace, or as part of a unit on current events. Over time, the teacher pre-selects and copies short reading texts (reflecting students' interests, life experiences, and maturity) that can be found in many magazines and newspapers.[2] These texts range from 50 to 150 words in length and can cover a variety of topics (e.g., abortion, legalization of marijuana in Amsterdam, pollution in China compared to Canada). Students work individually and have approximately 15 minutes to read through their text (each student has a different text). The task requires students to present a one-minute oral summary of the content of the text, and the student must offer an opinion on the social commentary presented by the author. If they wish, students may make notes as a support during the oral presentation.

It is clear that the principal focus of this activity is reading. Writing may be a secondary focus if students choose to take notes. In our experience, core French students often feel a need to make notes to help them with an oral presentation. When this activity moves to the oral presentation, the principal focus is speaking and we hope that most students are listening to their peers' summaries!

Although this activity was first used in a Grade 12 core French class with students whose language skills were at an intermediate level, it seems clear that it would also be appropriate for a secondary French immersion class or a university-level context where the students are not beginners.

Now let's consider adaptations to this activity that would work for these classes or another Grade 12 core French class.

Adaptation one

As many of us know, the cultural component of second and foreign language teaching tends to be relegated to the back burner. This text summary activity does not include any deliberate focus on culture. Choosing texts with cultural content, for example, that focus on anglophone or francophone attitudes about abortion, the importance of music and art for young Vancouverites, the use of Ecstasy at raves in North America, and so on, would easily add the cultural dimension to the text summary activity, thus adding a solid bullet in the bottom right hand corner of our framework.

Adaptation two

Many theoreticians (e.g., Piaget, 1959; Vygotsky, 1967), researchers (e.g., Holt, 1993; Swain, 1995, 2000), and classroom teachers agree that students can develop their second language skills and hone their social skills by working with their peers. It is therefore important to vary one's grouping strategies from time to time. When learners work in groups, they have more opportunities to speak and listen to the target language. Swain (1985, 1995) also argues that when students are pushed to speak or write, they extend and develop their language knowledge and communicative competence.

We can adapt the text summary activity whereby two students share the oral presentation (one might do the summary and the other might share their opinions). This could also be done as a jigsaw activity (Holt, 1993) where a group of four or five students reads the same text and prepares its summary and commentary in expert groups. After preparing this summary and commentary collaboratively, all students go to pre-assigned home groups in which there are peers who have read different texts. Students then present their summaries and opinions, playing the role of experts or teachers for those particular texts. The teacher could also give all students a multiple choice quiz on the content of all texts to ensure that all students have taken their tasks seriously, including having listened to their peers' presentations.

Example 2: Information gap activities

The basic premise of information gap activities is that two students work as a team to piece together information to complete a task: one person must have information that the other does not. Therefore, there is a true information gap. Moreover, all of the information the students hold collectively is required for successful completion of the task.

Our information gap activity has been used with both core French and ESL students at the beginner level and involves speaking, listening, and drawing. Each student receives a different drawing of familiar objects such as fruits of varying sizes (e.g., apples, oranges, bananas). Each student also receives a blank sheet of white paper and coloured markers. The pair of students sits back-to-back so that neither can see the other's picture. One at a time, each student describes, in the target language, his/her picture to his/her partner who attempts to replicate the drawing. The artist is encouraged to ask his/her partner questions for clarification. This short activity is generally an amusing way to review basic vocabulary, colours, sizes, directions (right, left, above, below, etc.) and clarification questions.

Our sample information gap activity involves a principal communicative and experiential focus, allowing students to engage in real speaking and listening to complete a task. Since the students also practise specific vocabulary, colours, sizes, directions, and clarification questions, this activity also has a subsidiary Language/Speaking/Listening focus.

Adaptation one
Another version of the information gap, appropriate for most grade levels and in most programs, requires the teacher to cut out and photocopy the 'world weather' section from any newspaper (or any accessible and age-appropriate document, printed or virtual). Before class, the teacher makes two copies of the

weather section (version A and version B) and whites out different elements on the two copies. The idea is to have two versions of the same weather forecast. However, each version lacks different information, thus creating an information gap. In class, an activity focusing principally on speaking and reading unfolds. Students work in pairs; one student receives version A of the weather forecast and the other student works with version B. The students must first identify the missing information on their version of the forecast and they then proceed to ask one another questions (a subsidiary focus on question formation) so that they are both able to complete their version of the weather forecast.

Adaptation two

Our second adaptation is quite a different type of information gap activity. In fact, our alternative retains little from the original activity except the information gap concept. This alternative provides an example of complex activity adaptation.

This alternative is communicative, experiential and authentic, and would be suitable for students in a secondary, post-secondary, or adult ESL program. The activity involves planning to attend a local film festival (e.g., the annual Toronto Film Festival). The teacher splits the Festival program into sections (depending on the number of students, we recommend no more than three students per group to make this activity manageable). Students work together with their assigned section of the program to decide which films they would like to view and why. Then the groups of students present their information orally to the class, while trying to convince their peers that the choices they have made from their section of the program are the best (hence the information gap). A vote to choose the films to be seen is held after all teams have presented. Following the in-class decision-making process, students arrange to attend four films (more or less depending on time and resources, and possibly as a class activity in the evening) on different days during the Festival.

This Film Festival activity transforms the basic information gap activity (drawing fruits) to include real, communicative and experiential activity with speaking, listening, and reading as principal foci, and writing and cultural awareness as subsidiary foci. Of course, when the students actually go to the cinema, cultural awareness may become a principal focus, depending on the nature of the films chosen.

Concluding comment

This book provides teachers with a number of activities that have been created and used by experienced language teachers. The focus of this introduction has been to describe and illustrate an organizational framework, based on a balanced and multidimensional curriculum, drawing on current theories of language learning and teaching. Our purpose is to help teachers use our conceptual framework to identify and adapt classroom activities required to achieve a balanced, multidimensional curriculum and to respond to students' capabilities, interests, and needs. We hope that we have provided the theoretical parameters and tools to do so successfully within the diverse and complex teaching situations where our readers find themselves.

Notes

1   Stern's original label for the communicative syllabus did not include the word 'experiential'; the latter term was added by the team of researchers and educators working on the *National Core French Study* (see LeBlanc, 1990). In our scheme, we have also taken many of the ideas Stern developed for his General Language Education syllabus, and incorporated them into our column entitled Language and Learning Awareness (see explanation in text).

2   For example, this activity was originally done using suitable and interesting texts from the last section (*En commençant par la fin*) of each issue of *l'Actualité*, a Québécois periodical available in most magazine shops in Canada or on-line at www.actualite.com.

References:

See page 28

Pour commencer : un cadre théorique pour les activités d'apprentissage des langues secondes en salle de classe

Introduction

Nous, les enseignants, sommes toujours désireux d'identifier les activités intéressantes et captivantes qui nous permettront d'offrir de riches expériences langagières à nos élèves. Puisque aucune classe n'est vraiment semblable à une autre, les activités qui réussissent dans l'une ne conviennent pas toujours pour la classe au bout du corridor, ou encore moins pour celle qui se trouve à l'autre bout du pays. Le niveau de compétence des élèves, l'âge, les besoins, les intérêts et les antécédents linguistiques doivent être pris en considération. Un curriculum obligatoire ou la pression des examens peuvent également influencer notre choix d'activités. Notre propre expérience d'enseignant et notre facilité dans la langue cible vont aussi influer sur notre choix, ainsi que l'accès à des locuteurs natifs, aux textes en langue cible ou aux ressources électroniques.

Les enseignants faisant face à des situations aussi complexes ont besoin de moyens rapides leur permettant de reconnaître la valeur des activités suggérées, et d'une façon d'évaluer le rôle joué par ces activités dans un curriculum bien équilibré qui touche à tous les aspects du développement langagier. Une activité peut très bien aider les apprenants à développer leur habileté d'écoute mais si elle n'est pas compensée par des activités s'adressant à d'autres besoins langagiers, elle devient rapidement inappropriée. Dans la plupart des programmes, un curriculum équilibré est multidimensionnel. Il comprend le développement de la facilité d'expression et de la précision dans tous les domaines d'habiletés, y compris le domaine réceptif (l'écoute et la lecture) et celui de la production (l'expression orale et écrite). De plus, les étudiants ont besoin d'aide pour utiliser convenablement la langue sur le plan culturel, et de stratégies pour leur permettre de fonctionner de façon indépendante quand ils n'ont plus le soutien de la salle de classe. Clairement, certains programmes tels que celui de l'Anglais à des fins académiques (*English for Academic Purposes*) exigent qu'une attention particulière soit portée à certains usages de la langue, et l'équilibre ici doit être compris dans ce contexte. Les apprenants apportent également à un programme des forces et des faiblesses dont l'enseignant doit tenir compte. Un curriculum équilibré pour les étudiants qui ont déjà de solides compétences en lecture et en écriture peut impliquer une concentration particulière sur le travail oral. Les efforts faits pour identifier et répondre à ces besoins caractérisent les cycles de planification des programmes d'études des enseignants, alors que ces derniers évaluent et adaptent de façon continue leurs activités en salle de classe pour s'assurer que les différentes composantes d'un programme de langue communicatif soient mises au point.

Afin d'aider les enseignants à évaluer la nature et la pertinence des activités présentées dans ce recueil par rapport à leurs objectifs à long terme, nous avons élaboré le cadre théorique et organisationnel suivant. Il offre un moyen de situer chaque activité selon son intérêt principal.

	Expression orale	Expression écrite	Écoute	Lecture	Prise de conscience linguistique et de l'apprentissage
Communicatif et expérientiel					
Langue					
Culture					

Ce cadre provient des discussions que nous avons eues lors de notre examen des nombreuses activités réunies dans cette collection ; nous avons essayé de nous assurer que notre cadre était suffisamment large pour contenir la grande variété des activités incluses et suffisamment pratique pour nous permettre de classer visuellement ces activités d'une manière accessible et utile.

Comprendre notre cadre théorique : l'axe vertical

Comme de nombreux enseignants vont le reconnaître, les catégories de l'axe vertical sont tirées du travail de H.H. Stern. Stern (1983 ; Stern, Allen et Harley, 1992) a élaboré une approche multidimensionnelle au curriculum de langue seconde comprenant les trois composantes inscrites dans la colonne de gauche : communicatif et expérientiel, langue, culture.[1]

Le communicatif et l'expérientiel

La plupart d'entre nous reconnaissons l'importance primordiale d'enseigner la langue pour communiquer. Nos étudiants doivent savoir commander un repas au restaurant, écouter un message enregistré au téléphone, lire un article de journal et en comprendre les points saillants ou écrire une lettre de demande d'emploi. De telles utilisations de la langue tombent carrément dans le domaine de la communication. Pour être vues comme expérientielles (voir p. ex., Allen, 1983 ; Luckmann, 1996), elles devraient être basées sur une langue authentique utilisée dans un contexte de vie réelle. Un étudiant qui accède à un site Web afin de trouver l'horaire des trains pour une future visite au zoo lit des renseignements dans un but authentique : planifier une réelle excursion pour la classe. Une telle activité est à la fois communicative et expérientielle. Si cette activité ne sort pas de la classe, la véritable dimension expérientielle est perdue, bien qu'une pratique de communication valable subsiste grâce à la composante de lecture.

Nous sommes conscients que les enseignants d'ALS au Canada anglais ont de nombreuses occasions d'offrir des activités expérientielles à leurs étudiants, alors que la situation est très différente pour ceux qui n'enseignent pas dans une communauté où l'on parle la langue cible. Ces derniers ne peuvent pas facilement organiser des excursions scolaires dans des milieux en langue cible, par exemple. Quand les éducateurs n'ont pas accès facilement à un tel environnement, ils peuvent s'efforcer d'incorporer une dimension quasi-expérientielle dans leur salle de classe en évoquant des contextes potentiels de vie réelle et en utilisant des documents authentiques, comprenant les ressources virtuelles disponibles sur le Web.

La langue

La composante « langue » d'un curriculum équilibré (voir p. ex., Hébert, 1990 ; Williams, 1995) nous est peut-être la plus familière car elle touche aux formes et aux fonctions de la langue comme objet d'étude. La construction de phrases grammaticales à partir d'« unités de base » plus petites fait certainement partie du syllabus langue. Mais tout système langagier est aussi plus complexe, allant bien au-delà de la grammaire, du vocabulaire et de la prononciation pour inclure les fonctions langagières telles que comment exprimer ses opinions, demander, réclamer poliment, exprimer ses émotions, etc. Analyser les variations de langue qui tiennent compte du contexte social particulier, y compris le côté relativement solennel de certaines situations, fait aussi partie de l'étude de toute langue seconde.

La culture

La composante « culture » (voir p. ex., Atkinson, 1999 ; Byram, 1997 ; Leblanc, Courtel et Trescases, 1990 ; Seelye, 1986) cherche à développer la prise de conscience culturelle, définie largement. Le caractère multiculturel de la société canadienne fournit un terrain fertile à l'exploration de l'ethnicité et des valeurs sociales et culturelles de nombreux groupes différents. L'étude de la littérature, de la musique ou de l'art émanant du groupe de langue cible peut informer et intéresser les élèves, et ces aspects de la culture sont généralement intégrés dans le curriculum. Il est important également d'examiner les usages culturellement appropriés de la langue et d'acquérir une compétence sociolinguistique. Pour utiliser une langue de façon culturellement appropriée, il faut comprendre comment les personnes communiquent dans la culture cible. Par exemple, nous pouvons faire une demande qui soit grammaticale, mais qui peut cependant offenser si elle n'a pas été exprimée avec suffisamment de politesse, étant donné le sexe, l'âge et la position sociale des interlocuteurs. Connaître la culture cible veut dire savoir s'il est convenable de poser des questions sur l'âge ou les revenus, comprendre les pauses silencieuses ou savoir à quelle distance il faut se tenir de la personne avec laquelle on parle.

Comprendre notre cadre théorique : l'axe horizontal

Passant à l'axe horizontal de notre cadre théorique, nous avons tenté à nouveau de rendre justice à la complexité de ce que veut dire utiliser une langue seconde. Bien des documents relatifs au curriculum et à l'évaluation (p. ex., Ministère de l'éducation de l'Ontario, 1998 ; Johansson, 2000) basent l'acquisition de la langue sur la division traditionnelle des quatre savoirs, mais bien qu'utile, cette approche présente cependant certains problèmes. Par exemple, où le vocabulaire se place-t-il dans les savoirs traditionnels : l'écoute, la production orale, la lecture et l'écriture ? Il est clair que la connaissance du vocabulaire fait partie à la fois des habiletés langagières de production et de réception. Savoir comment organiser un texte oral ou écrit (voir p. ex., Canale et Swain, 1980; Canale, 1983) est lié à l'écoute (prédire quels éléments d'information viendront par la suite), à l'oral (planifier ce que nous voulons dire), à la lecture (utiliser des indices tels que les relations logiques dans le texte pour aider la compréhension), ou à l'écriture (apprendre comment organiser un texte comme le fait quelqu'un écrivant dans sa langue maternelle).

Bien que nous reconnaissions les dangers d'une simplification excessive dans notre cadre organisationnel, nous avons trouvé que les quatre savoirs permettent de classer les activités dans cette collection d'une manière pratique et connue des enseignants. C'est pourquoi nous avons placé ces habiletés en haut de notre cadre : d'abord les habiletés de production orale et écrite, puis les habiletés de réception, l'écoute et la lecture.

Le dernier titre de notre axe horizontal est « Prise de conscience linguistique et de l'apprentissage ». Cette catégorie inclut le syllabus de formation langagière générale de Stern (voir aussi Hébert, 1990) et comprend des stratégies d'apprentissage de la langue (p. ex., Oxford, 1990), des stratégies de communication (Chamot et O'Malley, 1992) et la prise de conscience métalinguistique (Little, 1997 ; van Lier, 1996), parmi d'autres. Par exemple, les stratégies d'apprentissage de la langue peuvent inclure inscrire des règles grammaticales ou des listes de vocabulaire dans un cahier pour consultation future. Les stratégies de communication comprennent des techniques telles que la circonlocution pour contourner le manque de connaissance d'un élément de vocabulaire, la paraphrase, le recours au langage du corps et ainsi de suite. La prise de conscience métalinguistique entraîne la compréhension du fonctionnement de la langue et de sa mise en place. Elle comprend, par exemple, l'apprentissage des conventions d'un texte, l'étude des règles de formation des mots ou l'analyse de l'ordre typique des mots dans les phrases.

Comprendre notre cadre théorique : quelques exemples

Pour illustrer les catégories d'activités présentées dans ce livre, nous offrons les exemples suivants.

	Expression orale	Expression écrite	Écoute	Lecture	Prise de conscience linguistique et de l'apprentissage
Communicatif et expérientiel	Demander des renseignements à un agent de voyages pour un futur voyage	Écrire une lettre à l'éditeur d'un journal sur un sujet d'intérêt personnel	Écouter une émission sportive pour connaître les derniers résultats du base-ball	Lire les instructions pour installer un logiciel que l'étudiant veut utiliser	Se rappeler comment tirer de l'argent d'un distributeur automatique une fois à l'étranger
Langue	Pratiquer de faire des demandes en utilisant l'impératif	Changer au temps passé un texte écrit au présent	Discerner des éléments lexicaux particuliers dans une émission de radio	Lire un texte et en souligner les prépositions	Ranger des mots en catégories (p. ex., parties du discours, thèmes sémantiques) dans un cahier
Culture	Jeux de rôle conçus pour refléter des situations culturelles particulières	Rédiger une invitation d'une façon culturellement appropriée	Identifier l'âge et la position sociale probables de participants à des entrevues de radio sélectionnées	Lire un texte sur les attitudes relatives aux rôles assignés à chacun des sexes dans la culture cible	Discuter les stéréotypes culturels dans les émissions de télévision

Un grand nombre d'activités possibles peuvent être placées dans chaque case. Beaucoup d'activités incorporent parfois des éléments de plus d'une catégorie. Nous avons donc dû prendre certaines décisions concernant les objectifs principaux et secondaires, indiqués par des points noirs (●) et par des ronds (○) dans les cases appropriées.

Prenons un exemple précis. L'enseignant identifie une situation particulière et demande aux élèves de travailler en groupes de deux ou trois, de choisir des rôles et de mettre en scène la situation telle qu'ils l'imaginent. On peut demander aux élèves, par exemple, de commander de la nourriture dans un café. Au niveau le plus élémentaire, ceci est clairement une activité orale. Le but est de s'exprimer logiquement ou de communiquer ; nous mettrons donc un point noir dans la case de Communicatif et expérientiel / Expression orale. Les élèves doivent aussi s'écouter entre eux et répondre, donc l'activité comprend également une certaine pratique d'écoute. Cependant, s'ils ont eu la chance de préparer le travail, ils auront probablement une bonne idée à l'avance de ce qui va être dit, et le rôle de l'écoute sera donc moins important et cet objectif sera plus faible. Nous marquons ce rôle secondaire en utilisant un rond, comme indiqué ci-dessous.

	Expression orale	Expression écrite	Écoute	Lecture	Prise de conscience linguistique et de l'apprentissage
Communicatif et expérientiel	●		○		
Langue					
Culture					

Bien entendu, les enseignants attribuent rarement un jeu de rôle d'une façon aussi élémentaire. Ils peuvent demander aux élèves de travailler en groupes pour préparer leur texte, ajoutant ainsi à la tâche un objectif d'écriture important. Ils peuvent présenter un menu en langue cible à partir duquel les élèves doivent choisir, introduisant ainsi un élément de lecture. Ils peuvent demander à certains élèves de préparer leurs remarques seuls, afin que le garçon ne sache pas ce qui va être commandé et doit ainsi écouter plus attentivement. Ces variations vont augmenter la portée des habiletés pratiquées, mais continueront cependant à être classées dans les tâches communicatives et expérientielles, car elles s'appliquent toutes à transmettre et à comprendre le sens.

Cependant, l'enseignant pourrait penser que l'activité serait plus utile à une classe en particulier si on en cernait davantage l'objectif. Il est peut-être en train d'enseigner les formes modales telles que « peut / pourrait / voudrait » et aimerait que ses élèves en pratiquent l'usage pendant le jeu de rôle. Il peut fournir des phrases toutes faites exprimant des demandes et contenant les formes modales que les élèves doivent pratiquer avant le jeu de rôle. Pour augmenter les occasions d'utiliser ces formes modales, l'enseignant peut demander au garçon d'annoncer qu'aucun des plats déjà commandés n'est disponible, ou il peut exiger que les clients commandent trois plats ou plus. L'activité est maintenant centrée fortement sur l'usage correct de la langue, et elle sera codée comme suit :

	Expression orale	Expression écrite	Écoute	Lecture	Prise de conscience linguistique et de l'apprentissage
Communicatif et expérientiel	○		○		
Langue	●				
Culture					

Un autre enseignant peut penser qu'il est important pour ses élèves de se sentir à l'aise dans les restaurants de la culture cible, d'être capables de prédire la suite logique des événements et de commander avec la courtoisie voulue. Il peut donc fournir un simple schéma suivi d'un ensemble de phrases à inclure dans le dialogue. Cela ajouterait un élément culturel à l'activité et nous verrions des points noirs dans les cases de Culture / Expression orale (utilisation de la langue voulue sur le plan culturel) et Culture / Prise de conscience linguistique et de l'apprentissage (comprendre les façons de se comporter au restaurant), comme ci-dessous :

	Expression orale	Expression écrite	Écoute	Lecture	Prise de conscience linguistique et de l'apprentissage
Communicatif et expérientiel					
Langue					
Culture	●				●

Décider de l'objectif principal d'une activité n'est pas toujours aussi facile que l'on aimerait. En essayant d'organiser les activités présentées dans ce livre, nous avons eu le plaisir de quelques discussions intéressantes alors que nous tentions de nous mettre d'accord sur l'emplacement exact des points noirs. La plupart des meilleures activités semblent impliquer les élèves dans une variété de tâches, et l'on pourrait théoriquement placer un point noir dans presque chaque case. Mais ceci n'aiderait pas vraiment les enseignants dans leurs efforts pour obtenir un curriculum équilibré. Nous avons donc placé nos points noirs dans les cases qui nous paraissaient représenter l'objectif principal de l'activité telle qu'elle était conçue.

Les facteurs influençant la sélection des activités

En plus d'avoir codé les activités quant à leurs objectifs d'apprentissage linguistique principaux et secondaires, nous avons aussi indiqué d'autres facteurs qui pourraient aider les enseignants à sélectionner et à identifier les activités convenant à leur classe. Pour chaque activité, nous avons désigné le niveau scolaire auquel nous estimons que cette activité convient le mieux. Pour les apprenants adultes, nous avons fait la distinction entre les études universitaires et de formation continue, utilisant le terme « post-secondaire » pour les programmes collégiaux et universitaires, et le terme « adulte » pour les classes données dans la communauté.

De nombreuses activités exigent un degré de maturité et un certain niveau de compétence pour réussir. Par exemple, alors qu'une activité peut être à la portée d'un élève du niveau 4 à 6 sur le plan cognitif, elle peut également exiger un plus haut niveau de compétence linguistique dont vraisemblablement seuls les élèves des programmes d'immersion sont capables. Dans de tels cas, nous avons indiqué le programme approprié après le niveau scolaire.

Il est bien entendu impossible pour nous de connaître tous les détails de la situation dans laquelle se trouve l'enseignant. Nous ne pouvons donc pas offrir de suggestions définitives quant au meilleur moyen d'adapter les activités suivantes pour une classe en particulier. Nous encourageons donc les enseignants à réfléchir aux besoins et aux intérêts de leurs élèves, en gardant à l'esprit les questions telles que la langue maternelle, le degré d'hétérogénéité de la classe, les raisons pour lesquelles les élèves étudient, etc.

De plus, les classes se tiennent dans un contexte déterminé de temps et de lieu. Les activités qui conviennent au début de l'année peuvent sembler hors de propos quand les examens sont proches, et une tâche fascinante basée sur les résultats de baseball aura perdu tout intérêt après la fin de la Série mondiale. Le plan de l'école peut aussi influencer le choix. Les activités peuvent être trop bruyantes pour certains lieux ou exiger des ressources électroniques qui ne sont pas facilement disponibles. Les enseignants doivent être conscients des choix qu'ils font, et s'assurer qu'en réalité les activités choisies conviennent vraiment à leurs apprenants et à eux-mêmes. Ceci peut exiger une adaptation considérable du matériel publié.

Adapter les activités à des groupes d'élèves distincts

La tentation existe pour tous d'ignorer une idée parce qu'elle n'a pas été créée dans le contexte de la classe que l'on enseigne. Mais pourquoi ? Y a-t-il une raison valable de ne pas adopter une idée qui a eu beaucoup de succès dans une classe de français de base en 8e année, et de l'adapter pour qu'elle obtienne le même succès dans une classe de FLS pour adultes dans la communauté, ou une classe d'espagnol à l'université ?

Pour tenir compte des nombreuses différences en salle de classe (l'âge des élèves, les intérêts et besoins, la diversité linguistique et culturelle, les expériences précédentes, les styles d'apprentissage, le niveau de compétence des élèves, le choix du moment, etc.), nous proposons deux adaptations pour chaque activité dans notre collection. Nous espérons qu'après avoir travaillé avec notre cadre organisationnel et examiné les idées proposées, nos lecteurs comprendront comment utiliser le cadre et les activités pour combler les lacunes tout en s'efforçant de parvenir à un curriculum multidimensionnel équilibré dans leur salle de classe. Les cadres ci-dessous proposent aux enseignants un processus à quatre étapes à considérer quand ils réfléchissent à l'équilibre de leur curriculum et aux moyens d'adapter une activité à un groupe d'élèves en particulier.

Réfléchir à l'équilibre de votre curriculum et des activités en salle de classe

Quatre étapes simples
Étape 1 : La recherche d'une activité appropriée doit commencer avec les élèves, le curriculum et les objectifs de votre programme plutôt qu'avec une activité en particulier. Pensez aux buts de votre programme et aux progrès et habiletés de vos élèves dans la langue cible.
- Avez-vous besoin d'une activité pour aider vos élèves à atteindre un but particulier ?
- Votre curriculum manque-t-il d'une composante en particulier (p. ex., la culture) ?

- Vos élèves ont-ils des difficultés avec une certaine habileté ou tâche ?
- Y a-t-il des objectifs à court terme ou à long terme que vous aimeriez atteindre ou dont vous avez besoin ?

Si la réponse à l'une ou l'autre de ces questions est OUI, vous devez trouver une activité qui réponde à vos besoins. Vous pourriez créer votre propre activité, ou adapter l'activité de quelqu'un d'autre pour vos élèves Avant de choisir une activité, vous devez cependant examiner les questions de l'étape 2.

Étape 2 : Une partie du processus de sélection d'une activité en salle de classe comprend de poser les questions suivantes : Y a-t-il certains aspects de votre classe et de votre école que vous ne pouvez changer ? Quelle influence ont-ils sur votre choix d'activité ?
- Combien d'élèves avez-vous ? Quelle est la fréquence de vos rencontres ?
- Quel type d'apprenants avez-vous ? Quel âge ont-ils ? Quel est leur développement cognitif ?
- Combien de temps avez-vous ? Quelle est votre charge de travail ? Y a-t-il des contraintes physiques à considérer ? Partagez-vous une classe avec un autre enseignant ? Avez-vous accès aux ordinateurs ?
- Quel genre de budget avez-vous ?

Étape 3 : Sélection d'une activité initiale
En tenant compte des étapes 1 et 2, choisissez une activité possible pour l'adapter. Autant que possible, elle devrait répondre aux critères requis afin de minimiser le nombre d'adaptations nécessaires. Un collègue peut suggérer une activité. L'activité choisie peut aussi provenir d'un remue-méninges ou bien vous l'avez trouvée en consultant ce livre.

Étape 4 : Ajustez l'activité choisie
Après avoir choisi une activité qui va vous aider à combler une lacune de votre curriculum, et avoir pris en considération les facteurs sur lesquels vous avez peu ou pas de contrôle, vous devrez peut-être ajuster l'activité choisie selon votre groupe d'élèves.
- Devez-vous adapter l'activité pour la rendre plus ou moins difficile sur le plan linguistique pour vos élèves ?
- Devez-vous adapter l'activité pour répondre aux intérêts et au développement cognitif de vos élèves ?
- Voulez-vous adapter l'objectif linguistique de l'activité ? Devez-vous porter davantage votre attention sur la facilité ou la justesse d'expression de vos élèves ?
- L'activité reflète-t-elle la composition de votre classe sur le plan culturel ? Pourriez-vous l'adapter pour la rendre plus appropriée ?
- Avez-vous des élèves avec des difficultés d'apprentissage pour lesquels vous devrez adapter l'activité ?
- Pourriez-vous adapter l'activité pour répondre aux intelligences multiples de vos élèves ?

Nos adaptations

Pour créer nos adaptations, nous avons fait le tour des activités que nous avons utilisées dans les diverses classes que nous avons enseignées et en avons exploré la valeur dans d'autres contextes de langue seconde et de langue étrangère. Nous avons d'abord « codé » chaque activité selon notre cadre organisationnel, décrit ci-dessus dans la section « Comprendre notre cadre théorique : quelques exemples » (p. 18) ; nous avons réfléchi également à d'autres contextes d'enseignement et aux facteurs qui influencent le succès d'une activité dans une vraie salle de classe. Pendant notre remue-méninges, nous avons essayé d'étendre le champ de chaque activité en changeant les objectifs principaux ou secondaires ou en en ajoutant d'autres. Nous avons aussi tenté de trouver divers moyens d'adapter l'activité pour la rendre utile à différents types d'apprenants dans différents programmes. Les exemples suivants, qui présentent des activités de résumés de textes et d'écart à combler, ainsi que les adaptations s'y rattachant, aideront à clarifier ces processus.

Exemple 1 : résumés de textes

À l'origine, cette activité de résumé de texte a été conçue pour une classe de français de base de 12e année. On pourrait l'utiliser comme mise en train, pour introduire une certaine variété, ou comme faisant partie d'une unité sur les affaires courantes. Au fil du temps, l'enseignant choisit et copie de courts textes de lecture (reflétant les intérêts des élèves, les expériences vécues et la maturité) que l'on peut trouver dans n'importe quel journal ou magazine.[2] Ces textes comptent de 50 à 150 mots et peuvent couvrir une variété de sujets (p. ex., l'avortement, la légalisation de la marijuana à Amsterdam, la pollution en Chine comparée au Canada). Les élèves travaillent individuellement et ont environ 15 minutes pour lire leur texte en entier (chaque élève a un texte différent). Les élèves doivent alors présenter un résumé oral d'une minute du contenu du texte et donner une opinion sur le commentaire social offert par l'auteur. Les élèves peuvent prendre des notes s'ils le désirent pour s'aider pendant leur présentation orale.

Il est clair que l'objectif principal de cette activité est la lecture. L'écriture peut être un objectif secondaire si les élèves choisissent de prendre des notes. Nous savons, par expérience, que les élèves de français de base ressentent souvent le besoin de prendre des notes pour s'aider dans leur présentation orale. Quand l'activité en arrive à cette présentation, l'objectif principal devient l'expression orale, et nous pouvons espérer que la plupart des élèves écoutent les résumés de leurs pairs!

Bien que cette activité ait été utilisée d'abord dans une classe de français de base de 12e année dont les élèves avaient des habiletés langagières de niveau intermédiaire, il semble évident qu'elle conviendrait également pour une classe d'immersion française au niveau secondaire ou dans un contexte universitaire où les étudiants ne sont pas des débutants.

Examinons maintenant les adaptations qui pourraient être apportées à cette activité pour qu'elle réussisse dans ces classes ou dans une autre classe de français de base de 12e année.

Adaptation n° 1

Comme beaucoup d'entre nous le savons, la composante culturelle de l'enseignement de la langue seconde et étrangère est souvent reléguée aux oubliettes. Cette activité de résumé de texte n'a pas délibérément de centre d'intérêt culturel. Choisir des textes avec un contenu culturel, touchant par exemple aux attitudes des anglophones et des francophones à propos de l'avortement, de l'importance de la musique et de l'art pour les jeunes de Vancouver ou de l'usage de l'ecstasy dans les raves en Amérique du Nord, apporterait facilement une dimension culturelle à l'activité de résumé de textes, ajoutant ainsi un point noir en bas à droite de notre cadre.

Adaptation n° 2

Bien des théoriciens (p. ex., Piaget, 1959 ; Vygotsky, 1967), des chercheurs (p. ex., Holt, 1993 ; Swain, 1995, 2000) et des enseignants en salle de classe s'accordent pour dire que les élèves peuvent développer leurs aptitudes en langue seconde et perfectionner leurs compétences sociales en travaillant avec leurs pairs. Il est donc important de varier de temps à autre les stratégies de groupement. Quand les apprenants travaillent en groupes, ils ont davantage l'occasion de parler et d'écouter la langue cible. Swain (1985, 1995) présente aussi l'idée que lorsqu'on pousse les élèves à parler ou à écrire dans la langue cible, ils augmentent leurs connaissances langagières et leur compétence de communication.

Nous pouvons adapter l'activité de résumé de textes en faisant partager la présentation orale par deux élèves : l'un peut faire le résumé et l'autre exprimer leur opinion. Ceci peut être fait également comme activité de casse-tête (Holt, 1993) où un groupe de quatre ou cinq élèves lit le même texte et prépare le résumé et le commentaire, agissant en groupes d'experts. Après avoir préparé ce résumé et ce commentaire en collaboration, tous les élèves joignent le groupe de base qui leur a été assigné à l'avance et dans lequel des pairs ont lu des textes différents. Les élèves présentent alors leurs résumés et leurs opinions, jouant le rôle d'experts ou d'enseignants dans le cadre de ces textes. L'enseignant peut aussi donner aux élèves un test à choix multiple sur le contenu de tous les textes pour s'assurer que les élèves ont pris leur tâche au sérieux et ont écouté les présentations de leurs pairs.

Exemple 2 : activités d'écart à combler

Le but principal de ces activités, c'est que deux élèves travaillent en équipe pour rassembler des informations afin de compléter une tâche ; une personne doit avoir des informations que l'autre n'a pas. Ainsi, il y a un réel écart à combler. De plus, toutes les informations que les élèves ont en commun sont nécessaires pour réussir à compléter la tâche. Notre activité d'écart à combler a été utilisée avec les élèves du français de base et avec ceux de l'ALS au niveau débutant, et elle concerne l'expression orale, l'écoute et le dessin. Chaque élève reçoit un dessin différent représentant des objets familiers tels que des fruits de taille diverse (p. ex., pommes, oranges, bananes). Chaque élève reçoit aussi une feuille de papier blanc et des marqueurs de couleurs. Les deux élèves se tournent le dos afin que ni l'un ni l'autre ne puisse voir le dessin de l'autre. L'un après l'autre, dans la langue cible, chaque élève décrit son dessin à son partenaire qui essaie de le reproduire. On encourage l'artiste à poser des questions de clarification à son partenaire. Cette courte activité est en général un moyen amusant de revoir le vocabulaire de base, les couleurs, les tailles, les directions (à droite, à gauche, au-dessus, en dessous, etc.) et les questions de clarification.

Notre échantillon d'activité d'écart à combler comprend un objectif principal expérientiel et de communication, permettant aux élèves de parler et d'écouter de façon réelle pour compléter une tâche. Les élèves pratiquant également un vocabulaire spécifique, les couleurs, les tailles, les directions et les questions de clarification, cette activité a aussi un objectif langagier secondaire d'expression orale et d'écoute.

Adaptation n° 1

Dans une autre version de cette activité, convenant à la plupart des niveaux et des programmes, l'enseignant découpe et photocopie le bulletin météorologique mondial publié dans les journaux (ou tout autre document disponible et correspondant à l'âge des élèves, imprimé ou virtuel). Avant la classe, l'enseignant fait deux copies du bulletin météorologique (version A et version B) et efface différents éléments sur les deux copies. L'idée est d'avoir deux versions des mêmes prévisions météorologiques, mais dans chaque version des informations différentes sont omises, créant ainsi un écart à combler. En classe, une activité se déroule basée principalement sur l'expression orale et la lecture. Les élèves travaillent par groupes de deux ; un élève reçoit la version A du bulletin météorologique et l'autre la version B. Les élèves doivent d'abord identifier les informations qui manquent sur leur version du bulletin, puis commencer à se poser mutuellement des questions (un objectif secondaire porte sur la formulation de questions) afin que tous deux puissent compléter leur version du bulletin météorologique.

Adaptation n° 2

Notre seconde adaptation est une activité d'écart à combler d'un genre très différent. En fait, peu de chose subsiste de l'activité originale sauf le concept d'écart. Notre alternative offre un exemple d'adaptation complexe d'une activité.

Cette alternative est communicative, expérientielle et authentique et pourrait convenir aux étudiants du niveau secondaire, universitaire ou d'un programme d'ALS pour adultes. L'activité consiste à planifier d'assister à un festival du film local (p.ex., le Festival annuel du film de Toronto). L'enseignant partage le programme du festival en sections (selon le nombre d'étudiants par groupe ; nous recommandons de ne pas avoir plus de trois étudiants pour mieux gérer l'activité). Les étudiants travaillent ensemble avec leur section du programme pour décider quels films ils aimeraient voir et pourquoi. Puis, les groupes d'étudiants présentent oralement leur information à la classe, tout en essayant de convaincre leurs pairs que le choix qu'ils ont fait à partir de leur section du programme est le meilleur (d'où l'écart à combler). Lorsque toutes les équipes ont fait leur présentation, on passe au vote pour choisir les films à voir. À la suite du processus de prise de décision en classe, les étudiants s'organisent pour aller voir quatre films (plus ou moins selon le temps et les ressources et peut-être la classe toute entière en soirée) au cours de journées différentes pendant le festival.

Cette activité du festival du film transforme l'activité de base (dessiner des fruits) en une activité réelle, communicative et expérientielle dont les objectifs principaux sont l'expression orale, l'écoute et la lecture, avec comme objectifs secondaires l'expression écrite et la prise de conscience culturelle. Il est évident que lorsque les étudiants vont réellement voir les films, la prise de conscience culturelle peut, selon la nature des films choisis, devenir un objectif principal.

Conclusion

Ce livre offre aux enseignants de langue un certain nombre d'activités créées et utilisées par des enseignants chevronnés. Cette introduction a pour but de décrire et d'illustrer un cadre théorique, fondé sur un curriculum équilibré et multidimensionnel, et s'appuyant sur les théories actuelles d'apprentissage et d'enseignement des langues. Notre but est d'aider les enseignants à utiliser notre cadre théorique pour identifier et adapter les activités nécessaires pour avoir un curriculum équilibré et multidimensionnel dans leur salle de classe, et répondre aux aptitudes, intérêts et besoins des élèves. Nous espérons avoir fourni les paramètres théoriques et les outils nécessaires pour réussir à cette tâche malgré la complexité des diverses situations auxquelles nos lecteurs ont à faire face.

Notes

1   Le terme choisi à l'origine par Stern pour le syllabus communicatif ne comprenait pas le mot « expérientiel » ; il fut ajouté plus tard par une équipe de chercheurs et d'éducateurs travaillant sur *L'Étude nationale sur les programmes de français de base* (voir Leblanc, 1990). Dans notre projet, nous avons également adopté beaucoup d'idées que Stern avait élaborées pour son syllabus de formation langagière générale, et les avons incorporées dans notre colonne intitulée « Prise de conscience linguistique et de l'apprentissage »

2   Par exemple, cette activité était faite à l'origine en utilisant les textes appropriés et intéressants de la dernière section (*En commençant par la fin*) de chaque numéro de *L'Actualité*, un périodique québécois disponible dans la plupart des magasins de journaux au Canada ou en ligne à www.actualité.com.

References

Allen, P. (1983). A three-level curriculum model for second language education. *Canadian Modern Language Review, 40*, 23–43.

Atkinson, D. (1999). TESOL and culture. *TESOL Quarterly, 33*, 625–654.

Byram, M. (1997). *Teaching and assessing intercultural communicative competence.* Clevedon, UK: Multilingual Matters.

Canale, M., & Swain, M. (1980). Theoretical bases of communicative approaches to second language teaching and testing. *Applied Linguistics, 1*, 1–47.

Canale, M. (1983). On some dimensions of language proficiency. In J. W. Oller Jr. (Ed.), *Issues in language testing research.* Rowley, MA: Newbury House.

Chamot, A., & O'Malley, M. (1992). *Building bridges: Content and learning strategies for ESL.* Boston: Heinle & Heinle.

Hébert, Y. (1990). *Syllabus formation langagière générale.* Ottawa: Canadian Association of Second Language Teachers.

Holt, D.D. (1993). *Cooperative learning: A response to linguistic and cultural diversity.* Washington: Center for Applied Linguistics.

Johansson, L. (2000). *Canadian language benchmarks 2000: ESL for literacy learners.* Ottawa: Centre for Canadian Language Benchmarks.

LeBlanc, R. (1990). *National core French study – A synthesis.* Ottawa: Canadian Association of Second Language Teachers.

LeBlanc, C., Courtel, C., & Trescases, P (1990). *Le syllabus culture.* Ottawa: Canadian Association of Second Language Teachers.

Little, D. (1997). Language awareness and the autonomous language learner. *Language Awareness, 6*, 93–104.

Luckmann, C. (1996). Defining experiential education. *Journal of Experiential Education, 19*, 6–7.

Ontario Ministry of Education. (1998). *Ontario curriculum, Grades 1–8.* Toronto: Queen's Printer for Ontario (www.edu.gov.on.ca).

Oxford, R.L. (1990*). Language learning strategies: What every teacher should know.* Rowley, MA: Newbury House.

Piaget, J. (1959). The language and thought of the child (3rd ed.). London: Routledge & Kegan Paul.

Seelye, N. (1985). *Teaching culture.* Lincolnwood, IL: National Textbook Co.

Stern, H.H. (1983). *Fundamental concepts of language teaching.* London: Oxford University Press.

Stern, H. H., Allen, P., & Harley, B. (Eds.) (1992). *Issues and options in language teaching.* Oxford: Oxford University Press.

Swain, M. (1985). Communicative competence: Some roles of comprehensible input and comprehensible output in its development. In S.M. Gass & C.G. Madden (Eds.), *Input in second language acquisition* (pp. 235–254). Rowley, MA: Newbury House.

Swain, M. (1995). Three functions of output in second language learning. In G. Cook & B. Seidlhofer (Eds.), *Principle and practice in applied linguistics.* (pp. 125–144). Oxford: Oxford University Press.

Swain, M. (2000). The output hypothesis and beyond: Mediating acquisition through collaborative dialogue. In J. P. Lantolf (Ed.), *Sociocultural theory and second language learning* (pp. 97–114). Oxford: Oxford University Press.

van Lier, L. (1996). *Interaction in the language curriculum: Awareness, autonomy and authenticity.* London: Longman.

Vygotsky, L.S. (1965). Thought and language. (E. Hanfmann and G. Vakar, Eds., Trans.) Cambridge, MA: MIT Press.

Williams, J. (1995). Focus on form in communicative language teaching: Research findings and the classroom teacher. *TESOL Journal*, 4(4), 12–17.

The Use of E-mail as a Tool to Enhance Second Language Education Programs: An Example from a Core French Classroom

Geoff Lawrence

	Speaking	Writing	Listening	Reading	Language & Learning Awareness
Communicative & Experiential		●		●	
Language					
Culture					○

Notes

Grade levels and programs: 4 to 12 immersion, 7 to 12 core French, ESL
Equipment required: Computer with e-mail access
Preparation: Establish connections for e-pals with target language schools or individuals

Editors' Introduction

Lawrence describes how language students can enhance their reading, writing, and computer skills through the use of e-mail as they write to target language speakers. Students are motivated to participate in the exchange because it involves student-centred interaction and because many enjoy using the technology itself. In addition, e-mail communication does not require an immediate response and therefore allows students more time to plan their responses. While one-on-one e-mail exchanges are valuable, a number of different forms of communication are available through e-mail such as collaboration on projects with students in another class or school or international discussion lists. Lawrence stresses the need to give purpose to these exchanges by integrating them into the curriculum rather than leaving them as an optional extra-curricular activity. If there is no real purpose for the correspondence, there is a considerable danger that it will wither away with neglect.

It has been said that an ideal second language classroom involves student-centred, authentic and meaningful communication, collaborative and constructivist tasks, interaction with native and near-native speakers, and access to a variety of second language input-promoting opportunities for extensive second language output (Brown, 1994; Stern, 1992; Swain, 1993). E-mail and related forms of computer-mediated communication (CMC) afford the second language teacher the necessary tools to approximate such an ideal second language learning environment. This article will outline reasons why e-mail, and specifically e-mail exchanges, are valuable tools to promote authentic target language interaction in the second language classroom. Recent research examining the use of e-mail exchanges on the second language learning process will then be outlined, followed by one specific example of an e-mail exchange in a secondary core French classroom. This will be followed by advice on how best to use such technology to enhance second language learning.

Why does it make sense to use e-mail and e-mail exchanges in the second language classroom?

The use of e-mail as a teaching tool can ground the study of second and foreign languages in a learner-centred, authentic communicative context, and can offer interaction with first language speakers, yielding insight not only into the target language but also the target culture (Turnbull & Lawrence, 2001; Warschauer, 1998). E-mail can be used by teachers to create motivating, engaging and dynamic second language learning environments that simultaneously address linguistic and cultural learning objectives. The use of e-mail gives all classroom students a voice and an audience other than through the teacher, thereby motivating learners to interact with each other in a collaborative, complementary and personally meaningful manner. The use of e-mail encourages participation from all learners including those more reluctant to participate in a face-to-face learning environment (Beauvois, 1998). Learners are often motivated by the use of such computer-mediated educational mediums as they attain collaborative working strategies and learn timely and relevant computer and communication skills in the process of learning a second language – acquiring skills that are highly marketable in today's networked societies (Warschauer, 1996).

Of all Internet tools, e-mail is one of the most accessible and commonly used and is relatively simple to orchestrate within the classroom context. When used in exchanges with first language speakers, e-mail gives learners the opportunity to communicate with target language speakers along with their peers and teachers, summoning linguistic and socio-cultural knowledge to make themselves understood. This collaborative, content-driven interaction encourages the sharing of culturally-based ideas and values, thereby contributing to learners' cultural and linguistic knowledge (Kaufman, 1998). E-mail exchanges with target language speakers from different cultures is a form of collaborative learning that allows learners to construct personally meaningful knowledge of the second language and culture following a truly constructivist approach (Warschauer, 1997).

What has research revealed about the effectiveness of e-mail and e-mail exchanges in second language learning?

E-mail exchanges create a versatile, student-centred forum prompting second language production that can be orchestrated to target a range of linguistic and cultural learning objectives. Such collaborative forums offer second language learners the opportunity to directly interact with first language speakers from a range of target language communities, providing a variety of contextualized second language exposure that may be quite different from that presented by the teacher. Research has shown that the use of e-mail communication among second language classroom students encourages increased learner-centred interaction, often dramatically reducing teacher-based dialogue and in turn dramatically increasing student-centred discussion and second language output (Pratt & Sullivan, 1994; Warschauer, 1995). Research suggests that the use of e-mail can result in improved second language writing and reading skills and can prime second language learners with the necessary tools to enhance their oral communication abilities (Appel & Vogel, 2001; Pratt & Sullivan, 1994; Warschauer, 1995; Weininger & Shield, 2001). Due to its asynchronous nature (communication that does not occur simultaneously), e-mail affords second language learners the time necessary to reflect upon and analyze interpersonal communication, thereby encouraging a focus on target language form in addition to fluency (Warschauer, 1997). E-mail exchanges with first language speakers in tandem learning environments, in which learners are paired up to learn each other's first language, reportedly promote second language learners' use of first language speakers' grammatical and vocabulary knowledge (Appel & Vogel, 2001). In such exchanges, first language partners act as target language models whose linguistic forms are often adopted by second language learners. In addition, exposure to target language communities through e-mail exchanges can promote increased cross-cultural awareness and interest among second language learners in the target language communities (Moore, Morales, & Carel, 1998). One of the most potentially exciting, long-term benefits of e-mail exchanges (reported anecdotally) is that learners are motivated to use the second language long after the institutional learning process, having established contacts and friends in the target language community (Turnbull & Lawrence, 2001).

Organizing an e-mail exchange for your class

When selecting an appropriate exchange for a classroom context, it is important to consider its potential pedagogical advantages and limitations, and the range of second language learning outcomes the exchange will meet. E-mail exchanges can be established where learners in one class communicate directly with learners in another class (abroad or within the same school) at different proficiency levels using a tandem learning approach – where learners are paired to learn each other's first language through project-based tasks – to discuss classroom topics, collaborate on project-based tasks, or simply exchange personal information. Teachers can also set up team teaching partnerships, where classes from different schools or different levels work together to share information and complete certain tasks or projects. It is also possible for students to join international discussion lists to collaborate on group projects and report on these discussions to their class.

One must, however, be conscious of two significant problems with e-mail exchanges, as reported by teachers: inadequate response from e-mail participants, and a lack of purpose behind the e-mail interaction (Warschauer, 1995). One approach to avoiding such reported problems is to integrate the e-mail interaction into the course curriculum, ensuring that all students involved are accountable for their participation while encouraging them to take some control over the direction and outcomes of the interaction. The following project-based example, taken from a secondary classroom observed as part of a recent study related to core French teachers' uses of technology in their teaching (Turnbull & Lawrence, 2001), succeeds in integrating e-mail interaction directly into the curriculum.

The use of e-mail exchanges in secondary core French: Canada-Haïti-France

I observed one Canadian teacher who used a student-designed online newsletter to prompt interaction between secondary core French students and students in two other French-speaking nations (Turnbull & Lawrence, 2001). The newsletter featured a variety of sections ranging from editorial, sports, and an advice column, to student articles, and links to partnered schools. This teacher established an online relationship with classes in these partnered schools, one in France and one in Haïti, and had students prepare articles on self-selected topics related to Canadian music and culture to be posted in the newsletter. Articles on French or Haïtian music and culture were simultaneously prepared by students in the partner schools so that eventually all students' articles were posted online, in categories, and then read by students in all three schools. All students from participating classes were then responsible for sending a minimum number of comments on the articles directly to individual writers' e-mail addresses (listed at the bottom of each article), and these students were responsible for responding to each message. After a period of time, all students were responsible for summarizing their discussions for evaluation purposes. Students summarized the issues that were raised and prepared an analysis of the cultural similarities and differences in the area of music and culture.

The topic of music was chosen as a relatively neutral topic for the first round of articles prepared by the students to facilitate non-threatening interaction and ease learners into cross-cultural communication. As learners become more accustomed to interacting in this type of exchange, they will likely require more stimulating and potentially controversial topics to motivate future discussions. Such projects can be integrated into the curriculum, ensuring all students involved post a minimum of contributions to the conference and undertake some sort of related assignment summarizing their participation for evaluation, such as working in groups to summarize, and presenting to their class the discussion that occurred online.

Such an activity is an example of a team teaching activity where teachers work together with other classes in different schools (or even within the same school) to complete a group task. To ensure participation, students can work collaboratively with multiple e-mail partners and complete tasks such as preparing and publishing an online newsletter, doing comparative evaluations surveying students, families or individuals online or in their communities, and preparing reports on issues including the environment, economics, society, or politics. In this way, students have the opportunity to work with multiple partners, increasing their target language exposure and production. One benefit of this type of interaction pattern is that students involved in online collaborative group projects have been shown to adopt the broader linguistic speech patterns of the entire online community rather than the more individual patterns from working alone with a single partner (Appel & Vogel, 2001). This more dynamic approach contrasts with the traditional tandem learning approach where students work with one other student and are therefore exposed to a much more limited variety of target language and have more restricted opportunities for acquisition.

Teachers can have students participate in international discussion lists on a range of topics including music, cinema, sports, science and technology, and learning a second language. This can be a great venue to introduce students to target language speakers, encourage potential e-pal connections, and allow students to research and explore a variety of topics. Such discussion lists can be integrated into the curriculum by having each student join a specific list, write a minimum number of postings each week to the discussion, and prepare a paper or presentation summarizing what happened and what was learned from this activity (Warschauer, 1995, p. 52).

General tips on the use of e-mail exchanges

Second language teachers interested in exploring e-mail exchanges can find a number of exchange web sites linking schools and teachers by conducting a search using major Internet search engines for 'international e-mail exchanges' or 'second language e-mail exchanges.' Here are some relevant web sites:

Kidlink: http://www.kidlink.org/index.html: A global networking portal for children around the world including links to discussion groups in several languages and links to kids' discussion groups, forums, educational projects, and chat.

E-Pals.com: http://www.epals.com: The world's largest online classroom community and leading provider of 'student-safe' e-mail with links to e-pals in English, French, Spanish, German, Portuguese, and Chinese

International E-mail Classroom Connections: http://www.iecc.org: This site links teachers and classrooms from around the world from a range of teaching contexts (primary/secondary schools, adult, and higher education), and includes links to discussion lists for students and teachers, and a list of publications on online learning. This site also has a useful international research link to an list of previously conducted student surveys and a link for students to create their own surveys.

International EFL/ESL E-mail Student Discussion Lists: http://www.latrobe.edu.au/education/sl/sl.html: These lists were established in February 1994 to provide a forum for cross-cultural discussion and writing practice for college, university, and adult students in English language programs around the world. There are currently ten student lists on a range of topics, but more may be added as demand increases.

Linguistic Funland: http://www.linguistic-funland.com/addapal.html: Links to student e-pals along with a site listing messages from second language teachers searching for partner classes.

International Tandem Learning: http://www.slf.ruhr-uni-bochum.de/email/ infen.html: Comprehensive site on tandem learning approaches, with links to discussion lists, tandem learning projects, and participating institutions.

When conducting projects using e-mail exchanges, it is important to discuss and agree on terms of participation and curriculum integration with the partner teacher, so that both groups of students are participating and being evaluated on similar terms. If students have never used e-mail before, it is important to instruct students on appropriate language and e-mail terminology in the target language along with 'netiquette' rules to facilitate the communication process. It is important to model sample messages and responses and have students send practice messages to others within the class before sending e-mails to potential e-pals. In order to track student participation, students can be asked to copy teachers on some of their messages, submit a file of all correspondence, summarize correspondence, or keep a contribution log listing the date of each message composed and received, the name of the sender or receiver, and the number of lines in the message (Robb, 2001).

Like any new approach, effectively using e-mail within second language classrooms will take time and practice. It is wise to start with small, focused projects integrated into the curriculum to familiarize students and teachers with the medium before moving on to more complex and varied tasks. Once students have been exposed to this type of authentic communication it is likely they will want to use it more (Robb, 2001). E-mail is a versatile teaching tool that can make the study of a second language meaningfully alive and real.

References
Appel, C., & Vogel, C. (2001). Investigating syntax priming in an e-mail tandem language learning environment. In K. Cameron (Ed.), *CALL: The challenge of change* (pp. 177–184). Exeter, UK: Elm Bank Publications.

Beauvois, M.H. (1998). E-Talk: Computer-assisted classroom discussion: Attitudes and motivation. In J.Swaffar, S. Romano, P. Markley, K. Arens (Eds.). *Language learning online: Theory and practice in the ESL and L2 computer classroom* (pp.99–124). Austin, TX: The Daedalus Group, Inc.

Brown, H. D. (1994). *Principles of language learning and teaching*. Englewood Cliffs, NJ: Prentice Hall Inc.

Kaufman, L. M. (1998). Email keypals in zone of proximal development. *ERIC Digest* [On-line]. Available: http://www.ed.gov/databases/ERIC_Digests/index/.

Moore, Z., Morales, B., & Carel, S. (1998). Technology and teaching culture:

Results of a state survey of foreign language teachers. *CALICO Journal, 5*(1–3), 109–128.

Pratt, E., & Sullivan, N. (1994). *Comparison of ESL writers in networked and regular classrooms.* Paper presented at the 28th Annual TESOL Convention, Baltimore, MD.

Robb, T. (2001). *Email keypals for language fluency.* Available:http://www.kyoto-su.ac.jp/~trobb/keypals.html

Stern, H.H. (1992). *Issues and options in language teaching.* Oxford: Oxford University Press.

Swain, M. (1993). The output hypothesis: Just reading and writing aren't enough. *Canadian Modern Language Review, 50,* 158–164.

Turnbull, M., & Lawrence, G. (2001). *Core French teachers and technology: Classroom application and belief systems.* Report prepared for the Canadian Association of Second Language Teachers.

Warschauer, M. (1995). *Email for English teaching.* Alexandria, VA: TESOL.

Warschauer, M. (1996). Comparing face-to-face and electronic discussion in the second language classroom. *CALICO Journal, 13 (2),* 7–26.

Warschauer, M. (1997). Computer-mediated collaborative learning: Theory and practice. *Modern Language Journal, 81 (4),* 470–481.

Warschauer, M. (1998). Computers and language learning: An overview. *Language Teaching, 31,* 57–71.

Weininger, M. J., & Shield, L. (2001). Orality in MOO: Rehearsing speech in text: A preliminary study. In K. Cameron (Ed.), *CALL: The challenge of change* (pp. 89–96). Exeter, UK: Elm Bank Publications.

Adaptation One: Strengthening content of e-messages

	Speaking	Writing	Listening	Reading	Language & Learning Awareness
Communicative & Experiential		●			
Language					○
Culture	○				

Notes

Grade levels and programs: 7 to 12 core French, 2 to12 immersion, ESL
Grouping strategy: Individual and small groups
Equipment required: Computer with Internet connection
Preparation required: Establishing connections for e-pals with target language schools

This adaptation explores ways to ensure that the content of e-messages is substantive. One way to start the correspondence is to have students work in class to create their first message – a sort of autobiography developed through a writing process, including peer- and self-correction. The second message might involve a series of questions for their e-pals. The teacher starts this process by engaging students in a brainstorming session to create questions the students would like to ask. If appropriate, this process might become a review of interrogative forms, hence the subsidiary emphasis in the Language/Language & Learning Awareness cell above. Another session could involve asking questions of a cultural nature prepared in advance through a similar brainstorming process. Ideally, the students will eventually engage in their own dialogues with their e-pals and create a portfolio of messages and responses. There could also be special class time set aside to allow students to check their e-mail. At this time, the teacher would circulate to help students decode the messages they received from their e-pals.

Web sites useful for establishing connections:

Cyberpals
A data base for students (teenagers) to exchange messages with students who have similar interests.
http://www.cyberpals.studentcenter.org/

KS Connection Penpal Box
A network for students (ages 6 to 16), teachers and classes to connect with pen pals. For all ages.
http://www.ks-connection.org/penpal/penpal.html

L'Escale
A Québécois site for school exchanges in over 15 countries for students ages 4 to 15 years. Multimedia and Internet activities as well as resources for teachers and parents:
http://www.globetrotter.net/escale/corresp9.htm

Student Letter Exchange
An American-based organization that matches students and classes all over the world for letter writing exchanges. Can register and order information on-line.
http://www.pen-pal.com/

Freinet
A French site that offers correspondence exchanges for all ages and levels in France and abroad.
http://www.freinet.org/corinter/

Canada's SchoolNet
A government website for students, educators, and the general public which provides hundreds of links to national and global learning resources, exchanges and programs:
http://www.schoolnet.ca

Keypals
A site for establishing e-exchanges between students, parents and educators:
http://www.teaching.com/keypals

Adaptation Two: Electronic *Flat Stanley*[1]

	Speaking	Writing	Listening	Reading	Language & Learning Awareness
Communicative & Experiential	○	●		●	
Language					
Culture					●

Notes

Grade levels and programs:	2 to 3 immersion, 5 and 6 core French, ESL
Equipment required:	Optional computer with e-mail access
Preparation required:	Establishing connections with target language schools

This adaptation for primary immersion or junior core French students concerns the fictional character from the popular children's book, *Flat Stanley*. The teacher explains (in French for FSL students, in English for ESL classes) to the students that Stanley got his name because a bulletin board fell on him. Flat Stanley now goes around the world in an envelope, but he can also travel by e-mail. If the students want, they can change Flat Stanley's name and create another fictional character (e.g., Bugs Bunny Plat) and give the Stanley or the new character a Canadian identity. The objective of this activity is to send an e-mail or a letter in the target language to a relative or friend or another class in Canada or abroad who understands the target language. In their e-mails, students describe Flat Stanley or another fictional character. They may draw and colour Stanley if they wish, scan it into their e-mails or draw him in their letters. The students may also ask their correspondents to design and describe their own Flat Stanley or other character in their return e-mail or letter.

Students assist each other to edit the e-mails or letters and the teacher does one final check before they are sent out. When the e-mails and letters are answered, the students will have a collection of different Flat Stanleys from Canada or around the world. The students orally describe to the class the other Flat Stanleys or characters that their e-pals have told them about. They might also create a display of their Flat Stanleys in class or in a prominent location in the school.

Note

1   Brown, Jeff. (1968). *Flat Stanley*. London: Methuen & Co.

Un gars, une fille: plaidoyer pour la culture avec un 'petit *c*' dans un cours de français langue étrangère

Catherine Black

	Speaking	Writing	Listening	Reading	Language & Learning Awareness
Communicative & Experiential			○		
Language			●		○
Culture					●

Notes

Grade levels and programs:	9 to12 immersion, post-secondary, adult
Equipment required:	Videotape and television
Preparation required:	Videotaping television program, preparing list of idioms

Editors' Introduction

Black describes how the Québec television sitcom, *Un gars, une fille*, can be used in a post-secondary (or advanced immersion) setting to teach culture, language awareness, and listening skills. The program uses everyday language with many idioms, slang, unfamiliar linguistic structures, and a variety of realistic situations that resonate with students. The natural language and events in the program show authentic examples of Québec culture and contrast with the artificiality of some post-secondary texts and videos. In the chart above, we have indicated these foci with solid bullets in the Language/Listening and Culture/Language & Learning Awareness cells. The hollow bullets in the Communicative & Experiential/Listening and Language/Language & Learning Awareness cells indicate the subsidiary focus on these components.

Dans un article récent, Lussier (1997, p. 236) affirmait que la culture doit être perçue comme une vision du monde à découvrir par le biais de la langue et des interactions des locuteurs qui utilisent cette langue. Si l'on souscrit à cette opinion, l'émission de télévision *Un gars, une fille* mettrait assez bien en évidence le fait que langue et culture sont étroitement liées et que, par conséquent, le visionnement et l'exploitation de ce matériel, dans un cours intermédiaire de français au niveau universitaire, ne pourrait avoir qu'un impact positif sur les apprenants en développant leur compétence de communication. Afin de démontrer cela, nous avons divisé cet article en trois parties distinctes : une brève description de l'émission et des thèmes abordés, une justification théorique et pédagogique avec des suggestions d'activités possibles et enfin les difficultés ou défis à surmonter lorsqu'on utilise ce genre de matériel dans la salle de classe.

Contenu culturel et thématique de l'émission

Fruit de l'imagination de Guy Lepage et de Sylvie Léonard (comédiens québécois), *Un gars, une fille* est diffusé sur les antennes de Radio-Canada[2] depuis 1997 et met en scène un jeune couple montréalais. Chaque diffusion comporte une série de quatre saynètes d'une durée de quinze minutes chacune dans lesquelles Guy et Sylvie (et depuis récemment Anakin, leur fille) vivent leur vie de couple/famille de tous les jours avec ses joies, ses colères, ses peines et ses moments de tendresse. Les thèmes abordés sont multiples mais celui qui domine concerne surtout les relations interpersonnelles entre hommes et femmes dans les situations qui testent justement ces relations. Ainsi, voit-on les personnages évoluer dans leur milieu professionnel, en famille, pendant leurs loisirs (au cinéma, en discothèque, au restaurant, au chalet, en voyage) ou encore dans leurs interactions avec d'autres corps de métier (dans les commerces : à la pharmacie, au dépanneur, à la banque, dans une librairie, dans un magasin de sports, etc.). Bref, il s'agit du milieu quotidien de monsieur et madame tout-le-monde, dans lequel les téléspectateurs peuvent se retrouver et rire d'eux-mêmes. Or, c'est exactement ce contenu culturel avec un « petit *c* » qui nous est apparu intéressant à exploiter en classe de langue car « son » langage colle à la réalité linguistique de monsieur et madame tout-le-monde. Les expressions idiomatiques, l'argot, les structures familières non standard–tout cela contribue au bagage linguistique et culturel de l'apprenant qui désire communiquer de façon appropriée dans le contexte socio-culturel de la langue étudiée.

De plus, comme l'affirme Bufe,

> la vie quotidienne banale de la culture-cible (C2) peut être valorisée dans la per-
> spective de l'enseignement/apprentissage à partir de la culture de départ (C1). Ce
> qui est familier aux Français ne l'est pas forcément aux apprenants [anglophones
> ou allophones] de la culture française et inversement. (2000, p. 85)

Ce type de culture est ce que Mehl (1992, p. 89 *sq*) appelle la « culture ethnographique » et c'est elle qui nous intéresse dans le cadre de cet article. Elle renseigne non seulement sur la langue de la majorité de la population de la culture-cible, mais aussi elle présente ses habitudes, ses particularités linguistiques et sociologiques. C'est dans cette optique que nous avons préféré l'utilisation de *Un gars, une fille* dans la classe de langue plutôt que les supports vidéo qui accompagnent les manuels de français L2. Pourquoi ce choix ? Comme justification, examinons brièvement ce que les programmes intégrés ont à offrir à l'apprenant en langue.

Si l'on consulte la plupart des manuels de français langue seconde publiés récemment et utilisés dans plusieurs universités canadiennes, il en ressort que la culture y a certainement une place proéminente. Or, un examen plus approfondi révèle que le plus souvent il s'agit de la culture avec un « grand *C* » ou comme l'appelle Mehl (1992) « la culture cultivée ». Prenons à titre d'exemple le cas de *Bravo* (Muyskens, Harlow, Vialet et Brière, 1998) qui est le manuel adopté par notre institution. Dans l'introduction du livre, le lecteur apprend que les étudiants vont apprendre à connaître la vie quotidienne des Français et des membres de la francophonie. À cet effet, les auteurs ont divisé en deux parties l'aspect culturel. La première catégorie, les *Liens culturels*, stimule l'intérêt de l'apprenant en lui présentant sous forme de vignettes des éléments culturels spécifiques à la France ou au monde francophone (par exemple, les médias, les loisirs, les relations, les achats, etc.) sans pour autant noyer cet apprenant sous les détails. L'autre catégorie, l'*Intermède culturel*, propose des extraits littéraires, des articles de presse, des photos concernant l'art et l'histoire. Il existe aussi un site sur la Toile de l'information qui présente des activités guidées pour l'exploitation de la Toile culturelle francophone.[3] On retrouve également ce format dans *À votre tour !* (Vallette et Vallette, 1995) et dans *À bon port* (Compain, Courchêne, Knoerr et Weinberg, 1998). Toutefois, il convient de faire remarquer que, dans les trois manuels, il existe aussi des mini-dialogues qui donnent un aperçu de la langue parlée. Dans *Bravo*, les auteurs ont voulu aussi montrer les variantes lexicales et syntaxiques du « joual », tâche tout à fait louable mais l'explication donnée avant le texte ne facilite en rien la compréhension des étudiants. Dans ces cas-là peut-être vaudrait-il mieux s'abstenir !

Ce panaché culturel donne un aperçu un peu figé de la culture française. Certes, on nous parle des jeunes, de leurs intérêts, mais on présente aussi à l'étudiant cette culture française actuelle de façon passive, par exemple : lisez l'article suivant sur les jeunes et la culture des cafés en France et répondez aux questions ci-dessous. Un tel format n'est guère favorable à l'apprentissage de langue-culture puisqu'il ne met pas l'apprenant en contact avec le discours des jeunes qui fréquentent les cafés. La dimension linguistique de la langue courante est généralement absente ou présentée sous forme de dialogues d'imitation.

D'autre part, ce qui est présenté dans les manuels de langue comme étant la culture avec un « grand *C* » n'est en fait qu'un ramassis des événements historiques et artistiques qui ont façonné la France et la francophonie. On peut alors se poser la question : pourquoi intégrer ce contenu de façon fragmentaire dans le cours de langue alors qu'il a plus sa place dans un cours de civilisation/ culture où il sera exploité de manière approfondie ?

Dernier aspect du « paquet » qui accompagne le manuel de langue : les vidéo-cassettes dans lesquelles on voit des Français ou des francophones évoluer dans leur environnement quotidien (maison, bureau, restaurant, etc.). Ce qui frappe l'enseignant qui utilise ces « pseudo » documents authentiques, c'est le fait que les vidéos manquent d'authenticité. Certes, le contexte culturel est respecté mais les participants manquent de spontanéité. On observe aussi, chez les sujets filmés, des phénomènes d'autocorrection dans les domaines de la grammaire, de la phonétique et des niveaux de langue, ce qui nuit encore à l'authenticité des documents exploités. Ce sont principalement toutes les raisons mentionnées ci-dessus qui sont à l'origine de notre choix.

Justification pédagogique

Si l'on se place du point de vue pédagogique, les situations qui apparaissent dans *Un gars, une fille* font partie des thèmes traités dans la plupart des manuels de français L2 comme il a déjà été mentionné. On y retrouve les relations interpersonnelles, la famille, le monde du travail, le logement, les loisirs, les voyages, la nourriture. Les relations interpersonnelles et les situations relatives présentent un intérêt culturel dans la mesure où elles sont assez représentatives du milieu décrit. En effet, Guy et Sylvie, les « héros », représentent un couple typique de jeunes Québécois de classe moyenne. Ils travaillent tous les deux, ont leur petit intérieur, sortent avec leurs amis, vont au cinéma ; ils vivent en union libre et viennent de fonder une famille ; Guy a des problèmes avec sa « presque » belle-mère et Sylvie est jalouse des collègues de travail féminines de Guy, et de plus tous les deux sont assez versés sur la question du sexe. Bref, ce petit train-train quotidien filmé à Montréal est une mine de ressources culturelles. À travers la vie des personnages, les étudiants découvrent la vie en milieu francophone, et ils peuvent la comparer à leur propre environnement et à leur vie journalière acquérant ainsi un plus grand bagage culturel. D'autre part, ce qui différencie cette émission des vidéos dites authentiques qui accompagnent les manuels, c'est le fait que les personnages sont des acteurs professionnels et non des individus choisis par les auteurs des livres de français L2. Mais ne pourrait-on pas argumenter que de vrais Français ou Québécois filmés dans leur milieu sont plus authentiques que des acteurs ? Certes, mais il faut aussi considérer que les premiers manquent généralement de naturel et sont souvent gênés par la caméra ; de plus, ils sont aussi coupables d'autocorrection ou d'hypercorrection linguistique (nous avons remarqué que cela apparaît surtout chez des locuteurs plus âgés, mais un peu moins chez les jeunes). Or, ce phénomène va à l'encontre de l'authenticité tant recherchée par les promoteurs de l'approche communicative. Dans *Un gars, une fille*, l'authenticité est respectée dans la mesure où les comédiens vivent la situation qu'ils ont à jouer d'après le scénario tout en conservant une part d'improvisation ; le jeu est naturel, les comédiens ne sont pas gênés par la caméra, la langue n'est pas châtiée, le débit est normal, voire rapide dans certains cas. Tout cela contribue, selon nous, à un excellent entraînement au niveau de la compréhension, de l'acquisition de vocabulaire courant, ainsi qu'à l'étude de la communication non-verbale de membres d'une culture francophone.

Examinons à présent le contenu linguistique de *Un gars, une fille*. Avant toute chose, il serait bon de mentionner que les scénarios sont écrits par des comédiens et de jeunes auteurs québécois. Ces derniers ont le souci de rendre l'émission le plus authentique possible. Les mots, les expressions sont donc choisis avec soin pour faire rire ou sourire, mais aussi pour que le public puisse s'identifier aux protagonistes. Par conséquent, la langue doit nécessairement refléter le parler de la tranche de société décrite. C'est en cela que l'émission nous paraît bénéfique pour les apprenants de FLE. En effet, ces derniers sont d'abord confrontés à un niveau de langue différent de celui du professeur ; ensuite, la langue parlée comporte toutes sortes d'altérations : telles que la disparition de la particule « ne » dans la négation, la modification des pronoms « elle, il » en « a, i' », l'apparition du fameux « t'sé » que Yvon Deschamps appelle « la mouche syntaxique » ; on peut citer aussi la diphtongaison du [E] en [ai], du [a] en [au], du [œ] en [œy] pour ne citer que les plus courantes au Québec. Ce sont souvent ces modifications qui causent des problèmes d'incompréhension chez les apprenants lorsqu'ils se retrouvent en milieu natif.

Si l'on se place du point de vue du vocabulaire, l'émission est une mine d'expressions idiomatiques et populaires telles que : « t'es don ben plate », « ç'a pas d'allure », « t'es donc fin », « chu tanné, t'sé », « Hé maudit ! T'as tu don la tête dure », « T'es ben trop poche » et « maganné » « à soir » pour n'en citer que quelques unes. *Un gars, une fille* expose aussi les apprenants aux anglicismes et aux emprunts qui se sont glissés dans la langue populaire : « triper », « chauffer l'boat », « l'freezer » et « pitcher ». La langue de *Un gars une fille* est loin d'être aseptisée et en cela est bien différente de celle enseignée dans la plupart de cours de langue. Mais il n'y a pas que la langue qui soit loin d'être aseptisée ; le contenu des scènes gravite aussi parfois autour des relations sexuelles comme nous l'avons dit plus haut. Ainsi, il n'est pas rare d'entendre certaines expressions vulgaires telles que : « fourrez quelqu'un » ou encore « C'est ton QI qu'il aime mon père, sans le I », mais qui font partie de la réalité linguistique locale. Nous sommes convaincues qu'il est indispensable que nos apprenants sachent reconnaître ou même utiliser dans un contexte « approprié » ces expressions qui appartiennent à la langue familière voire populaire.

Applications pratiques

Avant de passer à ces applications, il serait bon de situer le contexte dans lequel nous avons utilisé *Un gars, une fille*. Il s'agit d'un cours de français L2 de deuxième année universitaire : *la langue à travers la culture populaire.* Ce cours de cinq heures par semaine (trois avec le professeur, une de conversation avec un assistant et une au centre multimédia avec un moniteur) explore la langue à l'aide de divers média (chansons, textes, vidéos, articles de journaux en-ligne, visite de la Toile de l'information). Lorsque les étudiants sont au centre multimédia avec le moniteur, ils visionnent des vidéos du *Français dans le Monde* et naviguent sur la Toile. Toutes les deux semaines, ils visionnent l'émission *Un gars, une fille*.

Voici comment nous avons procédé : dans un premier temps, nous avons choisi avec le moniteur[4] les scènes à montrer en classe. Ensuite le moniteur les a visionnées afin de vérifier la qualité du son, le débit des acteurs, leur articulation. Il a ensuite compilé une liste de toutes les expressions idiomatiques et des québécismes qui apparaissent dans les scènes choisies. Une fois en classe, il a donné cette liste aux étudiants, leur demandant de les expliquer et de donner un exemple de situation dans laquelle on pourrait les utiliser. Puis, il a montré la scène sans le son et a demandé aux étudiants de relever tous les détails qui les ont frappés sur les lieux, l'habillement des personnages et leur comportement. Ils ont ensuite fait une mise en commun en essayant de voir s'il y avait des différences par rapport à leur propre milieu. Les étudiants ont ensuite vu la vidéo deux fois.

La seconde fois, ils ont dû repérer le contexte dans lequel les expressions étaient employées ainsi que le comportement non-verbal qui les accompagnait. Un échange a eu lieu ensuite pour demander aux étudiants quel aurait été leur propre comportement dans une situation identique. La dernière phase de l'activité consistait à faire utiliser les expressions relevées dans des mini-contextes/saynètes tout en prenant soin d'imiter l'intonation ou la prononciation des acteurs.

Détail intéressant à noter : si l'on veut exploiter la version écrite du sketch, il suffit de se rendre sur le site de l'émission où l'on trouvera la transcription. Une autre activité que nous n'avons pas testée mais qui pourrait être intéressante serait de créer un forum de discussion dans lequel les étudiants pourraient parler en français au sujet des réactions des personnages et les comparer aux leurs en pareille situation. Une autre activité possible serait de diriger les étudiants vers le site de l'émission où ils pourraient poser directement des questions aux comédiens ce qui serait un excellent exercice de communication réelle.

Difficultés ou défis à surmonter

Le plus grand défi à surmonter est d'avoir un moniteur consciencieux car, avec ce genre de cours, il y a peu de place pour l'improvisation. Les étudiants passeraient un bon moment devant la télévision sans en retirer grand chose. De plus, le moniteur doit être formé à l'utilisation en classe de la vidéo. Il doit rendre le visionnement interactif par ses commentaires, son rôle étant toutefois plus celui d'un animateur que celui d'un dispensateur de savoir. Il doit aussi bien connaître la culture québécoise pour compléter avec des détails culturels ce que les étudiants voient. Enfin, il doit avoir une bonne formation en phonétique pour sensibiliser les étudiants aux variations phonétiques de la langue familière. Cela dit, il est tout à fait envisageable que l'enseignant fasse ce genre d'activités sans l'aide d'un moniteur.

Conclusion

Après ce rapide examen du contenu de l'émission télévisée *Un gars, une fille*, pouvons nous dire que ce genre d'émission a sa place dans un cours de langue. Non seulement est-elle divertissante mais elle est aussi linguistiquement et culturellement éducative car elle permet aux apprenants en français L2 de s'ouvrir sur le monde francophone. Du point de vue pédagogique, cette émission est une mine de ressources. Elle peut être utilisée dans un cours de langue intermédiaire/avancé en raison des différents niveaux de langues présentés, ainsi que du vaste champ sémantique qu'elle explore. Dans un cours de phonétique, elle permettrait l'étude approfondie des traits de prononciation caractéristiques du français québécois parlé. Dans un cours de langue et culture, elle servirait de support à l'analyse du comportement non-verbal des francophones ; elle pourrait aussi contribuer au repérage des anglicismes et des québécismes. Nous avons vu plus haut que l'émission a son propre site sur la Toile qui contient la transcription des scripts. Ne serait-il pas possible dans un cours de traduction d'utiliser ce matériel riche en expressions populaires ?

Nous avons aussi mentionné que les droits d'auteurs avaient été achetés par plusieurs pays européens dont la France et la Belgique. Ces pays vont conserver les situations mais les adapter à la couleur locale. Pourquoi ne pas se servir de ces émissions pour effectuer des comparaisons culturelles, linguistiques et gestuelles entre la France, la Belgique et le Québec ? Bufe suggère que : « la culture médiatique au sens large du terme, accompagnée d'une pédagogie de la rencontre, pourra contribuer à un renouveau de l'apprentissage des langues étrangères » (2000, p. 93). Nous adhérons entièrement à cette idée et *Un gars, une fille* se prête parfaitement à cette pédagogie de la rencontre car l'émission stimule la compétence interculturelle, procure un accès direct à la culture de langue-cible, stimule la compréhension de la langue spontanée et encourage l'utilisation de la langue orale et de la gestuelle de la culture C2–autant d'aspects que l'on a encore trop tendance à ignorer dans les cours de français langue étrangère.

La réaction des étudiants a été positive comme le montrent les réponses au questionnaire que nous avons fait circuler à la fin du cours (voir Appendice). Du point de vue de la langue, il ressort que l'émission leur a paru utile, que la langue n'était pas trop familière, que les comédiens parlaient parfois trop vite, qu'il valait mieux étudier le vocabulaire avant de voir la scène et qu'ils avaient découvert un certain nombre d'expressions inconnues jusqu'alors. De plus, il n'était pas nécessaire d'avoir des questions pour faciliter la compréhension ; ils ont estimé que la présence des anglicismes n'était pas en soi un mal dans un cours de langue dans la mesure où le moniteur les avait mis en évidence. En ce qui concerne le comportement non verbal, les étudiants étaient tous d'avis qu'il facilitait la compréhension.

En ce qui concerne le contenu, les sujets traités présentaient un certain intérêt pour les apprenants; l'émission leur donnait une impression adéquate de la classe moyenne québécoise et en cela elle était véritablement culturelle ; le contenu « sexuel » de certaines scènes ne les avait pas choqués et, selon eux, était même acceptable dans un cours de langue au niveau universitaire. Par contre, les étudiants ne se sont pas identifiés aux protagonistes. Cela résulte peut-être de la différence d'âge qui existe entre eux et les personnages de l'émission (tous les deux dans la trentaine) ainsi que de leurs préoccupations qui semblent différentes de celles de nos apprenants qui n'ont pas encore tous vingt ans.

Cette année, nous nous proposons d'utiliser de nouveau *Un gars, une fille* dans le même cours, mais en nous assurant que le contenu pédagogique, tel qu'énoncé plus haut, sera respecté au pied et à la lettre. En fin de semestre, nous ferons une analyse des productions orales d'étudiants afin de voir s'il y a des résultats tangibles du point de vue linguistique et culturel. Et qui sait, serons-nous peut-être mieux en mesure de dire si les étudiants apprécient plus la culture avec un « petit *c* » ? À suivre….

Notes

1   Dans cet article, le masculin est employé de façon générique et englobe le féminin.

2   Plusieurs vidéo-cassettes, facilement accessibles, ont été produites depuis la création télévisée de l'émission. À ce propos signalons que l'institution dans laquelle le professeur de langue enseigne doit avoir le droit de visionner les cassettes. Pour cela il suffit d'écrire à Guy Lepage qui vous mettra en rapport avec la personne qui s'occupe des autorisations. Voici son adresse électronique : ungarsunefille@nm.radio-canada.ca.

3   Voir bravo.heinle.com/

4   Il faut préciser que le moniteur fait partie du Programme des moniteurs des langues officielles qui permet à un jeune Québécois qui étudie à plein temps dans une université ontarienne de partager sa culture en enseignant huit heures de conversation par semaine chaque trimestre. Pour nous, le moniteur est le candidat idéal pour faire ce travail sur l'émission, puisqu'il connaît bien la culture québécoise.

Réferences

Bufe, W. (2000). De la médiation technologique à l'apprentissage interculturel des langues étrangères. *Revue de didactologie des langues-cultures, 117*, 73–95.

Compain, J., Courchêne, R., Knoerr, H., et Weinberg, A. (1998). *À bon port.* Englewood Cliffs, NJ : Prentice Hall.

De Carlo, M., et Aquistapace, S. (1997). Civilisation / Culture : histoire du développement de concepts. *Revue de didactologie des langues-cultures, 105*, 9–13.

Lussier, D. (1997). Domaine de référence pour l'évaluation de la compétence culturelle en langue. *Revue de didactologie des langues-cultures, 106*, 321–246.

Mehl, D. (1992). *La fenêtre et le miroir : la télévision et ses programmes.* Paris : Payot.

Muyskens, J., Harlow, L., Vialet, M., et Brière, J-F. (1998). *Bravo ! Cahier d'exercices et Manuel de laboratoire* (3e ed.). Boston : Heinle & Heinle, 1998.

Un gars, un fille site de la Toile: www.radio-canada.ca/ungarsunefille/

Valette, J-P., et Valette, R.M. (1995). *À votre tour ! : Intermediate French.* Lexington, MA : DC Heath and Company.

Annexe

Français 251 / Questionnaire informatif

Cochez l'option qui correspond le plus à votre opinion.

L'émission *un gars, une fille* est utile dans un cours de langues.
☐ je suis d'accord tout à fait.
☐ je suis moyennement d'accord.
☐ je ne suis pas tout à fait d'accord.
☐ je ne suis pas du tout d'accord.

Les sujets traités dans un gars, une fille n'offrent pas d'intérêt.
☐ je suis d'accord tout à fait.
☐ je suis moyennement d'accord.
☐ je ne suis pas tout à fait d'accord.
☐ je ne suis pas du tout d'accord.

La langue est trop populaire pour un cours de langue.
☐ je suis d'accord tout à fait.
☐ je suis moyennement d'accord.
☐ je ne suis pas tout à fait d'accord.
☐ je ne suis pas du tout d'accord.

Les scènes sont difficiles à comprendre à cause du vocabulaire familier.
☐ je suis d'accord tout à fait.

☐ je suis moyennement d'accord.
☐ je ne suis pas tout à fait d'accord.
☐ je ne suis pas du tout d'accord.

Les acteurs parlent trop vite.
☐ je suis d'accord tout à fait.
☐ je suis moyennement d'accord.
☐ je ne suis pas tout à fait d'accord.
☐ je ne suis pas du tout d'accord.

La gestuelle (comportement non-verbal) des acteurs facilite la compréhension.
☐ je suis d'accord tout à fait.
☐ je suis moyennement d'accord.
☐ je ne suis pas tout à fait d'accord.
☐ je ne suis pas du tout d'accord.

Le contenu de certaines scènes n'est pas approprié pour un cours.
☐ je suis d'accord tout à fait.
☐ je suis moyennement d'accord.
☐ je ne suis pas tout à fait d'accord.
☐ je ne suis pas du tout d'accord.

Pour mieux comprendre la scène, il faudrait étudier le vocabulaire avant.
☐ je suis d'accord tout à fait.
☐ je suis moyennement d'accord.
☐ je ne suis pas tout à fait d'accord.
☐ je ne suis pas du tout d'accord.

Pour faciliter ma compréhension j'aimerais avoir des questions précises auxquelles répondre.
☐ je suis d'accord tout à fait.
☐ je suis moyennement d'accord.
☐ je ne suis pas tout à fait d'accord.
☐ je ne suis pas du tout d'accord.

Un gars, une fille est vraiment une émission culturelle.
☐ je suis d'accord tout à fait.
☐ je suis moyennement d'accord.
☐ je ne suis pas tout à fait d'accord.
☐ je ne suis pas du tout d'accord.
Un gars, une fille ne dépeint pas la société québécoise.
☐ je suis d'accord tout à fait.
☐ je suis moyennement d'accord.
☐ je ne suis pas tout à fait d'accord.
☐ je ne suis pas du tout d'accord.

Je m'identifie facilement aux deux héros de l'émission.
☐ je suis d'accord tout à fait.

☐ je suis moyennement d'accord.
☐ je ne suis pas tout à fait d'accord.
☐ je ne suis pas du tout d'accord.

J'apprends beaucoup d'expressions idiomatiques en regardant cette émission.
☐ je suis d'accord tout à fait.
☐ je suis moyennement d'accord.
☐ je ne suis pas tout à fait d'accord.
☐ je ne suis pas du tout d'accord.

Il y a trop d'anglicismes, on ne devrait pas montrer cette émission à des étudiants en langue.
☐ je suis d'accord tout à fait.
☐ je suis moyennement d'accord.
☐ je ne suis pas tout à fait d'accord.
☐ je ne suis pas du tout d'accord.

49

Adaptation One: Comparing French and English sitcoms

	Speaking	Writing	Listening	Reading	Language & Learning Awareness
Communicative & Experiential	●		●		
Language					○
Culture					●

Notes

Grade levels and programs:	10 to 12 immersion, post-secondary, advanced adult
Grouping strategy:	Individual or small groups
Equipment required:	Videotape and television
Preparation required:	Videotaping or previewing television program, preparing lists of idioms

This activity requires students to compare the themes and levels of language used in five-minute clips from *Un gars, une fille* and a popular, but quite different, English-language program such as *Friends*. Either the teacher or the students record the clips and they try to find similar situations in both programs, such as asking for a date, talking about fashion, doing household chores, teasing, etc. After viewing the clips, students present their analyses of language levels, vocabulary, body language, and/or cultural variations to the class.

Alternatively, over a period of several weeks, students listen to an English-language sitcom at home and *Un gars, une fille* in class. Other programs may be substituted if the teacher and students prefer. In the selected programs, they compare such cultural markers as degree of vulgarity, relationships between men and women, the language used by different people, the different types of greetings, etc. The analyses can be presented orally, but the teacher might encourage students' writing skills by asking them to keep a weekly journal of their observations.

Adaptation Two: Student-created sitcoms

	Speaking	Writing	Listening	Reading	Language & Learning Awareness
Communicative & Experiential	●	●	○		
Language					
Culture					

Notes

Grade levels and programs:	10 to 12 core French, 9 to12 immersion, adult French, secondary and adult ESL
Grouping strategy:	Small groups
Equipment required:	Videotape and television
Preparation required:	Videotaping television program, preparing lists of idioms

After watching an episode from *Un gars, une fille*, students, in groups of about four, write a short skit with an ending different from the one they have just seen or give a different twist to the plot. If they prefer, the students may devise an entirely different version with different characters and plot, or even write a parody of the original. The groups present their skits to the class.

To encourage a variety of skits, students may tape a variety of episodes of *Un gars, une fille* and work on their skits at home if classroom time is not available. Alternatively, students may prefer to transcribe or paraphrase parts of the show and then re-enact them.

Much the same type of skit activity can be accomplished with ESL classes using English-language sitcoms or other target-language television programs. The teacher brainstorms with the class as to which shows the students feel would be most suitable for them, and then proceeds in the way described above.

Portfolio langagier en français

Bernard Laplante et Helen Christiansen

	Speaking	Writing	Listening	Reading	Language & Learning Awareness
Communicative & Experiential					●
Language					●
Culture					

Notes

Grade levels and programs: Teacher education, possible in all languages
Grouping strategy: Individual

Editors' Introduction

The authors designed the language portfolio program described in this article for students in a four-year Teacher Education program to help them maintain and develop their own French-language skills, but it could be used in many language-learning programs.

Laplante and Christiansen found that keeping a portfolio encouraged students to become more aware of their progress in the target language, to help them take charge of their own learning, and to improve their communication skills.

The authors recommend that students form a three-part action plan: first, they must decide where they are in their language-learning curve; second, they clarify and fix their goals; third, they justify their plans to attain their goals. Students include in their portfolios a variety of documents that best reflect their progress toward these goals. It is also important that students attach a reflective note to each entry stating why that document was included. The authors also recommend that students include in their portfolios a reflective summary of how they have attained or worked toward their goals set out in the action plan.

Il semble, qu'après avoir passé cinq ou six ans à apprendre une langue seconde dans les classes d'immersion, certains élèves atteignent un plateau dans leur développement langagier. Il semble que ce soit également le cas de certains étudiants inscrits aux programmes de formation à l'enseignement en immersion, ainsi que de ceux inscrits au baccalauréat en français offerts par les universités canadiennes hors Québec. La situation est facile à comprendre. En milieu anglo-dominant, le français est souvent assez peu visible et les occasions de pratique sont peu fréquentes. Ainsi, un apprenant, s'il veut poursuivre le développement de sa compétence langagière, ne peut simplement se limiter à suivre quelques cours de perfectionnement en français. Il doit également mettre en œuvre de nouvelles stratégies d'apprentissage susceptibles de l'amener à se surpasser.

C'est dans un tel contexte et dans le but d'encourager le développement langagier des étudiants de première année du baccalauréat en éducation française de notre université que nous avons demandé à ces derniers de réaliser un portfolio langagier. La finalité du « portfolio langagier », et ce, en raison même de sa nature, est d'amener l'apprenant à devenir plus conscient de son apprentissage tout en lui permettant de développer une plus grande autonomie. C'est pour ces raisons que nous pensons que le portfolio langagier représente un outil des plus prometteurs. Dans les sections suivantes nous précisons ce qu'est un portfolio langagier, puis nous expliquons pourquoi il nous paraît important que les apprenants langagiers, ayant atteint un certain niveau de compétence, entreprennent la réalisation d'un tel portfolio. Puis nous décrivons les différents documents qui pourraient être inclus dans un premier portfolio langagier.

Qu'est-ce qu'un portfolio langagier ?

Un portfolio langagier est un dossier dans lequel un apprenant documente et illustre son développement langagier tout au long d'une période de temps. Ce dossier contient des documents résultant d'expériences langagières vécues par l'apprenant. Ces documents peuvent être des plus variés. Ils peuvent prendre la forme de textes écrits (lettre, composition, liste, travaux scolaires) ou d'enregistrements (lecture, présentation, leçon, conversation). Ils peuvent provenir d'expériences sur le vif ou en rétrospective. Chaque document doit incorporer une note réflexive dans laquelle l'apprenant précise la nature de celui-ci, et le pourquoi de son inclusion dans le portfolio.

Pourquoi réaliser un portfolio langagier en français ?

Dans le contexte qui nous est propre, un des buts de tout apprenant langagier est d'améliorer sa compétence de communication. Dans le cas d'apprenants qui se dirigent vers l'enseignement du français dans les écoles (immersion ou français de base), cela correspond au développement de leur compétence de communication afin, entre autres, qu'ils puissent devenir de véritables modèles langagiers pour leurs élèves.

Avant d'en arriver à ce point, la plupart des apprenants doivent, s'ils veulent constater une amélioration de certains aspects de leur compétence de communication, devenir plus conscients de leur propre apprentissage. Le résultat souhaité est qu'ils puissent reconnaître leurs forces et, plus particulièrement, leurs faiblesses au niveau de la langue. De plus, s'ils veulent être en mesure de bâtir sur leurs forces et prendre les moyens nécessaires pour remédier à leurs faiblesses, ils doivent devenir des apprenants plus autonomes. Cette démarche s'applique tant à ceux qui apprennent le français en tant que langue seconde qu'aux locuteurs natifs qui sont en voie de perfectionnement.

C'est dans ce sens que le portfolio langagier amène les apprenants langagiers à progresser et prend toute sa valeur. Dans la mesure où il inclut un plan d'action qui met en évidence les mesures mises en place pour remédier à certaines faiblesses et des documents choisis avec soin et comportant une dimension réflexive, le portfolio peut offrir à l'apprenant l'opportunité de se conscientiser vis-à-vis son propre développement langagier. Ce dernier peut ainsi en arriver à mieux gérer son apprentissage tout en développant une plus grande autonomie. Dans sa dimension affective, le portfolio permet également à l'apprenant de réaliser l'ampleur de ses réussites au niveau langagier et de célébrer son progrès. Il se prépare ainsi à faire face à de nouveaux défis.

Documents à inclure dans un premier portfolio langagier

Les documents suivants pourraient être inclus dans un premier portfolio langagier :

- Ma vie en français jusqu'à maintenant
- Mon plan d'action
- Documents relatifs à des expériences langagières vécues en classe
- Documents relatifs à des expériences langagières vécues hors classe
- Comment j'ai vécu mon plan d'action

La description de chacun de ces documents fait l'objet des sections suivantes. Nous faisons état de ces descriptions telles que nous les avons distribuées à tous nos étudiants de première année.

Ma vie en français jusqu'à maintenant

Ce premier document devrait prendre la forme d'un bref narratif (environ deux pages) dans lequel vous raconterez comment vous en êtes arrivé à parler français, ainsi que la place que le français occupe aujourd' hui dans votre vie. Les questions suivantes pourraient vous aider à composer ce texte :

- Qui suis-je ?
- Quelle est ma langue maternelle ?
- Où, quand et comment ai-je appris à m'exprimer en français ?
- Quelle a été ma première expérience en français ?
- Quelles autres expériences en français m'ont marqué ?
- Quelle place le français occupe-t-il dans ma vie maintenant ?
- Quels incidents décrivent la place du français dans ma vie ?
- Comment est-ce que je me sens en tant qu'apprenant langagier ?
- Comment est-ce que je me sens quand j'ai à m'exprimer en français ?
- Comment les expériences langagières que j'ai vécues m'ont amené à devenir l'apprenant langagier que je suis ?

Vous pourriez conclure ce narratif en réfléchissant sur ce que vous avez appris en le produisant et sur l'importance de l'inclure dans votre portfolio langagier.

Mon plan d'action

Votre plan d'action devrait comprendre trois parties distinctes. Premièrement, faites le point de façon à préciser où vous en êtes dans votre développement langagier. Deuxièmement, fixez-vous des objectifs en fonction des grands buts que vous désirez atteindre (entre autres : être un modèle langagier pour vos élèves, atteindre un certain niveau de compétence langagière, etc.). Et troisièmement, précisez et justifiez les moyens que vous prendrez pour atteindre vos buts.

Les questions suivantes pourraient vous aider à compléter votre plan d'action :

- Quels sont les éléments de ma compétence de communication en français (oral et écrit) qui représentent des forces ?
- Qu'est-ce que j'ai fait pour en arriver là ?
- Quels sont les éléments de ma compétence de communication en français (oral et écrit) sur lesquels je devrais travailler ?
- En tenant compte de mes forces, de mes faiblesses et des objectifs que je me suis fixés, où est-ce que j'aimerais me situer du point de vue développement langagier d'ici six mois ou un an ?
- Qu'est-ce que je compte faire pour combler, au moins en partie, chacune des faiblesses identifiées plus haut ?
- Quelles sont les ressources matérielles et humaines dont je dispose ?
- Comment est-ce que je les utiliserai ?

Vous pourriez conclure ce plan d'action en réfléchissant sur le rôle que peut jouer un tel plan dans votre développement langagier et sur l'importance de l'inclure dans votre portfolio.

Documents relatifs à des expériences langagières

D'autres documents servent à décrire certaines des expériences langagières que vous avez vécues tant en classe qu'en dehors de la classe. Ceux-ci doivent mettre en valeur la manière dont vous mettez votre plan d'action en œuvre. Le but n'est pas de tout inclure, mais plutôt de choisir des documents qui représentent le mieux votre développement langagier. Ces documents peuvent provenir de travaux que vous avez préparés pour vos classes, d'observations faites en classe, de lettres que vous avez écrites à un ami, et cetera. Ils peuvent également, si vous le souhaitez, être préparés spécifiquement pour le portfolio.

En guise d'introduction, et pour chaque document, vous devez préciser dans une note réflexive, la nature du document en question et expliquer pourquoi vous l'avez inclus (quelle compétence langagière illustre-t-il ?). Cet élément de réflexion est essentiel si l'un de vos buts est de devenir plus conscient de votre apprentissage.

Voici des exemples de documents à inclure dans votre portfolio :

- Enregistrement d'une présentation faite en classe
- Enregistrement de la lecture d'un texte ou d'un poème
- Résumé d'un film, d'un livre, d'une émission de télévision
- Extrait d'un journal qui décrit des expériences vécues en français
- Conversation avec un étudiant qui est dans un de vos cours
- Liste de livres lus avec le nouveau vocabulaire et les expressions intéressantes
- Dictionnaire avec des mots et expressions en contexte
- Ébauche et copie finale d'un travail avec analyse des changements

Comment j'ai vécu mon plan d'action

Ce document devrait prendre la forme d'un bref narratif (environ deux pages) dans lequel vous faites un retour en arrière sur votre plan d'action. En particulier, vous pourriez y discuter comment vous avez vécu votre plan d'action et dans quelle mesure vous avez atteint les objectifs que vous vous étiez fixés.

Les questions suivantes pourraient vous aider à compléter ce document :

- Quelles étaient les faiblesses identifiées dans mon plan d'action ?
- Qu'ai-je fait pour combler ces faiblesses ou lacunes ?
- Qu'est-ce qui a « bien marché » ? Qu'est-ce qui a « moins bien marché » ?
- Qu'est-ce que j'aurais pu faire différemment ?
- Dans quelle mesure suis-je parvenu à atteindre mes objectifs ?
- Comment est-ce que je me sens par rapport à mon progrès ?
- Où est-ce que j'en suis maintenant dans mon développement langagier ?
- Que me faut-il faire maintenant pour continuer à progresser ?

Vous pourriez conclure ce document en réfléchissant sur ce que vous tirez de votre expérience avec le portfolio langagier. Vous pourriez, entre autres, décrire comment ce portfolio vous a permis de devenir plus conscient de votre apprentissage, de le prendre en charge, et de développer ainsi votre autonomie en tant qu'apprenant langagier. Ce dernier document que vous devez inclure dans votre portfolio pourrait se révéler fort utile dans le développement de votre prochain plan d'action.

Conclusion

L'élaboration d'un portfolio langagier demande un effort de travail particulièrement important. Il est donc essentiel que, tout au long de l'année, les personnes qui s'engagent dans un tel effort soient soutenues. Dans notre cas, six semaines après avoir lancé le projet, nous avons organisé une rencontre avec les étudiants de première année afin de répondre à leurs questions et de calmer certaines de leurs inquiétudes. La plupart de leurs questions portaient sur la nature exacte des documents à inclure. En mars, soit environ un mois avant la date de remise des portfolios, nous avons organisé un atelier de travail qui a permis aux étudiants de partager et de finaliser le choix de documents qu'ils voulaient inclure dans leur portfolio. Il nous a paru particulièrement important d'insister pour que les apprenants en arrivent à faire le lien entre leur plan d'action et leur choix des documents. Cette rencontre nous a également permis de clarifier la teneur de la note réflexive qui doit accompagner chaque document.

Finalement, fin avril, nous avons organisé une dernière rencontre afin de permettre aux étudiants de présenter leur portfolio langagier et de célébrer leurs succès. Le but de toutes ces rencontres est de suivre et de soutenir les étudiants tout au long de leurs démarches et des quatre stages de la réalisation d'un portfolio : la frustration initiale, l'exploration, la démonstration et la célébration (selon Schultz, 2000).

À notre avis, il serait facile d'adapter le contenu d'un portfolio langagier afin de répondre aux circonstances particulières des apprenants langagiers qu'il s'agisse d'élèves de l'immersion au niveau intermédiaire ou secondaire, d'élèves en français de base ou même d'étudiants universitaires inscrits à des cours de langue ou littérature française. Comme nous l'avons précisé plus haut, il nous semble que les avantages de tels portfolios ne se limitent pas seulement aux étudiants qui apprennent le français en tant que langue seconde, mais aussi aux locuteurs natifs qui sont en voie de perfectionnement langagier.

Même si le portfolio que nous avons décrit ne constitue qu'un premier portfolio de travail, il n'en permet pas moins d'atteindre deux buts importants. D'abord, il amène l'apprenant qui le réalise à prendre conscience de son apprentissage tout en développant son autonomie. De plus, dans le cas d'étudiants en éducation, il peut servir de point d'entrée pour les initier à l'art du portfolio, puis devenir un volet important de leur portfolio professionnel (ce dernier étant une exigence dans plusieurs institutions universitaires).

Référence

Schultz, R. (2000, février). *Preparing your portfolio: A workshop for teacher candidates.* Atelier offert dans le cadre de la Conférence Westcast, Regina, SK.

Adaptation One: Portfolios for language learners

	Speaking	Writing	Listening	Reading	Language & Learning Awareness
Communicative & Experiential					
Language	●	●	●	●	●
Culture					

Notes

Grade levels and programs:	4 to 12 immersion , 11 to 12 core French
Grouping strategy:	Individual

While the use of portfolios to track writing skills is common in many first language classrooms, the focus of this adaptation is to encourage teachers and students in second language classrooms to use the portfolio to persuade students to practise *all* the language skills outside the classroom. It is easy to track improvement in student productive skills by putting samples of writing in the portfolio and by tape recording some oral work and placing the tapes in the portfolio. If they add to the tape from time to time, they can compare how their speaking skills have progressed.

Including a record of progress for the receptive skills (reading and listening) is more challenging. The teacher can encourage the students to make a commitment to practise these skills and to self-assess their progress. Learners should include in their portfolios a description of the tasks completed, reflections on the difficulties encountered and the strategies they used to understand the spoken or the written word. Students could also include an artefact related to the language event: a target language movie ticket, the cover of a video, etc. If the students include book reports or summaries, their progress in reading can be monitored as they progress from easier to more difficult books or stories.

It is a good idea for the teacher to encourage the students to review and to reflect upon the contents of their portfolios so they can see just how they have improved and their need for further progress. Teachers should make explicit their criteria for evaluating the portfolios. We suggest that teachers focus not only on skill performance and quality but also on reflections on the process, strategies developed, and Language & Learning Awareness.

58

Because students are generally assessed on their portfolios and will have a record of their progress (or lack of it), it is hoped that learners may become more motivated to seek outside-of-classroom opportunities for speaking, reading, writing, or listening to the target language. If teachers note in their portfolios the occasions when they were able to speak the target language outside of the classroom and share this with the students, they may be able to motivate their students to find the same or similar situations in their locality. Encouraging students to find e-pals or pen pals will help in the development of their reading and writing skills and help them to become more aware of their language learning.

Adaptation Two: Portfolios in non-academic programs

	Speaking	Writing	Listening	Reading	Language & Learning Awareness
Communicative & Experiential					
Language	○	●			●
Culture					

Notes

Grade levels and programs:	All, including adult ESL
Grouping strategy:	Individual
Equipment required:	Audiotape

Portfolios are particularly valuable in non-academic programs that often lack formal evaluation processes. While summative testing may be quite inappropriate in programs such as community ESL, there is still a need for students to be able to recognize and assess their progress, and for teachers to have the necessary information to adjust their curriculum and teaching approach, if necessary. For students at a lower level of language skills, including adult ESL students, the portfolio can be a critical component of an ongoing self-evaluation process. Typically, the portfolio will be paired with regular one-on-one sessions with the teacher in which students complete a number of self-evaluation tasks. For those whose writing skills are very limited, simple scale measures can be adopted by which students rank their performance on a range of tasks. Adult ESL students, for example, might assess on a scale of one to ten their ability to ask directions. The portfolio holds such self-assessments and allows for progress to be tracked without the emotional element of grades with their implicit risk of failure. The portfolio is thus a gentle evaluation process that can help students to appreciate their improving language skills.

Traditionally, portfolios have been used to monitor writing skills. Students place selected pieces of their writing in a portfolio, and, from time to time throughout the year, they compare their early efforts with their later ones. Often it is the students' choice as to which pieces are saved. However, the teacher may designate specific compositions for placing in the portfolio. By revisiting the early compositions and comparing them with later ones, students and teachers can track the progress made. By revisiting submissions at different points during the year, students may wish to edit earlier submissions in hopes of improving their texts.

A portfolio can also be used to help students track their oral development. Typically, students would make a tape recording at the beginning of the year. Depending on level, they might read a passage aloud, or they might make a short impromptu speech about themselves. As the year proceeds, they review the original entry, and add material to the tape demonstrating their increasing fluency and improved pronunciation.

Exploring Reading-Writing Connections Through a Pedagogical Focus on 'Coherence'

Icy Lee

	Speaking	Writing	Listening	Reading	Language & Learning Awareness
Communicative & Experiential					
Language		●		●	●
Culture					

Notes

Grade levels and programs: 11 and 12 immersion, post-secondary FSL and ESL
Grouping strategy: Whole class
Equipment required: Optional computers (word processing)

Editors' Introduction

Because second language learners tend to focus at the word or sentence level in reading and writing, Lee finds that they may miss the importance of coherence in a paragraph or longer text. She describes the reading and writing tasks that she used in her post-secondary ESL classes to enhance the concept of coherence by moving students' attention beyond grammatical and lexical correctness to showing students how coherence functions in different types of texts. Coherence is a teachable and learnable concept if students are able to recognize and understand a number of essential elements that Lee has identified. These elements in a text include: its purpose, audience, the context of situation, its macrostructure, how information is distributed, how ideas are developed, the devices that make a text cohesive, and the linguistic devices that help produce a reader-friendly text. Through the teaching of the elements of a coherent text, Lee believes that reading and writing can be taught as integrated skills where reading is an essential element of students' composing skills, and writing helps them prepare for, respond to, and comprehend reading selections more effectively.

Research on reading and writing has demonstrated that these two skills are interconnected. Writers read and reread their own drafts in order to improve them. Readers, on the other hand, paraphrase and summarize in writing what they have read. Thus, reading and writing are 'integrally connected' (Reid, 1993, p. 64). For both readers and writers, meaning does not reside solely in the texts; instead, they engage themselves actively in the texts, interpreting and constructing meaning at the same time. Nystrand (1986) spells out the connectedness between reading and writing by explicating the roles of the readers and writers as interdependent of each other. Writers `write on the premises of the reader' (p. 46), gearing their texts towards readers' expectations. Readers, on the other hand, 'read on the premises of the writer' (p. 49), since their goals and expectations are directly influenced by those of the writers. Thus, Ferris and Hedgecock (1998) suggest that ESL instruction should include reading and writing tasks that will prepare learners for the demands of their academic disciplines.

This paper describes a range of reading-writing tasks that I tried out in a first-year university ESL classroom[1] with a view to helping students understand better the concept of coherence, which is crucial to both reading and writing. Meta-awareness of 'coherence' (i.e., explicit knowledge of 'coherence') is believed to be able to enhance the comprehension process and equip students with strategies to go about their own writing. In both reading and writing, ESL students tend to focus on word and sentence levels rather than the whole discourse (such as the organization of texts) (Bamberg, 1984; Grabe & Kaplan, 1996; Ferris & Hedgecock, 1998). The pedagogical endeavour described in this paper involves a range of reading-writing coherence awareness-raising tasks that shift students' attention away from the low level of texts and sensitize them to how coherence functions in different text types. Although the pedagogy was implemented in a Hong Kong classroom, it is believed that the pedagogical principles of coherence are applicable to similar teaching and learning contexts and possibly to other second and foreign languages.

The pedagogy is based on an understanding of coherence as a teachable and learnable concept, which embodies the six elements listed below. These elements are explained and exemplified in the following list.

1. Purpose, audience, and context of situation (Halliday & Hasan, 1976).
2. Macrostructure, that is, the overall structure of texts (Hoey, 1983; Swales, 1990; van Dijk, 1981).
3. Information distribution, that is, how information is distributed in texts (Danes, 1974; Firbas, 1975).
4. Propositional development, that is, how ideas are developed in texts (Kintsch & van Dijk, 1978; Mann & Thompson, 1992).
5. Cohesion, that is, devices that make a text cohesive (Halliday & Hasan, 1976).
6. Metadiscourse, that is, linguistic devices in texts that help writers produce reader-friendly texts (Cheng & Steffensen, 1996; Crismore, Markkanen, & Steffensen, 1993; van de Kopple, 1985).

These elements draw together text- and reader-based features of coherence, beginning with a concern with the *purpose of writing* that is governed by the *context of situation* and *audience* expectations. The purpose draws students' attention to the social aspects of writing and brings the readers' needs and expectations to the forefront of the act of writing. The framework then characterizes coherence in terms of the overall text structure, taking into account the communicative purpose, context of situation, et cetera, and how these social aspects of writing help shape the *macrostructure*. Coherence is then conceptualized in terms of the way information is distributed (i.e., given and new information) and the way the *distribution of information* in a text contributes to the development of the discourse topic. The framework also draws students' attention to the propositional content of writing, how the underlying assertions are linked and developed in order to produce coherence (i.e., *propositional development*). It then describes coherence at a more local level in terms of *cohesion*, that is, the connectedness between sentences and clausal units, such as references, conjunctions, and lexical cohesion. Finally, the framework focuses on *metadiscourse*, some linguistic materials in texts which help the readers organize, interpret, and evaluate information so as to make the texts more reader-friendly, such as logical connectors, announcements, code glosses.

For each coherence topic, I selected a range of short texts, mostly authentic and student texts, and designed some reading-writing tasks which engaged students in (a) text analysis, (b) critique, and (c) text improvement. Each coherence concept was explained both when the tasks were discussed and in the handouts that I prepared. Some of the tasks that I designed for each coherence topic are illustrated below:

1. Purpose, audience and context of situation
I asked students to read a text and analyze its purpose, its intended audience, and the context in which the text might appear. This could sensitize students to important issues such as reader expectations and the fact that writers adapt their writing (including style and register) to their specific audience. Students were also asked to read some extracts of student texts, identify the purpose, audience, and context, and rewrite the texts to improve the clarity of these elements.

2. Macrostructure
Students were asked to read jumbled texts and rearrange the order so that the texts would make sense in terms of their overall structure. Students also read some texts with problematic macrostructure and worked in small groups to improve the texts.

3. Information distribution
Students read two versions of the same text with the given and new information inverted in the doctored version. They discussed the readability of the texts and revised the information distribution of the doctored version to make the text more coherent.

4. Propositional development

Students read texts with parts of sentences blanked out and completed the missing parts by paying specific attention to the development of the propositions. They also read some texts with illogical information or with missing illustrations or exemplification and worked in small groups to improve the texts.

5. Cohesion

Students learned about different kinds of cohesion (see Halliday & Hasan, 1976) and analyzed the cohesive devices used in texts. They also read some student texts and improved the use of cohesion in them.

6. Metadiscourse

Students learned about different types of metadiscourse (see Crismore, Markkanen, & Steffensen, 1993) and analyzed the use of metadiscourse in authentic texts. They also read student texts with overuse or underuse of metadiscourse, evaluated the effectiveness of the texts, and improved the use of metadiscourse.

This pedagogical framework is versatile because it can be exploited to sensitize students to the genre-specific nature of coherence, that is, how the various elements of coherence may vary with different text types or in different disciplines. For instance, the macrostructure of a research article would be different from that of a course textbook, and the use of metadiscourse would differ in informative and in persuasive writing.

To conclude, reading and writing can be and should be taught as integrated skills. Through a pedagogical focus on 'coherence,' the connections between reading and writing are demonstrated, with 'reading' being seen as `an essential and positive contributor to ESL students' emerging composing skills' (Ferris & Hedgecock, 1998, p. 42) and 'writing' being used to 'help students prepare for, respond to, and comprehend reading selections more effectively' (p. 43).

Note

1   The students, between 19 and 20 years of age, completed Form 7 (i.e., Grade 13) and passed the subject Use of English (a pass is estimated to be equivalent to TOEFL 500–550 or above) at the Hong Kong Advanced Level Examination (a university entrance examination).

References

Bamberg, B. (1984). Assessing coherence: A reanalysis of essays written for the National Assessment of Education Progress. *Research in the Teaching of English, 18*(3), 305–319.

Cheng, X., & Steffensen, M.S. (1996). Metadiscourse: A technique for improving student writing. *Research in the Teaching of English, 30*(2), 149–181.

Crismore, A., Markkanen, R., & Steffensen, M.S. (1993). Metadiscourse in persuasive writing: A study of texts written by American and Finnish university students. *Written Communication, 10*(1), 39–71.

Danes, F. (1974). Functional sentence perspective and the organisation of text. In F. Danes (Ed.), *Papers on functional sentence perspective* (pp. 106–128). The Hague: Mouton.

65

Ferris, D., & Hedgecock, J.S. (1998). *Teaching ESL composition: Purpose, process, and practice*. Mahwah, NJ: Lawrence Erlbaum.

Firbas, J. (1975). Some aspects of the Czechoslovak approach to problems of functional sentence perspective. In F. Danes (Ed.), *Papers on functional sentence perspective* (pp. 11–37). The Hague: Mouton.

Grabe, W., & Kaplan, R.B. (1996). *Theory and practice of writing*. London: Longman.

Halliday, M.A.K., & Hasan, R. (1976). *Cohesion in English*. London: Longman.

Hoey, M. (1983). *On the surface of discourse*. London: George Allen and Unwin.

Kintsch, W. , & van Dijk, T.A. (1978). Toward a model of text comprehension and production. *Psychological Review, 85*, 363–394.

Mann, W.C., & Thompson, S.A. (1992). Rhetorical structure theory and text analysis. In W.C. Mann and S.A. Thompson (Eds.), *Discourse description: Diverse linguistic analyses of a fund-raising text* (pp. 39–78). Amsterdam: John Benjamins.

Nystrand, M. (1986). *The structure of written communication: Studies in reciprocity between writers and readers*. London: Academic Press.

Reid, J.M. (1993). *Teaching ESL writing*. Englewood Cliffs, NJ: Prentice Hall Regents.

Swales, J.M. (1990). *Genre analysis: English in academic and research settings*. Cambridge: Cambridge University Press.

Vande Kopple, W.J. (1985). Some exploratory discourse on metadiscourse. *College Composition and Communication, 36*, 82–93.

Van Dijk, T.A. (1981). *Studies in the pragmatics of discourse*. The Hague: Mouton.

Adaptation One: Cohesion markers in academic texts

	Speaking	Writing	Listening	Reading	Language & Learning Awareness
Communicative & Experiential					
Language		●		●	●
Culture					

Notes

Grade levels and programs: 11 and 12 immersion, post-secondary, ESL
Grouping strategy: Whole class
Preparation required: Appropriate text in target language

This adaptation, designed for advanced academic students, helps them recognize how cohesion markers function in a text. To begin this task, the teacher gives the students a short story or other suitable piece of prose that is already cohesive, and talks them through the elements that hold it together, showing them, for example, how the choice of words allows the reader to predict what is coming next, or how ideas in the text are linked to each other using temporal or logical conjunctions or other devices. In this way, relationships among parts of the text are explicitly spelled out.

With this knowledge and model text in mind, students then construct their own texts on a topic of interest. Instructor and students ensure that these texts are truly reader-friendly by the addition of certain markers such as the introduction of an advance organizer paragraph and key phrases such as 'the first argument in favour of this' so that readers get some explicit help in their comprehension of the text.

Next, the students move to an analysis of their texts and then to a process by which they focus in each draft on a different feature of cohesion or a cohesive device. They also analyze the improvement in their texts for such aspects as reader-friendliness and consider how the revisions have improved their texts.

Adaptation Two: Discovering coherence in genre writing

	Speaking	Writing	Listening	Reading	Language & Learning Awareness
Communicative & Experiential					
Language		●		●	●
Culture					

Notes

Grade levels and programs:	7 to 10 immersion, 10-12 core French, ESL
Grouping strategy:	Whole class and small groups
Preparation required:	Appropriate texts in target language

In this adaptation, we focus on the fact that each genre of writing has a recognizable structure and certain patterns of organization. For example, in a newspaper story, the first paragraph usually gives the information to answer the 'who,' 'when,' 'what,' 'how,' and 'where' questions. The rest of the story builds on and provides more details about this information. The task for students would be to look at the key features that make a genre recognizable and coherent. Examples could be letters to an advice columnist and the responses to them, recipes, instructions for assembling something like a model airplane or a piece of IKEA furniture, etc. Students try to analyze the features that distinguish each genre, for example, the sequencing or the print conventions, and then in small groups, compare their findings. Finally they generate a short example (a letter, recipe, news item, want ad, etc.) to illustrate each of the genres that they had identified. The emphases in this activity are, as indicated in the chart above, on Language/ Reading, Writing, and Language & Learning Awareness.

Écouter/visionner des messages publicitaires: démarche et propositions pédagogiques

François Lentz, Robert Campbell, Annick Carstens, Henri Péloquin et Hélène Roy

	Speaking	Writing	Listening	Reading	Language & Learning Awareness
Communicative & Experiential	○	○	●		●
Language			○		
Culture					○

Notes

Grade levels and programs:	7 to 12 immersion, 10 to 12 core French, adult
Equipment required:	Audiotape or videotape, television
Preparation required:	Taping of commercials

Editors' Introduction

We know that many students spend considerable time watching television and listening to the radio. The authors of this article give many examples of ways teachers can exploit these media in the target language to teach Listening and Language & Learning Awareness skills in the context of the Communicative & Experiential mode as indicated in the chart above. The authors provide detailed practical suggestions for teaching students how to analyze the various elements of television and radio commercials, and they give guidelines for discussions to take place both before and after seeing the commercials. If students write and act out their own commercials, as suggested by the authors, they will be able to practise their target language writing and speaking skills.

Brève mise en contexte

Cet article présente une démarche et avance des propositions pédagogiques relatives à l'écoute / au visionnement de messages publicitaires en français langue seconde. Ces propositions, initialement construites pour des élèves en immersion française de 9e année,[1] conduisent les élèves à porter sur les messages publicitaires un regard critique, par le biais d'écoutes/visionnements successifs orientés par des critères spécifiques. Plus largement, ces propositions s'inscrivent dans le champ des réflexions pédagogiques menées actuellement en immersion.

Cependant, cette démarche et ces propositions sont susceptibles d'être utilisées dans un contexte plus large que celui qui a présidé à leur élaboration ; c'est ainsi qu'elles pourraient être mises en œuvre, avec d'éventuels ajustements, auprès d'un public d'apprenants de français langue seconde, étudiants en français de base, ou adultes au niveau universitaire. C'est dans une telle perspective qu'elles sont ici offertes.

Ces propositions, enfin, sont ici avancées comme un ensemble d'activités d'apprentissage possibles portant sur l'écoute/le visionnement de messages publicitaires : une sorte de menu qui donne lieu à des choix, mais où les ingrédients sont rassemblés par une démarche, qui les oriente. Plus fondamentalement, il s'agit ici d'illustrer, d'une part le potentiel pédagogique des messages publicitaires, et d'autre part un travail pédagogique visant à habiliter l'apprenant à « reconstruire du sens ».

Le travail pédagogique proprement dit

Le travail pédagogique mené sur l'écoute/le visionnement de messages publicitaires met essentiellement l'accent sur le développement, par l'apprenant, d'une analyse critique des messages publicitaires, comme l'atteste le résultat d'apprentissage suivant : « L'[apprenant] sera capable d'analyser certains éléments d'une publicité tels que trame sonore, slogan, répétition, montage, caractérisation, humour ».[2]

Les suggestions pratiques qui suivent sont articulées selon une démarche pédagogique en trois temps (voir, parmi d'autres, Lentz, 1995) : chacun de ces trois temps est brièvement décrit ci-après.

Pré-écoute/Pré-visionnement

Pourquoi la pré-écoute/la pré-visionnement ? : pour établir une préparation et contextualisation :

1. établir des liens avec le vécu de l'apprenant;
2. mettre en place la situation de communication et l'intention de communication de l'apprenant-récepteur : écouter/visionner pour faire quelque chose;
3. mettre en évidence les connaissances (référentielles, discursives, stratégiques, etc.) que les apprenants ont à leur disposition;
4. sensibiliser l'élève au discours : éventuelles prédictions de contenu et anticipitations de la structure discursive.

Quelques suggestions :

1. Animer une discussion sur le monde de la publicité : but, fonction, besoins à satisfaire, public cible, formes, moyens, types, valeurs, etc. ; solliciter les

expériences des apprenants sur le sujet ; amener les apprenants à adopter sur la publicité un double point de vue : analyse et prise de position.

2. Proposer aux apprenants d'écouter/de visionner des messages publicitaires, hors du contexte de l'apprentissage, selon diverses modalités :
- différentes chaînes de télévision (francophones, anglo-canadiennes, ainsi qu'américaines générales et spécialisées) ;
- à un temps fixe pendant une période déterminée ;
- une même campagne sur différentes chaînes ;
- proposer également l'écoute de publicités radiophoniques.
- animer une discussion sur les diverses observations effectuées et notées lors de ces divers écoutes/visionnements.

3. Centrer la discussion sur une double composante de l'écoute/du visionne-ment de messages publicitaires :
- les caractéristiques du message publicitaire : slogan, images, textes (valeur dénotative et connotative des informations), trame sonore, montage, caractérisations, ton, etc. ;
- les stratégies mises en œuvre par les apprenants qui écoutent/visionnent un message publicitaire pour en reconstruire le sens : écoutes/visionnements successifs orientés par des focus spécifiques, prise en compte des caractéristiques du message publicitaire, mise à profit des rapports textes/ images, attention portée à la récurrence de certaines informations importantes, non-nécessité de comprendre le sens de chaque mot du message, habileté à comprendre des messages homologues dans une autre langue, anticipations du contenu et de la forme du message à partir du thème et de l'intention de celui-ci, etc.[3]

Écoute/Visionnement

Que faire pendant l'écoute/le visionnement ? La réalisation, l'exploration :

1. dégager des information générales :
- éventuelle vérification d'hypothèses
- collecte de données générales

2. dégager des informations spécifiques :
- effectuer des tâches spécifiques portant sur divers aspects du discours.

Quelques suggestions pratiques :
1. L'écoute/le visionnement de messages publicitaires gagne à s'effectuer en plusieurs étapes, chacune d'elles étant orientée par un focus spécifique, par une intention d'écoute/de visionnement particulière (voir la grille d'écoute/ de visionnement générique de messages publicitaires[4] proposée à l'appendice B) :
- *première étape* : écouter/visionner pour prendre connaissance du message en général (voir critère 1 de la grille d'écoute/de visionnement) ;

- *deuxième étape* : écouter/visionner pour
  - spécifier les éléments constitutifs de la trame sonore (voir critère 2 de la grille)
  - spécifier un slogan approprié au message (voir critère 3 de la grille)
  - spécifier les moyens utilisés pour convaincre (voir critère 4 de la grille) ;
- *troisième étape* : écouter/visionner pour
  - spécifier l'intention de communication qui correspond au message (voir critères 5 et 6 de la grille)
  - spécifier les procédés mis en œuvre (voir critère 7 de la grille) ;
- *quatrième étape* : écouter/visionner pour
  - spécifier les besoins satisfaits par le message publicitaire (voir critère 8 de la grille) – on jugera si cette quatrième étape doit s'appuyer sur une écoute/un visionnement spécifique ou si le critère 8 de la grille peut être travaillé en s'appuyant sur les trois écoutes/ visionnements précédents.

(On pourra, en fonction en particulier des publicités choisies et de l'habileté des apprenants, procéder à d'autres regroupements de critères par étape : ainsi, le critère 7 pourrait orienter à lui seul une étape.)

2. Après chaque étape, animer une discussion sur les stratégies qu'ont mises en œuvre les apprenants pour accomplir les tâches d'écoute/de visionnement, en faisant établir un lien avec la discussion intervenue sur ce point en fin de pré-écoute/pré-visionnement.

3. Variante de la modalité d'écoute/de visionnement : proposer aux apprenants, dans un premier temps, de prendre connaissance, collectivement, des messages publicitaires et de dégager ainsi le sujet de ceux-ci (ce premier temps correspond à la première étape présentée ci-dessus) ; dans un second temps, diviser la classe en trois groupes (ou en multiple de trois) et assigner respectivement à chacun d'eux, lors d'une deuxième écoute/d'un deuxième visionnement, les tâches correspondant aux deuxième, troisième et quatrième étapes indiquées ci-dessus ; chaque groupe construit une « réponse de groupe » qu'il partage ensuite avec les autres groupes ; une troisième écoute/un troisième visionnement permet aux élèves, en s'appuyant sur les informations apportées par les groupes, d'affiner la reconstruction du sens des messages publicitaires.

4. On pourra ajouter d'autres critères à la grille ou utiliser ces critères comme points de départ à un décodage plus approfondi des messages publicitaires ; exemples :
- spécifier le public cible visé ;
- relever les informations à valeur dénotative (faits présentés), à valeur connotative (émotions, sentiments évoqués par ces faits) et incitatives (qui poussent à agir) ;
- spécifier le ton du message ;
- qualifier les ressources visuelles et sonores : telles qu'utilisées, incitent-elles à agir? Sont-elles appropriées au message ?

- dégager les ressources linguistiques utilisées : qualifications et caractérisations, registres de langue (populaire, familier, courant, soutenu).

5. On animera également une discussion entre les apprenants, répartis en triades, sur l'impact qu'ont eu sur eux les messages publicitaires écoutés/visionnés : effet, ap-préciation générale, évaluation de la pertinence des moyens linguistiques, discursifs et visuels mis en place au regard de l'objectif affiché/perçu du message, etc.

6. On pourra également mettre en place des interventions portant sur des aspects spécifiques des messages publicitaires :
- Public cible : à partir de messages publicitaires, proposés aux apprenants ou identifiés par eux, faire recomposer, en dyades, le message publicitaire en fonction d'un autre public cible ;
- Rapports texte/images : proposer aux apprenants d'écouter/de visionner des messages publicitaires, d'une part en supprimant le son, d'autre part sans regarder les images, pour préciser les rapports texte/images :
  - le texte complète l'image : l'un et l'autre sont nécessaires à la compréhension du message ;
  - le texte et les images se répètent : les images, comme le texte, suffisent à faire comprendre le message ;
  - les images sont plus importantes que le texte : le texte, écouté sans regarder les images, ne porte pas le message ;
  - le texte est plus important que les images : les images, muettes, ne suffisent pas à faire comprendre le message ;
  - faire commenter ces quatre rapports texte/images en fonction des messages publicitaires retenus.
- Vocabulaire à valeur positive (souligne les qualités du produit ou du service) et à valeur connotative (évoque des émotions ou des sentiments favorables) : dans des messages publicitaires, proposés aux apprenants ou identifiés par eux, faire relever les mots et expressions qui relèvent de ces deux dimensions; faire commenter les effets produits.
- Slogans et procédés linguistiques : à partir de slogans de messages publicitaires, proposés aux apprenants ou identifiés par eux, faire mettre en évidence quelques procédés linguistiques – par exemple, jeux de mots, allitérations et assonances, paradoxes, créations de mots – et faire commenter l'impact de ces procédés linguistiques sur la réception des messages publicitaires. Exemples de slogans publicitaires se prêtant à une analyse des procédés linguistiques :[5]
  - « En tête de file, le fil Caspa »
  - « Misez avec cœur, choisissez la marque Cartatou »
  - « Employer la peinture Sico, c'est Siconnaître! »
  - « Buvez du lait, c'est vachement bon! »
  - « La cécité, ça regarde tout le monde »
  - « La LABATT, y'a rien qui LABATT »
- Techniques cinématographiques : à partir de messages publicitaires, proposés aux apprenants ou identifiés par eux, faire dégager certaines techniques cinématographiques telles que plan et mouvement de caméra ; discuter avec

les élèves des effets de sens produits par ces techniques (par exemple : un gros plan dramatise une situation ou un objet, met en valeur certaines qualités).

Post-écoute/Post-visionnement

Pourquoi la post-écoute/le post-visionnement ? Pour effectuer l'intégration, l'élargissement :

1. Effectuer un retour sur l'intention de communication : la pratique de compréhension a-t-elle effectivement permis de faire quelque chose ?
2. Objectiver la pratique de compréhension : les étapes, les modalités et les stratégies mises en œuvre pour reconstruire le sens : les difficultés et les facteurs facilitateurs ;
3. Prolonger et élargir : d'autres pratiques de compréhension et/ou de production, des transferts à d'autres situations d'apprentissage.

Quelques suggestions pratiques :

1. Certaines activités d'apprentissage réalisées lors de la post-écoute/du post-visionnement consistent en des activités de production, qui visent à permettre aux apprenants de réinvestir le travail d'analyse de messages publicitaires mené lors de l'écoute/du visionnement ; par exemple,

- Faire créer, en triades, un produit/un service et le présenter à la classe : les critères utilisés lors de la phase d'écoute/de visionnement servent à la fois de critères de production (pour l'équipe productrice) et de critères d'évaluation (pour les autres élèves) ; cette production peut se présenter sous la forme d'un vidéoclip ; ajuster la publicité selon son lieu de diffusion : journal ou revue, radio, télévision, panneau publicitaire.
- Faire créer, en dyades, un produit/un service et le présenter en utilisant des moyens faisant appel à l'humour.
- Faire créer, en petits groupes, une campagne publicitaire visant à agir sur certains comportements dans le contexte social d'apprentissage (exemple : école) ; cette campagne se composerait de plusieurs messages publicitaires s'étalant sur une certaine durée.

2. Proposer aux apprenants, répartis en triades, de construire une grille présentant les constituants nécessaires d'un « bon » message publicitaire : élaboration et justification des constituants. Faire comparer les grilles ainsi construites, pour, par exemple, élaborer « une » grille. Celle-ci pourrait être alors utilisée pour la production de messages publicitaires, dans une perspective d'évaluation tant formative que sommative.

3. Proposer aux apprenants de porter, sur les messages publicitaires oraux, audiovisuels et écrits, un regard plus large ; exemples :

- Chercher des messages publicitaires autour d'un même thème les assembler selon un ordre à établir et les présenter.
- Comparer divers messages publicitaires portant sur un produit/service/comportement, voire le même message publicitaire, présentés selon divers modes : oral, audiovisuel et écrit.
- Analyser le corpus de messages publicitaires publiés, durant une année ou une saison, dans un même lieu (revue pour la jeunesse, revue d'informations générales, etc.).

4. Réactiver les discussions intervenues lors des phases de pré-écoute/pré-visionnement et d'écoute/de visionnement sur les stratégies mises en œuvre par les apprenants pour appréhender et décoder les messages publicitaires : écoutes/visionnements successifs orientés par des intentions de communication spécifiques, mise à profit des rapports textes/images, attention portée à la récurrence de certaines informations importantes, transferts d'habiletés développées dans une autre langue, anticipations du contenu et de la forme, etc.

5. Proposer aux apprenants d'inviter des personnes francophones travaillant dans le domaine de la promotion publicitaire et, plus largement, médiatique : préparation de la venue de telles personnes, déroulement de leur venue et suivi.

6. Mettre sur pied des discussions et des débats reliés à quelques dimensions sociales de la publicité ; par exemple, son omniprésence dans notre société (et sa quasi-absence dans certains pays), la publicité portant sur certains produits tels que le tabac et l'alcool, la publicité visant les enfants, le sexisme dans la publicité, la publicité dans les médias électroniques et la presse écrite.

Ces discussions et ces débats pourraient s'appuyer sur des enquêtes menées par les élèves au sein même du contexte social d'apprentissage, par exemple, l'école : établissement d'un questionnaire visant à sonder le point de vue du groupe choisi sur le sujet retenu, entrevue avec certaines personnes, compilation des données recueillies et présentation.

7. Dans la perspective d'un travail plus large sur les médias, proposer aux apprenants de créer collectivement une « publicampagne »[6] : choisir un sujet d'intérêt général (par exemple, tabagisme ou alcoolisme chez les jeunes) ou plus spécifiquement lié à une situation particulière (par exemple, soirée de fin d'année à l'école), identifier la clientèle visée par la campagne, déterminer les objectifs de la campagne et les moyens les plus adéquats (utiliser des médias écrits et électroniques), monter et présenter la campagne.

Notes

1 Les propositions pédagogiques avancées dans cet article renvoient au travail curriculaire mené actuellement en français langue seconde – immersion au cycle secondaire par le Bureau de l'éducation française d'Éducation et Formation professionnelle Manitoba. Pour de plus amples informations sur ce travail curriculaire, on pourra se reporter à Dufresne, Lavoie, Lentz et Wright (1997).

2 Un résultat d'apprentissage décrit les habiletés, les connaissances et les attitudes – observables et, dans la mesure du possible, mesurables – qu'un apprenant a acquises au terme d'une situation d'apprentissage. Un résultat d'apprentissage n'est donc ni un objectif ni une stratégie d'enseignement ni une norme établissant une performance attendue de la part de l'élève. Dans une telle optique, c'est l'apprenant qui est au centre du dispositif pédagogique, c'est vers lui que convergent les interventions pédagogiques.

3 Ce qu'il est convenu d'appeler la compétence stratégique constitue une dimension très importante de l'apprentissage du français langue seconde (voir, parmi bien d'autres, Cyr, 1996, 1997 ; Papen, 1993 ; Lentz, 1999).

4   Cette grille d'écoute/de visionnement de messages publicitaires est adaptée de celle
     présentée dans l'ensemble didactique *Solstice* (1996, p. 303) ; elle s'inspire également
     d'autres informations sur les messages publicitaires présentées dans cet ensemble aux
     pages 348–352. L'autorisation en a été accordée par l'éditeur.
5   Ces slogans sont extraits de *J'y pense donc j'en parle* (1986, pp. 8–11).
6   D'après une activitée présentée dans l'unité « Flashmédia » de la ressource *En Direct 2*
     (1995, p. 186).

Références

Cyr, P. (1996). *Le point sur les stratégies d'apprentissage d'une langue seconde.* Anjou :
     Les Éditions CEC
Cyr, P. (1997). Les stratégies d'apprentissage d'une langue seconde. *Le Journal de
     l'Immersion Journal*, 21(1), 27–32.
Dufresne, J., Lavoie, J., Lentz, F., et Wright, I. (1997). Une vision commune de
     l'apprentissage du français en immersion pour l'Ouest et le Nord canadiens.
     Le Journal de l'Immersion Journal, 20(2), 15–22.
En direct 2. (1995). Toronto : Prentice Hall Canada.
J'y pense donc j'en parle. (1986). Toronto : Holt, Rinehart and Winston.
Lentz, F. (1995). La démarche à trois temps en compréhension et en production de
     discours : de quelques implications pédagogiques sur l'apprentissage et
     l'enseignement. *Le Journal de l'Immersion Journal*, 19 (1), 10–15.
Lentz, F. (1999). Des résultats d'apprentissage en compétence stratégique. *Le
     Journal de l'Immersion Journal*, 22 (1), 11–15.
Papen, R. (1993). Le rôle des stratégies d'apprentissage dans le processus
     d'appropriation d'une langue seconde. *La Revue de l'AQEFLS*, 14 : (2–3), 11–26.
Solstices [ensemble didactique]. (1996). Moncton : Éditions d'Acadie.

Appendice A

Ressources d'apprentissage possibles
On trouvera une section consacrée au message publicitaire – y compris une
vidéocassette présentant des messages publicitaires – dans l'ensemble didactique
Solstice (Éditions d'Acadie, 1996).

Autres ressources d'apprentissage :
*   les chaînes de télévision francophones (consulter leur site Web)
*   la série de 26 émissions *Fous de la pub* (Société de radio-télévision du Québec,
    1991/1992) – chacune de ces émissions a une durée de 26 minutes
*   les chapitres pertinents (en particulier le 6e consacré à la publicité) de
    l'ouvrage *Médias à la une* (Éditions de la Chenelière, 1994), ouvrage
    accompagné d'un *Guide d'enseignement*
*   les chapitres pertinents – en particulier la section consacrée à la publicité – de
    l'ouvrage *La compétence médiatique* (Ministère de l'Éducation de l'Ontario et
    Éducation et Formation professionnelle Manitoba/Bureau de l'éducation
    française, 1989, 1995)
*   la série *Vers une compétence médiatique*, qui comprend quatre volets : *Du
    communiqué à la une, La voix des ondes, Écrire avec la lumière, Plein d'images en*

    plan ainsi qu'un *Guide pédagogique* (Centre franco-ontarien de ressources pédagogiques, 1994, 1995)

- les activités pertinentes de *A Touch of... Class! Practical Teaching Tips for Second Language Teachers at the Secondary Level (3rd Collection)* (La Revue canadienne des langues vivantes, 1994)
- Le *Journal de l'Immersion Journal, 13*(3), mai 1990, numéro spécial intitulé « La compétence médiatique », *19*(3), juin 1996, numéro spécial intitulé « L'informatique et les compétences médiatiques en FLS »

Appendice B

Grille d'écoute/de visionnement générique de messages publicitaires

Critères	Messages publicitaires 1 2 3 n
Le sujet du message publicitaire	
Les éléments de la trame sonore : • musique • narration, dialogues • chanson (ou air fredonné) • bruitage, effets sonores • autre (à préciser)	
Le slogan approprié au message : • slogan... • slogan... • slogan... • autre slogan...	
Les moyens utilisés pour convaincre : • usage de slogan • témoignage d'une personne crédible ou d'un spécialiste • référence à des personnalités connues • forme humour • autre (à préciser)	
L'intention de communication qui correspond au message : • vendre un produit • accroître la notoriété d'une marque • sensibiliser le public à une cause • faire adopter un comportement ou une idée • promouvoir un service • autre (à préciser)	

L'objectif visé par le message est • commercial • culturel • social • autre (à préciser)				
Critères	Messages publicitaires			
	1	2	3	n
Les procédés mis en œuvre : • argumentation (présenter des arguments) • description (décrire les caractéristiques) • narration (raconter une histoire) • évocation (créer une atmosphère) • humour ou fantaisie (chercher l'adhésion par le biais de procédés humoristiques ou fantaisistes)				
Les besoins satisfaits par le message : • boire et manger • affection • confort • sécurité • désir de savoir, d'apprendre • bien-être • divertissement • sentiment d'appartenance • autre (à préciser)				

79

Adaptation One: Looking critically at commercials

	Speaking	Writing	Listening	Reading	Language & Learning Awareness
Communicative & Experiential	●	○	●	●	
Language					●
Culture					○

Notes

Grade levels and programs:	7 to 12 immersion, 11 and 12 core French, advanced adult ESL
Grouping strategy:	Small groups
Equipment required:	Audiotape or videotape, television
Preparation required:	Taping of commercials

While the authors of this article have suggested many activities, in this adaptation we focus on points 4, 5, and 6 in the section 'Quelques suggestions pratiques' in the article (see pages 73 & 74). These suggestions emphasize a critical media perspective most suitable for advanced students. For this activity, the teacher or students tape a number of television or radio commercials in the target language that are aimed primarily at the age group of the students. Advertisements for pizza would be an example that is targeted at teenaged students. After listening to the tapes (a number of times, if necessary), students discuss in groups and write (individually or as a group) about what they like or do not like about the advertisements, why they have these feelings, and what effect the commercials may have on consumers (for example, do they feel manipulated?). Their discussions can lead to a broader consideration, oral and/or written, of the role of advertising in our society, its benefits, and its downsides.

Adaptation Two: A critical comparison of print advertisements

	Speaking	Writing	Listening	Reading	Language & Learning Awareness
Communicative & Experiential	○			●	
Language					●
Culture					●

Notes

Grade levels and programs:	11 and 12 immersion and core French, postsecondary, adult
Grouping strategy:	Small groups
Equipment required:	Print advertisements from magazines or newspapers
Preparation required:	Selection of advertisements for the same product in L1 and in the target language

This adaptation focuses on reading and the critical analysis of print advertisements found in magazines or newspapers. As a pre-activity, students might discuss their favourite advertisements, either on television or from magazines or newspapers. In addition, the teacher might ask students to predict whether they think print advertisements for the same product will be the same or different in their first language compared to the target language. Following this preparation designed to activate the learners' prior knowledge, students work in small groups of four to five. Using print advertisements for the same product in both the target and first languages, students analyze the similarities and the differences between the two versions, confirm their predictions made during the pre-activity, and try to decide why the similarities and differences exist. Why, for example, did the developers of the advertisements not use a direct translation from either the English or the French? Why do the advertisers think that using the same situations and direct translations would not sell their products in the two cultures? Moreover, students note any slang or non-standard language used by the marketers in each language. Following this analysis, the groups report their findings either orally or in writing in the target language.

Writing to Think: Activities for Teaching Literature in a Second or Foreign Language

Elizabeth M. Knutson

	Speaking	Writing	Listening	Reading	Language & Learning Awareness
Communicative & Experiential	○	●	○		
Language					○
Culture					

Notes

Grade levels and programs: 10 to 12 immersion or core French, post secondary, adult ESL

Grouping strategy: Individual and small groups

Editors' Introduction

Knutson suggests a wide range of activities for use with secondary or post-secondary level students to help them improve their critical thinking and writing skills by using the study of literature as a starting point. We have indicated this focus with a principal emphasis in the Communicative & Experiential/Writing box. As many of Knutson's activities involve group work, possibilities also exist for students to develop their listening and speaking skills. Some of the suggested activities encourage students to become conscious of their language learning strategies, hence the subsidiary emphasis under Language/Language & Learning Awareness.

For many years now, the teaching of writing as a process has been a dominant paradigm in the field of English composition studies. Many of the approaches advocated by process theorists can be applied successfully to the teaching of literature in a second or foreign language at the secondary and university levels; expressivist approaches are particularly applicable to writing in a second or foreign language because of their emphasis on generating ideas and on freedom of form. While writing per se is not the focus of a literature course, writing can be used effectively not only as a vehicle for response to texts but also, and less conventionally, as a way to stimulate interest in a text, prompt the exploration and generation of ideas, and focus students' thoughts prior to discussion. Because writing provides time to think, it can also contribute to increased class participation.

Theoretical background

Peter Elbow and others who espouse an expressivist approach have argued that reading has traditionally held a privileged place in the literature classroom, while writing has played a secondary role. Most frequently writing has taken place after reading to help interpret, explain, or make comparisons between texts, reflecting the principle that input should take precedence over, and chronologically precede, output (Elbow, 1993, pp. 10–11; Zamel, 1992, p. 468). However, writing can be viewed, to the contrary, as a means to discover and explore ideas. Expressivists encourage classroom activities, such as freewriting, that promote writing fluency and allow students 'to think without the constraints of audience, register, or convention' (Blau, 1991, p. 290). Writing of this nature resembles inner speech, or conversation with oneself, and its purpose is to generate rather than to transmit meaning and knowledge.

In the foreign or second language literature classroom, writing can facilitate the reading process by helping students to formulate questions, explore interpretations, and begin to articulate what they don't understand. Expressive writing, because of its close resemblance to speech, is an accessible form of writing for most second or foreign language literature students. In addition, writing as a form of planned speech can be particularly useful for students who have difficulty expressing their ideas spontaneously when speaking in the target language. A few minutes of writing prior to discussion allows students a much-needed opportunity to reflect and to articulate a few thoughts that they can then contribute to whole group conversation.

In-class writing activities

A number of very brief in-class writing tasks in the target language can be assigned to facilitate thinking and discussion about any text under study.

List writing

List writing is a form of brainstorming on paper, a few minutes' work that can be used as the basis for longer writing pieces or for discussion. For example, when I teach Le Père Goriot, I generally ask students to write a list of memorable scenes or episodes in the novel. Comparing students' lists in small group or whole group discussion leads to a consideration of similarities and differences: which episodes are essential to a summary of the text, which are not, and why? Or, after reading *Madame Bovary* and before viewing a film adaptation of the novel, I ask students which scenes they would definitely include in a film version and which scenes they would consider dispensable (Donaldson-Evans, 1995, pp. 116–117). Other lists relating to *Madame Bovary* might include dominant imagery (horses, water, window views), symbolic objects (wedding cake, bridal bouquet, cigar box, riding crop), or themes (failure and inadequacy, escape, blindness and vision, appetite, food, and digestion).

Focused freewrites

The focused freewrite is a versatile in-class exercise in which students write for several minutes without pausing in order to produce a paragraph or two of text. A time limit is given (3–5 minutes, for example), and students are directed to write spontaneously, without planning, revising, or erasing. Freewrites are enjoyable precisely because they allow for a free flow of thought without any particular organization. An added benefit is that each student, having invested time in the effort, not only has something to say, but has a certain stake in the discussion that follows. I discovered the value of this kind of writing when teaching *Madame Bovary.* Prior to viewing the death scene in a film version, I asked a student to read aloud the passage in which Emma Bovary looks at herself in the mirror and hears the blind beggar sing. Next, I instructed the class to reflect on the significance of the mirror scene and the beggar as we watched the end of the movie. Students then spent five to seven minutes writing down their thoughts, after which they turned their papers in and spoke about their reactions. The discussion moved at a good pace, with many hands going up. I believe that the success of this simple sequence of activities was due, to a large extent, to the fact that students were able to think through the question in and by writing. After class, I read the freewrites and underlined one or more thoughts in each one that struck me as interesting in some way. At the beginning of the following class session, I read aloud the phrases or statements I had underlined. The uptake of student input that this kind of written exercise affords is an effective way to bring all student voices into classroom discussion (Dysthe, 1996, p. 409).

Writing pauses

A few minutes of silent writing can function as a means of focusing discussion at the beginning of class, or as a short thinking pause if discussion breaks down in the middle of class (Fulwiler, 1987, pp. 17–19). Students simply respond in writing to a question, which can originate from either the instructor or a student. The instructor asks a few students to read aloud or speak from what they've written, or students use their notes to continue discussion in small groups. In this way, student texts become the springboard for further thought and talk (Dysthe, 1996, pp. 417–418). Alternatively, at the end of class, students can take a few minutes to write down an idea of interest to them that emerged from class discussion. The instructor can collect these notes or not, as she desires; it is interesting to do so at least occasionally, for they afford valuable access to the thoughts of each student. Students, for their part, usually want to know beforehand whether what they write will be collected, and it is appropriate to give them this information.

84

Written conversational chains
In this activity (Pradl, 1996, pp. 110–117), students write a short response or reaction to a text and pass it along to the next student, who then writes in the margins his or her response to the first student's thoughts, elaborating, questioning, contradicting, agreeing, and so on, until the circle ends. This kind of writing provides solitary space for thought but also connects students and opens venues for discussion after the chain is complete.

Note-taking
The traditional activity of note-taking can be used in a non-traditional way: to help students think while listening. The instructor can suggest a particular focus; for example, students can be directed to take notes on any part of the class discussion that relates to narrative structure, to imagery, or to a particular theme or character. As a more open-ended task, students can take notes on an issue that is of interest to them. The instructor states that he'll be collecting the notes at the end of class. Before the notes are collected, each student exchanges papers with a classmate, who elaborates or comments on them in some way.

Out-of-class writing activities
A number of longer informal writing tasks can be assigned as homework.

Pre-reading exploratory papers
Short writing assignments can serve to introduce thematic or formal concepts *prior to* reading. In a survey course on the French novel or in a seminar on a particular kind of novel (for example, the French 'new novel' of the 1950s), generic questions to which students can respond in writing might include 'How would you define a novel?' 'How are literary narratives different from other kinds of fiction?' 'What makes a narrative interesting or compelling?' 'What makes a novel easy or hard to read?' 'What is the role of description in narrative?' 'What works *for* narrative, and what works *against* it?' 'What are the functions of dialogue?' Questions of this nature help the instructor learn what students already know and think about novelistic structures (Reagan, 1994, p. 85) and, at the same time, alert students to a frame of reference for the reading to follow. More specific questions can be asked as preparation for the reading of a particular text. For example, before assigning the reading of *Tristan et Iseut*, I ask students to write their own definition of romantic love, and we spend time during the first class, before my introduction to the text itself, exchanging definitions and finding common elements among them. Examples of other possible topics are the definition of a hero for *La Chanson de Roland*, women and marriage for Molière's *L'École des femmes*, the potential conflict between passion and social obligations for Madame de Lafayette's *La Princesse de Clèves*, or the nature of happiness for Rousseau's *Rêveries du promeneur solitaire*.

Reading journals
Out-of-class journals are a form of private conversation between student and instructor. In French literature classes, I require students to write one entry of continuous prose in their journal each time they read 20 to 30 pages of text. I

instruct them to use the journal to ask questions, note down story elements they don't understand, interpret the story or character motivations, anticipate what will happen next, or organize thoughts for a paper topic. On occasion I ask students to read passages from their journals to one another in pairs as a prelude to whole group discussion. I collect the entries at the end of each class session, read them, respond in the margins to what students have written, and return the journals at the following session. Yet another option is to have students exchange journal entries, or photocopy selected journal entries and distribute them among classmates (Fulwiler, 1987, p. 25). The student readers can be asked to write in the margins their responses to the ideas expressed.

Students for whom journal writing is a new task, or who feel little affinity for the task, need considerable guidance with respect to the purpose and possibilities of the exercise. One way to provide guidance is to assign journal writing regularly as an in-class activity, so that students understand exactly what to do and really acquire the habit of undistracted silent writing (Fulwiler, 1987, p. 15). Once they are comfortable with the activity, they can go on to write journal entries at home.

Writing in the margins

A very simple but effective way to assure entry into classroom discussion and retention of reading is to ask students to write as they read by highlighting passages in the text and commenting in the margins or on a separate piece of paper. If each student comes to class having thought about at least one passage, there is ample material for exchange of ideas in classroom talk. I may also ask students to select one passage from their reading – the most difficult passage, the most interesting or compelling, the passage that best conveys a message or contributes to a theme, for example – and write a paragraph explaining their selection.

On-line newsgroups

An on-line newsgroup or electronic message board provides a means for students to generate questions or try out ideas as they read assignments and get responses from classmates. The instructor can initiate talk by asking questions or by inviting students to write a list of some kind. Students can engage in collective quote gathering, looking through a text to find passages or quotes that support an argument or relate to a system of imagery. The newsgroup can be a forum for exploring and refining paper topics, or it can be used for more creative writing tasks such as imitation or parody of an author's style, rewriting an ending, or retelling story events from a different point of view. Students can easily print out these messages, collecting them in a portfolio and possibly saving them for use in a longer writing piece.

Responding to student writing

Research on error correction in both first and second language writing underscores the need for teachers to respond first and foremost to the meaning and substance of students' writing, and only secondarily to the form (Dvorak, 1986, p. 152; see also Semke, 1984; Barnett, 1989). In the case of exploratory writing, it is not necessary to assign grades, and it would be counterproductive to focus on correction of form. Comments on students' ideas, on the other hand, are always an appropriate form of feedback.

Most instructors would probably agree that reading final writing products – end-of-term essays, for example – is real work. By contrast, 'reading ... exploratory writing is like eating candy' (Wallace, 1994, p. 37). When I read a student's writing exclusively for meaning and respond to ideas rather than to surface text, the experience of reading is extremely enjoyable. I find that, upon returning from class, reading student journals or newsgroup comments is the first thing I want to do, rather than the last. Importantly, too, when a task is limited and focused, as most short writing tasks are, the chances the student writer will succeed – and by that I mean say something interesting – are greater.

Elbow (1993) has pointed out that 'whereas we usually have a spectrum of reading from high stakes to low stakes, most teachers fall unthinkingly into the habit of treating all writing as obligatory, high stakes work' (p. 19). He suggests assigning informal writing pieces that we collect and comment upon but do not grade, other pieces that we do not collect at all, and still others that are optional rather than required (pp. 19–20). Interestingly, he also outlines an analogous spectrum of instructor response to student writing, ranging from no response (lowest stakes) to 'critical response, diagnosis, advice (highest stakes)' (1997, p. 10). One of the more interesting aspects of reading informal student writing, such as journal entries, is that it is more natural to respond with parallel observations in the first person (e.g., 'I interpreted this passage in a similar way' or 'This makes me think of another passage ...'), than with the evaluative comments that often characterize the reading of formal essays (e.g., 'good introduction,' 'weak argument,' 'give more examples here'). First person responses reveal how the instructor reads both the journal itself and the literary text that is the subject of the journal. In this sense, they actually model the instructor's reading processes for the student.

Conclusion

The writing activities I have outlined are informal, sometimes fragmentary pieces that function to promote critical reflection, writing fluency, and successful classroom interaction. 'Writing to think' activities offer a number of advantages for both instructors and students. Freewrites and other short writing pieces can create interest in a text and facilitate reading comprehension by framing the reading in a particular way and activating background knowledge about the text topic. Writing can improve the quality and pace of classroom discussion by providing time to think. From a pragmatic standpoint, writing also provides variety in classroom interaction. Alternating between writing and speaking breaks up the class period and provides a welcome combination of private and public time. Frequent writing pieces promote writing fluency in the second or foreign language and afford the instructor access to what *all* students think, not just the most vocal in a group. The questions and comments students write in journals and other informal texts provide valuable, immediate feedback to the instructor on a regular basis and can be used to guide the instructor's course preparation. Lastly, and perhaps most interestingly, exploratory, informal writing is pleasurable – for the student, who records thoughts in an unconstrained, 'low stakes' manner and for the instructor, who is free to respond to the content of what students have to say.

References

Barnett, M.A. (1989). Writing as a process. *French Review, 63*, 31–44.

Blau, S. (1991). Thinking and the liberation of attention: The uses of free and invisible writing. In P. Belanoff, P. Elbow, & S.I. Fontaine (Eds.), *Nothing begins with N* (pp. 283–299). Carbondale, IL: Southern Illinois University Press.

Donaldson-Evans, M. (1995). Teaching *Madame Bovary* through film. In L.M. Porter & E.F. Gray (Eds.), *Approaches to teaching Flaubert's* Madame Bovary (pp. 114–121). New York: Modern Language Association.

Dvorak, T. (1986). Writing in the foreign language. In B.H. Wing (Ed.), *Listening, reading, writing: Analysis and application* (pp. 145–167). Middlebury, VT: Northeast Conference on the Teaching of Foreign Languages.

Dysthe, O. (1996). The multivoiced classroom: Interactions of writing and classroom discourse. *Written Communication, 13*, 385–425.

Elbow, P. (1993). The war between reading and writing – and how to end it. *Rhetoric Review, 12*, 5–24.

Elbow, P. (1997). High stakes and low stakes in assigning and responding to writing. In M.D. Sorcinelli & P. Elbow (Eds.), *Writing to learn: Strategies for assigning and responding to writing across the disciplines* (pp. 5–13). San Francisco: Jossey-Bass.

Fulwiler, T. (1987). *Teaching with writing*. Upper Montclair, NJ: Boynton/Cook.

Pradl, G.M. (1996). *Literature for democracy: Reading as a social act*. Portsmouth, NH: Boynton/Cook.

Reagan, D. (1994). The process of poetry: Rethinking literature in the composition course. In L. Tobin & T. Newkirk (Eds.), *Taking stock: The writing process movement in the 90s* (pp. 83–96). Portsmouth, NH: Boynton/Cook.

Semke, H.D. (1984). Effects of the red pen. *Foreign Language Annals, 17*, 195–202.

Wallace, M.E. (1994). How composition scholarship changed the way I ask for and respond to student writing. *Profession, 94*, 34–40.

Zamel, V. (1992). Writing one's way into reading. *TESOL Quarterly, 26*, 463–485.

Adaptation One: In-class publications

	Speaking	Writing	Listening	Reading	Language & Learning Awareness
Communicative & Experiential		●			
Language		●		○	○
Culture					

Notes

Grade levels and programs: 7 to 12 immersion, 11 and 12 core French, adult ESL
Grouping strategy: Individual and small groups
Equipment required: Optional use of computer with e-mail access
Preparation required: Suitable texts in the target language

For learners in less academic programs than those described in Knutson's article, teachers need to find predictable, accessible texts that will provide opportunities for the development of writing skills as students explore various common genres of language. Older learners might enjoy looking through target language items such as cookbooks (depending on students' interests), newspapers, shopping flyers, or travel guides. These everyday texts can lead to an in-class publication to which all students contribute. After browsing through a few cookbooks or other specialized texts to get a sense of the genre, learners begin by working in groups to list possible sections for a book they plan to write and possible material to fit into each section. They might try Knutson's idea of a 'focused free-write' (see page 84) to rough out the first draft of a favourite home recipe or other item that would then be revised or elaborated via a 'written conversational chain' (see page 85). 'Writing in the margins' (see page 86) would allow them to comment on each other's writing, and suggest possible variations or additions. The 'on-line news group' (see page 86) would make a wonderful forum through which the finished product could be shared. If facilities allow and if the students have produced a cookbook, trying out some of the recipes would be a good experiential activity.

Adaptation Two: Dialogue journals for beginners

	Speaking	Writing	Listening	Reading	Language & Learning Awareness
Communicative & Experiential		●		○	
Language		○			
Culture					

Notes

Grade levels and programs:	4 to 6 core French, 1 to 3 immersion, adult ESL
Grouping strategy:	Individual
Equipment required:	Possible use of computer with e-mail access

Students with limited language competency may have difficulty with literature in the target language, but can nevertheless benefit from writing activities in a communicative and experiential context similar to those suggested by Knutson.

Dialogue journals provide beginning writers with a safe place in which to try out their expressive skills. Younger children in the primary and junior grades, or beginners of any age, can use them. Each student is given a journal book in which they are required to write at least one sentence. For those who do not know where to begin on the first day, the teacher may offer a prompt such as 'What did you do on the weekend?' Later the teacher writes a short response to each entry. To maintain a sense of writing as real communication, it is important that this be done outside of class. Dialogue journals are not usually corrected because the focus is on encouraging students to recognize that they can communicate through print. Instead, many teachers try to incorporate an example of the correct form in their responses, as in the example below:

Student: My aunt come me see.

Teacher: That's nice that your aunt came to see you. Where does she live? Tell me about her.

Other teachers prefer to focus on getting the dialogue going by sharing information about themselves, such as: 'I have a favourite aunt who lives in Edmonton.' Students enjoy the sense that they are having a private conversation with the teacher and they soon begin to write more lengthy entries. Dialogue journals can also be done successfully as an on-line exchange if the students have access to the necessary technology.

Replying to each comment in a student's journal can be extremely time-consuming, especially for teachers who have many students. In such cases, students can make comments in each other's journals with occasional teacher review.

Le journal littéraire : une découverte

Christine Pelletier

	Speaking	Writing	Listening	Reading	Language & Learning Awareness
Communicative & Experiential		●		●	○
Language					
Culture					○

Notes

Grade levels and programs: 8 to 12 immersion
Grouping strategy: Individual and in groups
Preparation required: Selection of French novels or storybooks

Introduction

Pelletier discusses a problem encountered in her French immersion classes: students rarely read books in French for pleasure. The causes of this situation may be that most of the vocabulary taught is school-related and that students do not have the example of seeing adults reading French books for pleasure. In addition, teacher-assigned texts usually reflect the teacher's preferences and timelines. To counteract these problems, Pelletier designed an action research project to encourage her immersion students to read French novels for pleasure. Students were assigned a novel, given reading time in class, and were asked to keep a 'literary journal.' In these journals, the students would continuously record their reactions to and reflections on what they had been reading. At the end of the year, Pelletier asked students to evaluate their journals by comparing an early entry with a later one and by reflecting on what they had learned. She found from reading the journals that a number of her students had come to enjoy reading books in French.

La lecture en français : qu'est-ce que ça veut dire pour les élèves d'immersion ? D'après les recherches menées au cours des dernières années à ce sujet (Roy, 1996), les élèves lisent rarement pour le plaisir en français. Ce problème ne serait pas dû à un manque de compétence puisque des tests de lecture démontrent des habiletés satisfaisantes chez les élèves. De plus, on constate que la lecture spontanée et autonome en français est presque inexistante ; les élèves préfèrent les livres en anglais.

Comment expliquer ce problème ? Les études indiquent deux éléments importants. D'abord, tout le vocabulaire et les expressions que les élèves d'immersion apprennent sont reliés au contexte scolaire, le français n'étant présent qu'en salle de classe alors que l'anglais domine dans toute autre sphère d'activités. Ensuite, les élèves voient rarement des adultes lire pour le plaisir en français. Le français devient donc associé uniquement à l'école alors qu'on utilise l'anglais dans les loisirs et dans la « vraie vie ».

Ce malaise face à la lecture, je l'ai constaté dans ma salle de classe avec les élèves de la huitième à la douzième année. La lecture a toujours été une partie essentielle de ma vie. Même adolescente, je n'avais pas besoin d'encouragements pour lire. Je dévorais avidement toute littérature qui me passait sous la main. J'ai donc commencé à enseigner le français sans porter d'attention particulière à la lecture de romans qui m'apparaissait comme un acte naturel dont les élèves se chargeraient eux-mêmes de pleine volonté...

Au fil des années, je me suis rendue compte à quel point j'avais tort. Au début de chaque semestre je demandais aux élèves de répondre à un court questionnaire sur leur degré d'exposition spontanée à la langue française, que ce soit sous forme de lecture, d'écriture, d'écoute de la télévision ou de la radio, de conversation ou autres. Les réponses démontraient que les élèves ne faisaient que le minimum requis par les enseignants,[1] rarement plus. Évidemment, à chaque fois qu'on entreprenait la lecture d'une histoire en classe (récit, conte, nouvelle ou autres), la réaction générale s'avérait plutôt négative. Les élèves comprenaient peu le message et passaient à côté des subtilités de la langue. Suite à ces constatations et dans le but d'améliorer la compréhension et l'intérêt pour la lecture en français, je me suis mise à obliger les élèves à lire des livres de mon choix, tous à la même vitesse et dans le but de répondre aux questions qui me semblaient pertinentes. Où donc était passé cet acte naturel qui m'était si précieux ?

Ma perplexité et mon impuissance face à ce problème m'ont accompagnée jusqu'à ce que je découvre le concept de « journal littéraire ». Comme l'expliquent Kooy et Wells (1996), le journal littéraire (ou « Reading Response Log ») permet au lecteur de réagir et de réfléchir à sa lecture ; il ne se veut pas intime et privé mais plutôt personnel et public. Étant donné que chaque personne interprète un texte selon son expérience et ses connaissances propres, il n'y a pas de bonnes ou de mauvaises réponses mais des questions soulevées, des hypothèses discutées, des philosophies élaborées, et cetera. Réfléchir au contenu des romans, s'interroger sur leur signification tout en continuant à lire de façon naturelle et au rythme désiré : cela correspondait assez bien à ce que je fais moi-même en lisant ! Suite à cette découverte j'étais enthousiaste à l'idée d'essayer ce concept dans ma classe de français.

La recherche-action : une solution sur mesure pour les enseignants

À l'automne 1996, j'ai décidé de poursuivre un projet recherche-action portant sur le journal littéraire avec mes 22 élèves de onzième année (programme francophone). Le projet faisait partie d'un cours « Comète » offert par l'université Simon Fraser. Ces cours demandent aux participants d'identifier un changement pédagogique d'importance personnelle et professionnelle qu'ils aimeraient apporter à leur façon d'enseigner, de déterminer un plan d'action qui permettra d'effectuer ce changement, d'implanter et de contrôler le projet ainsi que d'évaluer l'impact du changement sur l'apprentissage des élèves. Tout au long du projet les participants sont amenés à réfléchir sur leurs valeurs et leurs croyances pédagogiques afin de préciser ce qui guide leur orientation pédagogique. Ils sont également encouragés à s'interroger sur l'impact des nouveaux comportements pédagogiques qu'ils essaient d'adopter et à déterminer l'impact de ces changements sur l'acte d'apprentissage. L'accent est mis sur le processus de réflexion professionnelle, d'analyse quotidienne et d'expérimentation.

La recherche-action m'offrait l'occasion de tenter l'expérience du journal littéraire dans un cadre universitaire structuré et supervisé. Les principaux avantages de ce genre de cours sont de permettre à l'enseignant d'apprendre à identifier ses besoins, d'établir ses objectifs de changement et de déterminer la démarche pour les atteindre. La recherche-action, grâce à la réflexion personnelle et professionnelle qu'elle génère et à son dynamisme, aide à sortir de l'enseignement statique qui consiste à répéter toujours les mêmes choses sans vouloir ou sans savoir comment s'améliorer. En fait de développement professionnel, la recherche-action est, de loin, l'expérience la plus enrichissante que j'ai vécue jusqu'à maintenant.

Le point de mire de mon projet consistait à utiliser le journal littéraire avec ma classe afin de favoriser la réflexion des élèves et de les encourager à lire en français. L'évaluation du journal s'est faite à l'aide d'une échelle de performance développée pendant l'été avec l'aide de Suzanne Simard, enseignante-bibliothécaire pour le conseil scolaire de Kamloops. Pour créer cette échelle nous avons utilisé principalement une description déjà existante du développement de la pensée critique. L'échelle devait servir de guide aux élèves afin qu'ils puissent eux-mêmes identifier leurs forces et leurs faiblesses et aussi qu'ils se fixent des objectifs d'apprentissage, c'est-à-dire qu'ils soient capables de déterminer comment s'améliorer. Établir clairement les niveaux et les critères d'évaluation en présentant l'activité du journal littéraire permettrait aux élèves de décider de leur performance. Cette échelle, on le verra plus loin, comportait plusieurs limitations qui apparurent pendant l'utilisation.

Début du projet en classe

En septembre, afin de présenter l'activité du journal littéraire, j'ai proposé aux élèves de faire la lecture d'un des deux romans suivants : *Le Petit Prince* d'Antoine de St-Exupéry et *Vendredi ou la vie sauvage* de Michel Tournier. En leur imposant ce choix, j'avais l'impression que je pourrais mieux les guider pour écrire leur journal puisque j'avais déjà lu ces deux livres et que j'en connaissais bien le contenu. Également, je voulais que les élèves se rencontrent une fois par semaine en petits groupes de trois ou quatre pour discuter de l'histoire, clarifier certaines parties plus difficiles, partager les entrées de leur journal, les comparer et identifier des façons de les améliorer. À la fin de leur discussion, d'une durée d'environ 20 minutes, chaque groupe devait avoir décidé du nombre de pages à lire avant la prochaine rencontre. Assez régulièrement, les élèves bénéficiaient de temps en classe consacré à la lecture ou à l'écriture du journal. Ils devaient écrire au moins deux entrées par semaine d'une longueur d'une demie-page à une page.

La recherche sur les habitudes de lecture des jeunes en immersion (Roy, 1996) a démontré à quel point il est important que l'enseignant serve de modèle. D'après Nancy Atwell (1987), l'enseignant, en tant que modèle, doit montrer son enthousiasme pour la lecture en parlant des livres qu'il a lus, aimés, détestés, abandonnés, et cetera. Atwell précise aussi l'importance de donner du temps en classe pour la lecture. Pendant que les élèves lisent, l'enseignant doit le faire également. Pour moi, cela apparaissait évident et dès septembre j'avais commencé à le faire. En tant que modèle et source première d'informations pour mes élèves, c'est également mon rôle de les informer des endroits où ils peuvent se procurer des livres en français et de discuter des différents auteurs susceptibles de les intéresser. De façon informelle, ou parfois par l'entremise du journal, je demandais aux élèves de me parler du type de livres qu'ils préfèrent (en anglais ou en français) et peu à peu, j'ai commencé à leur suggérer des livres que j'avais déjà lus et qui convenaient à leurs goûts et à leur personnalité. La plupart du temps le choix s'avérait judicieux et les élèves conseillés démontraient plus d'enthousiasme pour la lecture que les autres.

D'après Atwell (1987), il est naturel que chaque lecteur ait des intérêts particuliers et il est impossible qu'un livre imposé les « accroche » tous. Elle s'oppose donc catégoriquement au choix du livre par l'enseignant. Je ne peux que m'incliner devant un tel raisonnement, particulièrement si je le compare à mon expérience personnelle de lectrice. Cependant, je n'ai pas laissé le choix du premier roman aux élèves parce que je croyais qu'en lisant un livre en commun, ils pourraient ainsi partager leurs réflexions et se sécuriser face au processus d'écriture du journal. Kooy et Wells (1996) démontrent la valeur certaine de présenter un livre de classe :

> After much experimentation, I've learned that class novels are fundamental to building a community of readers, a crucial component of any response-based class. Reading a class novel is a shared experience that generates a common bond necessary for literary discussions. Students share the same points of reference and experience the response process together, learning as they go that we do not all think and feel alike when responding to literature (p. 56).

Donc, les opinions demeurent partagées à ce sujet. Pour ma part, je crois valable l'idée d'utiliser un roman de classe quand le partage des réflexions sur le contenu ou l'apprentissage d'un nouveau type d'activité (comme introduire le journal littéraire pour la première fois) sont les objectifs visés. D'ailleurs, les élèves ont pu constater que les réflexions variaient énormément d'un journal à l'autre et qu'il était important de personnaliser les entrées. En établissant eux-mêmes le nombre de pages à lire pour la prochaine rencontre, ils réalisaient un engagement avec les autres. La plupart du temps, ils exigeaient beaucoup plus que ce que j'aurais moi-même demandé. J'ai appris à leur faire confiance pour déterminer ce qu'ils peuvent faire.

Les premiers travaux d'élèves et l'évaluation critérielle

L'échelle de performance a été expliquée à toute la classe, puis j'ai montré des exemples concrets d'entrées de journal « exceptionnelles ». Les élèves devaient me remettre environ deux entrées par semaine. À mesure que je recevais leur journal, je répondais en écrivant leur note (*exceptionnel* 90 %, *très bien* 80 %, *satisfaisant* 64 % ou *qu'est-ce qui se passe ?* 55 %), des commentaires suivis d'un exemple de réponse que j'aurais moi-même écrite. À la fin du mois, je n'ai enregistré, pour leur note officielle, que les deux meilleures notes obtenues pour ne pas pénaliser les élèves en période d'apprentissage. Voici quelques exemples des premiers journaux recueillis :

Christy : C'est évident que Robinson a des visiteurs sur l'île. Selon la description, les Indiens ne sont pas des visiteurs plaisants... Le livre a plus de sens pour moi maintenant. Le vocabulaire n'est pas très difficile au moment. Je me demande la raison que les Indiens sont là ? C'est possible qu'ils vont rester là et former une sorte de colonie. Chapitre neuf : Robinson réapprend comment sourire. C'est la vérité que si tu es seule tu n'as personne pour rire avec sauf toi alors tu souris pas. Je me souviens d'un homme qui vit dans la forêt qui fait des recherches sur les loups. Il sourit pas non plus parce qu'il était seul pour une longue période de temps.

Mon commentaire : Satisfaisant (vérifie avec l'échelle pour avoir plus de détails sur ce que tu peux faire pour améliorer ta prochaine entrée). Tu résumes et tu expliques le livre. Je vois que tu comprends mais essaie de développer un aspect particulier. C'est bizarre l'idée du sourire. C'est une chose à laquelle je n'avais pas pensé. On peut perdre la faculté de sourire si on ne pratique pas nos muscles. Et c'est la même chose pour parler à voix haute. Je suis tellement habituée à être entourée de personnes que ça m'apparaît improbable que cela m'arrive. Et toi, qu'est-ce qui serait le plus difficile pour toi si tu étais seule sur une île ? Qu'est-ce qui te manquerait le plus ?

Sarah : « Les baobabs, avant de grandir, ça commence par être petit. » Cette phrase reflète bien notre société et notre pensée envers les jeunes. Il y a beaucoup d'adultes qui trouvent que parce que les enfants sont petits et savent moins qu'eux autres ils sont moins significatifs. Cette façon de penser est complètement ridicule ! On peut comparer ce que le Petit Prince avait remarqué des baobabs avec les adultes importants de notre société. Einstein, lui, a commencé par être jeune. Mozart, Bell, Colombus, Armstrong et même Hitler, eux aussi étaient jeunes. C'était pendant leur jeunesse que tous ces hommes importants ont appris comment être des adultes. La jeunesse est peut-être un des plus importants aspects de notre vie. C'est pendant la jeunesse qu'on décide si on veut pousser en grands baobabs ou en un beau sapin.

Mon commentaire : Très bien. Tu as tout à fait raison. Alors qu'est-ce qui se passe entre l'enfance et l'âge adulte ? Pourquoi les adultes oublient-ils qu'ils ont été jeunes? Comment se fait-il qu'on reconnaisse en théorie l'importance des enfants qui sont « les dirigeants de demain » mais que dans les faits notre société ne leur réserve qu'une place minime ?

Des défis : de la théorie à la pratique

Suite à ce premier essai en classe, j'ai dû réviser plusieurs aspects de mon activité. Premièrement, le concept de journal littéraire semblait totalement nouveau pour les élèves et j'ai éprouvé de la difficulté à expliquer clairement ce qu'ils devaient faire. De toute évidence, l'échelle de performance n'était pas complète ni assez détaillée puisque les critères n'étaient pas clairs. Les élèves eux-mêmes se sont plaints du fait que l'échelle ne leur donnait pas assez d'informations sur ce qu'ils devaient faire pour s'améliorer. L'échelle descriptive utilisée présentait plusieurs critères en même temps alors qu'en réalité un même élève peut se situer à différents niveaux selon le critère visé. Aussi, la classe n'était pas satisfaite des quatre niveaux correspondant aux lettres A, B, C et C-. Ils désiraient voir non pas une lettre et un pourcentage mais une lettre et une variation de pourcentage (par exemple, entre 73% et 86%). De plus, certains élèves écrivaient systématiquement une phrase ou deux répondant à chacun des critères mais sans articuler le tout d'une façon plus approfondie. J'ai donc réalisé que l'échelle devait subir des modifications pour inclure des critères sur la profondeur de la réflexion et sur la compréhension de la lecture. Suite aux commentaires des élèves, une seconde grille d'évaluation a été créée.

Deuxièmement, j'ai vite réalisé que le type d'effort intellectuel demandé ne correspondait pas à ce que les élèves sont habitués de faire en lecture. Comme mentionné précédemment, on leur demande en général de répondre à des questions relatives au contenu des livres ou des textes qu'ils lisent ou bien d'en faire un résumé, alors que le journal littéraire consiste en une réponse réfléchie liée au roman. Comment donner aux élèves des idées d'entrées pour leur journal sans leur dire directement quoi écrire ou sans imposer mes idées personnelles ? Habituer les élèves à réfléchir sur leurs lectures n'est pas une tâche facile. Plusieurs auteurs, dont Atwell (1987) et Cline (1993), semblent avoir rencontré le même problème. Au début, lorsqu'ils demandaient aux élèves d'écrire au sujet de leurs livres, ces derniers résumaient ou ne comprenaient pas exactement ce qui était attendu d'eux. Ils voulaient découvrir ce que l'enseignant désirait. Atwell, face à ce problème, écrit que l'enseignant ne doit jamais fournir la réponse. Elle propose une liste de questions ou d'idées pouvant amener les élèves à produire le type de réponses recherchées. Cline (1993) donne également vingt idées de sujets d'entrées pour les journaux littéraires, par exemple *(traduction libre)* :

- Quels étaient vos sentiments après le premier chapitre ? Au milieu du livre ? Après l'avoir fini ?
- Est-ce que ce livre vous a fait rire ? pleurer ? sourire ? Inscrivez quelques réactions.
- Y a-t-il des aspects communs entre ce livre et votre vie ? Quel personnage aimeriez-vous être ? Pourquoi ?
- Aimeriez-vous acquérir un trait de personnalité d'un des personnages du livre ? Décrivez ce trait et expliquez pourquoi vous l'aimez.
- Auriez-vous utilisé un nom différent pour l'un des personnages ? Quel nom et pourquoi ?
- Qu'est-ce qui vous fait réfléchir dans ce livre ?
- Qu'est-ce qui vous rend confus ?
- Y a t-il une idée qui vous a fait arrêter la lecture, penser ou vous poser des questions ? Identifiez l'idée et expliquez vos réactions.

- Quels sont vos passages préférés ?
- Quelles questions aimeriez-vous poser à l'auteur du livre ?
- Qu'est-ce que vous changeriez dans ce livre ?
- Que savez-vous maintenant que vous ne saviez pas avant ?
- À propos de quelles questions sur le livre aimeriez-vous obtenir des réponses?
- Qui d'autre devrait lire ce livre ? Pourquoi ?
- Qui ne devrait pas lire ce livre ? Pourquoi ?
- Aimeriez-vous lire d'autres livres du même auteur ? Pourquoi ?
- Si vous pouviez voir à l'intérieur du cœur d'un des personnages, que pourriez-vous voir ? Son âme ? Son cerveau ?
- Que pensez-vous qu'il arrivera dans l'histoire ? Pourquoi ?
- Qu'est-ce que les personnages feront 10 ans après la fin de l'histoire ?

Finalement, le désarroi persistant des élèves devant ce type d'activité m'a amenée à me questionner sur la validité des commentaires que j'écrivais pour chacune de leurs entrées. Lisaient-ils ces commentaires ? Y réfléchissaient-ils ? S'en servaient-ils comme point de départ ou de modèle pour écrire leur entrée suivante ? Est-ce que j'intervenais de la bonne façon ? J'ai posé ces questions directement aux élèves et certains m'ont répondu que les commentaires les aidaient, d'autres que non. Rien de très concluant ! Sur cette question, Swartz (1994) et Atwell (1987) proposent que l'élève adresse directement le journal à l'enseignant. Atwell appelle cela un journal de dialogue ; chaque entrée est une lettre qui commence par « Dear Ms. Atwell ... ». Ainsi les élèves sont tentés de répondre aux questions et commentaires et y voient l'occasion d'interagir plus activement avec l'enseignant.

Établir un cadre permanent

À partir du mois d'octobre, les élèves de ma classe ont eu libre choix quant au roman qu'ils désiraient lire. J'ai donc laissé tomber les rencontres en groupes puisque je ne voyais pas comment les poursuivre étant donné la disparité des livres lus. Je me suis rendue compte que je devais établir des règles mieux définies pour la lecture et l'écriture du journal. En lisant Atwell (1987, p. 156), j'ai trouvé des indications précises de règlements qu'elle utilise dans sa salle de classe pour la lecture. Ce sont les suivants :

Rules for using reading time

1. Students must read the entire period.

2. They cannot do homework or read any material for another course.

3. They must read a book (no magazines or newspaper) preferably one that tells a story.

4. They must have a book in their possession when the bell rings.

5. They may not talk or disturb others.

6. They may sit or recline wherever they'd like.

Je dois admettre que, même si ces règles apparaissent évidentes et faciles à suivre, ma classe les a toutes enfreintes les unes après les autres. Pour les encourager, Atwell donne des points aux élèves à chaque période pour qu'ils se conforment aux règles. Elle a développé un système particulier d'ateliers de lecture et d'écriture pour l'enseignement de l'anglais. Il serait difficile dans le contexte de l'immersion d'appliquer exactement le même modèle parce que nous devons réserver beaucoup de temps à l'expression orale et à la compréhension. Toutefois, son ouvrage a été pour moi une source d'inspiration sans égal et il est certainement à recommander pour quiconque s'intéresse à l'enseignement de la littérature. En plus des règles, j'ai donné des délais pour terminer les livres. Cela posait un problème car certains élèves avaient choisi un roman très court alors que d'autres s'étaient attaqués à des ouvrages plus volumineux. Évidemment, je ne voulais pas les encourager à choisir des livres plus petits et je voulais aussi éviter que les lecteurs rapides hésitent à débuter un nouveau livre, aussitôt le premier fini, pour ne pas avoir plus de travail à faire. Alors, j'ai établi un système dans lequel, peu importe le nombres de pages ou de livres lus, les élèves devaient produire un nombre fixe d'entrées de journal par semaine (généralement une seule). C'est ainsi que nous avons poursuivi jusqu'en décembre tout en utilisant la grille d'évaluation améliorée pour la correction (Tableau 1).

L'auto-évaluation des élèves

Le plus grand défi à ce point-ci concernait l'intérêt des élèves pour la lecture en français, ce qui me ramènerait à mon point de départ. Le choix des livres et leur disponibilité constituaient des problèmes, mais le cœur de la question tenait plutôt à se demander jusqu'à quel point les élèves ont le goût de lire en français et est-ce que l'activité du journal littéraire les aidait vraiment à développer ce goût ? Pour le vérifier, j'ai demandé comme exercice final que les élèves évaluent leurs propres progrès et leur expérience avec les journaux littéraires (voir Appendice A). Ils devaient comparer une entrée du début du semestre avec leur plus récente et noter leurs observations. Ensuite, je leur ai demandé de réfléchir à ce qu'ils avaient appris en faisant leur journal. J'ai été surprise par les réponses ; pour certains il apparaît clairement que les buts ont été atteints.

Chantel écrit :

> Durant l'activité du journal j'ai appris comment lire un livre en français, en comprenant en profondeur comme un livre en anglais sans penser au sens des mots, mais aux faits et idées. Maintenant je sens comme si « j'étais français écrivant comme un français » et non « un anglais écrivant comme un français » car j'utilise les expressions et les mots plus profonds, qu'avant je ne saurais pas d'en utiliser...

Janna remarque :

> Comme j'ai dit avant, mes entrées sont plus développées et plus personnelles. Je donne mes opinions et fais beaucoup de références et réflexions. Mes pensés en français ressemblent à mes pensées que j'ai en anglais. Ce que je veux dire, c'est que en anglais en faisant des journaux, je réussis des hautes notes. Si je compare mes

entrées d'anglais et de français, ils sont tous les deux structurés de la même façon. Mais en anglais c'est quand même un peu plus bon...

Est-ce que ces progrès ne touchaient que les meilleurs élèves ? Difficile à dire, mais je crois que non, puisque certains d'entre ceux qui éprouvaient plus de difficulté en français ont aussi exprimé des idées similaires. Cependant, il y a beaucoup de choses à changer, entre autres, la grille d'évaluation, encore une fois ! Suite aux commentaires des élèves, je m'interroge sur la pertinence des deux critères suivants : intérêt pour la lecture et conscience des difficultés. Comment puis-je évaluer ces deux aspects si les élèves ne les mentionnent pas directement dans leur journal ? Cela me semble bien subjectif...

Comment rendre l'évaluation du journal littéraire plus positive ?

Le semestre suivant, j'ai recommencé à utiliser le journal littéraire (avec une classe de onzième année en immersion) en apportant les changements nécessaires notés lors du premier semestre. Lire les entrées de journal des élèves constitue pour moi la partie la plus intéressante et stimulante. Ces jeunes ont des idées originales et des réflexions qui peuvent m'apprendre beaucoup sur leurs expériences, leurs valeurs, leurs philosophies. Parfois, les médias ou la société nous les dépeignent comme anonymes, sans idées (la « génération X »), mais est-ce que nous les encourageons à utiliser leur potentiel et à dépasser les limites ?

Mon but ultime, en utilisant le journal littéraire ou par d'autres moyens, est de communiquer mon amour pour la lecture et pour la langue française. L'auto-évaluation des élèves et les entrées de leur journal m'ont démontré, sans doute possible, que bien guidés les élèves peuvent aimer lire en français. Mais quel est le lien entre ce but et la note que je donnais à chaque élève pour chaque entrée de journal produite ?

L'évaluation des journaux est devenue ma préoccupation principale suite à cette expérience. Comment se sent un élève qui reçoit un 55% et « qu'est-ce qui se passe ? » comme commentaire ? Cleary-Miller (1990) remarque à quel point les commentaires ou les mauvaises notes peuvent affecter de façon permanente l'attitude des élèves face à l'écriture (ou à la lecture). Et comme le fait remarquer Guskey (1994) : « How can a teacher know, for example, how difficult a task was for students or how hard they worked to complete it ? ». Le cahier portfolio pourrait peut-être résoudre ce dilemme. Avec ce système, les élèves écriraient toutes leurs entrées dans un cahier utilisé uniquement à cette fin. Je lirais et je commenterais le journal à chaque semaine mais sans donner une note spécifique. Je demanderais également aux élèves, comme le fait Atwell (1987), d'établir eux-mêmes leurs propres objectifs de lecture à chaque semaine. À la fin du mois, ils pourraient s'évaluer eux-mêmes (par écrit ou lors d'une entrevue individuelle) en utilisant leurs objectifs et mes commentaires. La note finale ne serait donc pas un jugement rendu par l'enseignant mais une auto-évaluation de l'élève lui-même. L'écriture du journal littéraire est un processus qui se développe à mesure que l'élève lit et se familiarise avec des styles, des auteurs, des thèmes, et cetera, et l'évaluation devrait en être le reflet.

Note

1   Dans cet article, le masculin est utilisé de façon générique et englobe le féminin.

Références

Atwell, N. (1987). *In the middle : Writing, reading, and learning with adolescents.* Portsmouth (NH) : Boynton/Cook.

Cleary-Miller, L. (1990). The fragile inclination to write : Praise and criticism in the classroom. *English Journal, 79(2),* 22–28.

Cline, D.M. (1993). *Teachers are researchers : Reflection and action.* Newark (DE) : International Reading Association Publishers.

Guskey, T.R. (1994). Making the grade : What benefits students ? *Educational Leadership, 52(2),* 14–20.

Kooy, M., & Wells, J. (1996). *Reading response logs : Inviting students to explore novels, short stories, plays, poetry and more.* Markham: Pembroke Publishers.

Roy, M.R. (1996). *Reading for pleasure in immersion : Fantasy or reality?* Thèse de maîtrise inédite, Université Simon Fraser, Burnaby (C-B).

Swartz, L. (1994). Reading response journals : One teacher's research. Dans G. Wells (Réd.), *Changing schools from within : Creating communities of inquiry.* Toronto : OISE Press.

Appendice A

Auto-évaluation du journal littéraire

Veuillez répondre aux questions suivantes de la façon la plus complète possible afin de me fournir des informations pour améliorer l'activité du journal littéraire. Merci !

1. Qu'avez-vous appris en faisant cette activité ? Pouvez-vous mieux écrire en français ? Quels sont les obstacles qui nuisent ou facilitent votre expression en français ? Pensez-vous avoir amélioré votre compréhension ? Est-ce que l'utilisation du dictionnaire vous aide ? Avez-vous développé votre vocabulaire ? Pouvez-vous comparer vos habiletés en anglais et en français ?

2. Comparez une entrée de journal que vous avez faite au début du semestre avec une plus récente. Que remarquez-vous ? Y a-t-il des différences quant à la longueur ? Avez-vous réussi à développer vos idées plus en profondeur ? Est-ce que votre entrée récente est mieux structurée ?

3. Que pensez-vous de la méthode d'évaluation ? Croyez-vous que c'était juste ? Comment pourrait-on l'améliorer ?

Êtes-vous satisfait de la note obtenue ? Que devrait-on ajouter à la grille ? Croyez-vous que la grille représente bien vos apprentissages ? Pourrait-on ajouter d'autres méthodes d'évaluation (par exemple, des discussions sur les livres, des présentations orales, etc.) ?

4. Est-ce que vos habitudes de lecture ont changé ? Croyez-vous que le temps alloué en classe pour la lecture était suffisant ? Avez-vous fait des efforts pour lire à la maison ? Quel genre de livres préférez-vous ? Au cours du semestre, avez-vous découvert un nouvel auteur ou un style de livres que vous aimez particulièrement ?

TABLEAU 1
Grille d'évaluation modifiée pour le journal littéraire

	Excellent 4	Satisfaisant 3	Insatisfaisant 2	Faible 1
Clarté du message (x3) élève: /12 prof: /12	Idées exprimées de façon très claire et logique. Excellent choix de vocabulaire (précis et varié). Grammaire et structure impeccables.	Idées exprimées de façon assez claire. Grammaire et vocabulaire complexes et variés. Les différentes parties du texte sont bien reliées.	Les idées exprimées sont généralement claires. Parfois des erreurs de grammaire ou de vocabulaire rendent certaines parties floues – mais on peut quand même comprendre le sens de ta pensée.	Manque de variété et de précision du vocabulaire. Phrases simples. Erreurs fréquentes. C'est difficile à suivre.
Réactions à la lecture (x4) élève: /16 prof: /16	Références à ton expérience personnelle qui appuient ta réflexion. Détails et justifications des réactions traités en profondeur. Plusieurs aspects d'un problème sont explorés. Ton texte forme un tout qui démontre une réflexion de qualité supérieure.	Références pertinentes à ton expérience personnelle. Tu ajoutes des détails et justifies tes réactions. Plusieurs aspects d'un problème sont explorés. Tu pousses ta réflexion un peu plus en profondeur et en complexité.	Idées exprimées souvent de façon incomplète et superficielle. Réflexions manquant de détails. Tu fais preuve d'une certaine ouverture d'esprit. Les références à ton expérience personnelle n'aident pas toujours à préciser ta pensée.	Tu résumes le livre en faisant parfois référence à ton expérience personnelle mais sans approfondir ta pensée. Tu poses des questions par rapport au contenu du livre mais sans essayer d'y répondre ou d'explorer différentes possibilités.
Conscience des difficultés de la lecture (x2) élève: /8 prof: /8	Tu décris des difficultés rencontrées, tu expliques les causes. Tu proposes des solutions pertinentes que tu mets à l'épreuve et réévalues.	Tu décris parfois des difficultés que tu as rencontrées et tu proposes des solutions que tu essaies.	Parfois tu décris des difficultés rencontrées mais tu n'es pas capable de modifier ta méthode de lecture.	Tu expliques rarement les difficultés que tu as rencontrées.
Intérêt pour la lecture (x2) élève: /8 prof: /8	Enthousiasme évident pour la lecture. Les périodes de lecture en classe sont bien utilisées et tu lis à la maison aussi.	Tu démontres un intérêt pour la lecture. Les périodes de lecture en classe sont assez bien utilisées.	Tu fais un effort pour trouver quelques aspects intéressants à la lecture.	Attitude pas très positive pour la lecture en général et le livre que tu lis présentement en particulier.

Adaptation One: Book floods

	Speaking	Writing	Listening	Reading	Language & Learning Awareness
Communicative & Experiential	○			●	
Language					
Culture					○

Notes

Grade levels and programs:	1 to 12 immersion, 7 to 12 core French, ESL
Grouping strategy:	Individual
Preparation required:	Selection/provision of a wide range of reading material

Even in the younger grades, children should be encouraged to read for pleasure in the target language. This is unlikely to occur when the only text to which they are exposed is short passages in the textbook. A book flood is a form of extended reading program in which children are given access to a 'flood' of reading material in the target language, freedom to select their own choice of reading matter, and time in which to read it quietly. There are no tests of their performance to interfere with their reading pleasure. Instead, they assess the books and make recommendations to their peers.

Materials for the target language book flood might include a range of well illustrated children's storybooks, children's magazines, or non-fiction material on topics from dinosaurs to science experiments. Materials not specifically designed for children but which may attract interest because of the content should also be included, for example, reports of hockey games or programs from concerts. The requirement that students assess the interest level of the material for their peers is not intended to be an onerous exercise, but a chance to express the learner's thoughts about the reading, much as expert readers might recommend a book to a friend. The provision of simple assessment sheets, asking for 1 to 10 scores on a number of measures such as plot, readability, etc., will simplify this process.

Adaptation Two: Reading circles

	Speaking	Writing	Listening	Reading	Language & Learning Awareness
Communicative & Experiential	●	○	○	●	○
Language					○
Culture					

Notes

Grade levels and programs: 7 to 12 immersion, 10 to 12 core French, ESL
Grouping strategy: Small groups
Preparation required: Sets of short novels

An alternative method, similar to Pelletier's literary journal that emphasizes reading and speaking skills in the Communicative & Experiential context, is to create reading circles as a group activity. Groups of students select a short novel from the available sets. In each group, the students read the books together (either aloud or silently), and create a list of new vocabulary. At the end of each chapter or section they predict what they think will happen next, and discuss any problems of comprehension. When they have finished the book, the groups give their opinions of the story, commenting on the plot, characters, themes, and what they liked or disliked. These presentations can occur either orally in the target language in front of the class or in the form of a written book review or report for the teacher. Students should also indicate whether or not they would recommend the book they have read to others.

Dramatisation et gestuelle: découvrir la culture-cible

Catherine Black

	Speaking	Writing	Listening	Reading	Language & Learning Awareness
Communicative & Experiential	●			○	●
Language					
Culture					●

Notes

Grade levels and programs: 11 to 12 immersion and core French, post-secondary
Grouping strategy: Employs a range of grouping strategies
Preparation required: Selection of appropriate plays

Editors' Introduction

Many students love to act, and in her advanced FSL classes, Black has found that many levels of the spoken language can be taught through drama. Of equal importance, drama can be a useful vehicle for teaching the non-verbal language that native speakers instinctively use. Through the reading and re-reading of standard French plays and consultation with native speakers, post-secondary students in FSL discover that there are three kinds of gestures used by native speakers: gestures with a specific verbal meaning, movements primarily using hands and arms, and various other body movements. Students discover that body language can reinforce the meaning of the spoken word and that gestures and body language used by francophones may differ from those of anglophones.

Utiliser le théâtre dans les cours de langues à l'université, au collège et même à l'école primaire n'a rien de nouveau. En effet, de nombreux chercheurs se sont penchés sur la question et les résultats de leurs recherches ont montré les aspects positifs de l'intégration du jeu dramatique dans un contexte pédagogique (voir les travaux de Heathcote [1972] à ce sujet). Ce qui est plus nouveau, c'est de combiner les effets positifs de la dramatisation et de la gestuelle afin de faire découvrir la culture de la langue-cible. Ce dernier aspect est loin d'être négligeable.

En effet, l'apprenant qui se veut compétent en langue doit fonctionner verbalement et non-verbalement de façon appropriée au contexte culturel de la langue-cible (Hammerly, 1991). Cet auteur est convaincu que le non verbal (la gestuelle) devrait être enseigné en conjonction avec le comportement verbal qu'il doit accompagner. Cette notion de comportement approprié se retrouve chez Byrnes lorsqu'elle écrit : « instruction toward cross-cultural communicative competence is less concerned with getting learners to perform in highly specific ways than having them conduct themselves within a range of possibilities that are accepted and acceptable within the C2 culture » (1991, p. 208). L'étudiant en langue devrait donc apprendre à décoder la gestuelle propre à la C2 (culture seconde) afin d'adopter un comportement adéquat, évitant ainsi des impairs, lors de visites en milieu C2.

Quiconque est allé dans un pays étranger a pu noter des différences dans le comportement non verbal des habitants. En effet, si certains gestes sont identiques à ceux de la culture dont nous sommes issus, d'autres sont radicalement nouveaux et certains sont si subtils que l'on a tendance à ne pas les remarquer. Parfois, ils peuvent être très équivoques pour l'observateur, comme le fait remarquer Calbris (1990, p. 37) dans son ouvrage sur la sémiotique du geste. D'autre part, la gestuelle rend le discours plus compréhensible et plus vivant pour l'interlocuteur. Dans la communication chez les êtres humains, il y a un rapport étroit entre gestuelle et parole, comme l'ont démontré des psychologues et des neurologues qui ont fait des études avec des aphasiques (McNeill, 1970, p. 362). Le geste constitue donc un renforcement non codé du message.

La gestuelle constitue le dernier maillon de l'initiation à la communication, comme l'a dit Fancy (1991, p. 341). Ce sont ces mouvements et ces gestes propres aux natifs de la langue tels que la distance entre les individus, l'expression de la physionomie, qui sont autant de variables indispensables à une communication adéquate.

La gestuelle n'est pas uniquement une référence socioculturelle ; c'est aussi un moyen de traduire des émotions et des attitudes propres à la culture-cible. Si l'on enseigne les gestes et les postures ainsi que leurs charges émotives dans le contexte d'une pièce dans la langue-cible, l'apprenant est placé dans une situation réelle de communication et il augmente ses chances de comprendre et de s'approprier cette gestuelle propre à la culture de la langue qu'il étudie. C'est bien ce que vise la dramatisation.

Celle-ci est une pratique pédagogique particulière[1] qui permet de réaliser des objectifs culturels en utilisant les techniques de jeu de l'art dramatique telles que la compréhension du texte (au niveau lexical et syntaxique), la mémorisation, la prosodie, la diction et l'étude du comportement non verbal spécifique à la culture-cible.

Description du cours

Le cours d'expression orale offert en troisième année universitaire d'un baccalauréat en français L2 est un exemple de l'utilisation de la dramatisation. Il y a trois cours préalables, deux cours axés sur l'écrit et à forte concentration grammaticale et un cours d'expression orale. Les étudiants qui ont suivi le français de base ou l'immersion sont acceptés dans le cours s'ils ont les prérequis.

D'une durée de douze semaines, le cours est basé sur un travail intensif du français parlé tel qu'il apparaît dans la pièce qui sera représentée. Les pièces choisies sont des pièces françaises et québécoises[2]. Celles-ci doivent comprendre le français dit standard, mais aussi, dans la mesure du possible, différents niveaux de langue, d'une part afin d'y sensibiliser les apprenants et d'autre part parce que le niveau de langue est révélateur du milieu socioculturel des personnages ; d'où son importance pour découvrir et apprécier la culture C2. Un autre facteur de décision important pour le choix des pièces est le nombre d'étudiants inscrits au cours. Afin que chacun retire les mêmes bénéfices, il est indispensable qu'il y ait une certaine uniformité au niveau de la longueur des rôles.

Tout le travail de lecture, d'élaboration des personnages, d'interprétation, de mise en train physique et vocale, de répétition, de mise en scène, d'organisation du spectacle (la publicité, le choix des décors, des costumes et du maquillage), tout se fait en français. Le spectacle est donné plusieurs fois (trois en moyenne) au théâtre universitaire devant un public francophone ainsi qu'anglophone et francophile. Dans la mesure du possible, les étudiants donnent une ou deux représentations pour les élèves de 11e, 12e et 13e années des programmes d'immersion française des écoles secondaires locales et régionales. Le spectacle est payant (une somme minimale) afin de couvrir les frais encourus pour payer la publicité, les ingénieurs du son et les éclairagistes ainsi que pour la location des costumes et l'achat de maquillage, d'accessoires ou de matériel pour réaliser les décors. Toute l'organisation du spectacle contribue aussi à l'enseignement de la culture-cible. Ainsi, les décors peuvent faire référence à des lieux précis ou spécifiques à ceux de la culture-cible (les cafés, un intérieur d'appartement bourgeois ou au contraire populaire, un lycée, une université, etc.) Les costumes et le maquillage sont aussi porteurs de référents culturels. Tout donc est prétexte à l'exploration de la C2.

Déroulement du cours

Chaque cours commence par des exercices de relaxation qui permettent à l'étudiant-acteur de libérer son corps de toute tension musculaire afin de pouvoir jouer diverses situations allant de l'évanouissement à la colère en passant par la passion. Les jeux de contacts physiques sont importants dans la mesure où les étudiants vont devoir se toucher. C'est à ce niveau que l'on commence à parler des différences culturelles entre les francophones et les nord-américains en général. En effet, la société nord-américaine étant beaucoup moins attachée aux démonstrations physiques de certaines émotions, il peut en résulter une certaine gêne lors de contacts physiques. Afin de pallier ce problème, il est important de jouer à des jeux tels qu'on en trouve dans les camps d'été (le renard et le lièvre, touche-touche, le sculpteur, le miroir humain, le mime, etc.)

Viennent ensuite les exercices de respiration ainsi que ceux nécessaires à l'échauffement de l'appareil phonatoire. S'il y a trop de tension au niveau de la gorge et de la langue, la production orale est affectée et l'étudiant donne l'impression de parler avec des « patates chaudes » dans la bouche. Grâce à ces exercices, l'étudiant prend conscience du fait que parler est quelque chose de complexe ; il pourra moduler, projeter, jouer avec les intonations afin de capter l'attention du spectateur.

À ce point du cours, les étudiants sont détendus, focalisés, prêts à affronter le texte théâtral. Pendant la première semaine de cours, le texte est lu, relu, expliqué. Vient ensuite l'élaboration des personnages (d'où ils viennent, ce qu'ils aiment, ce qu'ils font dans la vie, leurs qualités, leurs défauts). Cette étape terminée, il convient de passer à l'étude de la gestuelle. Chaque personnage est disséqué du point de vue psychologique et social. Ce sont ces deux aspects qui vont guider son comportement non-verbal dans certaines situations. Les étudiants comparent leur propre comportement, leurs gestes dans le même contexte, avec ceux du professeur (natif ou non de la C2). Il est important de préciser ici que si le professeur n'est pas un locuteur natif et qu'il ne se sent pas à la hauteur pour décrire la gestuelle de la C2, il peut toujours essayer d'engager les services d'un étudiant étranger en stage d'études dans l'établissement. Il faut préciser à ce point que les gestes utilisés sont assez stéréotypés. Il existe quelques ouvrages qui traitent de cela en images (voir bibliographie). Le professeur peut toujours y avoir recours pour illustrer certains gestes moins courants.

La phase suivante consiste à faire mimer les gestes propres à la C2 dans le contexte de la pièce afin que les étudiants commencent à s'approprier ce nouveau bagage. Les semaines qui suivent, mimer les gestes se fera dans des contextes situationnels similaires afin de les rendre plus familiers. Lorsqu'on parle de gestes, le terme est trop vague, alors il est bon de les différencier. Eckman (1980, p. 89–98) a fait une taxonomie qui classe les mouvements du corps en plusieurs catégories : les emblèmes (actions symboliques dans lesquelles le geste a un sens verbal spécifique, connu de tous les membres de la culture ou de la sous-culture), les manipulateurs corporels (mouvements dans lesquels une partie du corps agit sur une autre partie du corps) et enfin les illustratifs (mouvements utilisant principalement les mains et les bras).

L'être humain a recours aux emblèmes pour des raisons de nature compensatoire : un environnement trop bruyant qui ne favorise pas la communication verbale (par exemple dans une usine avec le bruit des machines) ; ou bien la distance entre les interlocuteurs est trop grande et crier risquerait de gêner les autres personnes présentes (par exemple dans un théâtre lorsqu'on veut attirer l'attention de quelqu'un). Les emblèmes peuvent remplacer les mots eux-mêmes ou le message contenu dans les mots ; ainsi, on trouve le hochement de tête de bas en haut qui signifie oui et le mouvement de tête de droite à gauche qui indique la négation. Le geste de la main dans lequel le pouce et l'auriculaire sont en extension alors que les trois autres doigts sont repliés peut aussi évoquer l'objet « téléphone » ou alors le message: « je vais te téléphoner plus tard » . Un haussement d'épaules marque aussi bien l'ignorance que le manque d'intérêt.

On retrouve aussi des actions symboliques pour marquer le départ (index pointant vers l'avant, le pouce touchant le majeur et les deux autres doigts étant collés au majeur) ; ces gestes symboliques servent même à insulter (le poing fermé, l'avant bras replié). Dans cette optique, il est donc capital pour un enseignant de langue seconde ou étrangère de se familiariser avec les emblèmes les plus courants et d'initier les apprenants premièrement à les reconnaître et deuxièmement à les utiliser à bon escient dans le but de maximiser la communication et surtout ne pas commettre d'impairs. Signalons toutefois, que certains emblèmes se retrouvent d'une culture à l'autre, et qu'on peut parler alors d'emblèmes universaux (celui du téléphone par exemple, ou le geste de l'autostoppeur).

Si les emblèmes jouent un rôle important dans la communication, ce n'est pas tout à fait le cas des manipulateurs corporels. Ces gestes ne semblent pas vraiment porteurs de sens, il seraient plutôt mécaniques et dénoteraient l'inquiétude ou la gêne de la part du sujet ; par exemple il peut se gratter la tête, se frotter le nez, se tordre les mains, se lécher les lèvres, tenir un crayon dans une main et le faire frapper le plat de l'autre main ou la table. En général, ces gestes peuvent apparaître sans qu'il y ait réellement un rapport avec un message verbal.

Les illustratifs sont par contre intimement liés à la parole, au contenu du message et au débit. Eckman (1980, p. 98) en a identifié huit catégories. Ces mouvements qui « collent » à la parole diffèrent des emblèmes qui sont utilisés lorsque le locuteur choisit de ne pas parler ou est dans l'incapacité physique de le faire. Ils accompagnent la parole pour renforcer le message ; par exemple, lorsqu'on donne des directions dans une ville (pointer avec l'index, ou encore un mouvement de la main, doigts en extension, collés les uns aux autres, vers la droite ou la gauche pour indiquer un changement de direction). Toutefois, les illustratifs sont plus spontanés et ils ne font pas référence à une action précise porteuse de message comme le sont les emblèmes.

Nous avons vu plus haut que les emblèmes propres à une culture devraient être enseignés à tout apprenant de la langue-cible. Or, peut-on procéder de la même façon avec les illustratifs ? Le fait qu'ils soient plus spontanés rend la tâche plus difficile aux enseignants. Ceux-ci pourraient se trouver confrontés au problème de l'interférence. En effet, si l'apprenant a déjà tout un bagage gestuel personnel (venu du contexte socio-familio-culturel dans lequel il évolue) et si la langue qu'il étudie est proche de sa langue maternelle, il y a de fortes chances pour que cet apprenant effectue des transferts gestuels. Dans certains cas, les mouvements et les postures seront très similaires à ceux de la langue-cible, d'où la difficulté pour l'enseignant d'identifier ce qui est appris dans le contexte de la classe de langue et ce qui est « naturel » pour l'apprenant. Pourtant, il ne faudrait pas voir dans l'environnement socio-familio-culturel le seul facteur capable d'influencer l'utilisation de gestes et de postures chez les locuteurs.

Ainsi, nous nous rendons compte que la gestuelle est non seulement chargée d'émotions et d'attitudes sociales, mais est aussi un véhicule socioculturel important, d'où la nécessité d'en faire profiter les étudiants en langue. Cette prise de conscience du geste et de son sens devrait, selon nous, encourager l'apprenant à réviser sa façon de concevoir son apprentissage de la L2 et l'amener ainsi à modifier sa motivation d'instrumentale en intégrative. En effet, si l'apprenant néglige la gestuelle de la L2, il se contente seulement de communiquer verbalement. Si au contraire, il intègre la gestuelle (et même seulement certains gestes) propres à la culture de la langue qu'il étudie, son interlocuteur le considérera moins comme un étranger et il sera plus facilement intégré à la culture-cible. Nous sommes d'avis qu'une des faiblesses de l'enseignement des langues secondes et étrangères, à l'heure actuelle, est justement d'encourager uniquement la motivation instrumentale, c'est-à-dire l'attitude qui ne fait de la langue-cible qu'un outil de travail.

Nous croyons avoir montré l'importance de la dramatisation et de la gestuelle dans les cours de L2, mais il ne faut pas croire que ces principes pédagogiques soient réservés aux cours de langue en milieu universitaire. Il est tout à fait possible d'envisager de les adapter avec des élèves des écoles primaires et secondaires en immersion ou en français de base. Les mêmes techniques pédagogiques peuvent s'appliquer à d'autres langues (pour les cours d'anglais L2, voir Stern, 1980 ; Via, 1976, 1987 ; Wessels, 1987).

Les applications pédagogiques[3] sont nombreuses à qui veut donner son temps, son énergie, son enthousiasme pour faire de ses étudiants des locuteurs compétents et à l'aise dans n'importe quel contexte de la culture-cible.

Notes

1 Cette pratique d'une durée de 72 heures s'utilise seule et non en tant que procédé de renforcement. Ce nombre de 72 heures correspond au nombre d'heures auxquelles sont exposés les apprenants. Le nombre total peut varier en fonction du type de pièce présentée et du niveau de compétence en langue des étudiants. La moyenne par semaine est de quatre à six heures de contact.

2 Il n'est plus possible de consulter cette banque de données, mais le site www.magi.com/~dchartra/theat.htm comprend le centre des auteurs dramatiques du Québec, qui a un répertoire de 146 auteurs et environ 1000 textes ; le centre de documentation de Leloup théâtre à w1.neuronnexion.fr/~leloup/ fournit l'accès à une collection de 5000 textes dont certains sont en ligne.

3 Pour des idées pratiques, se référer aux ouvrages et articles indiqués dans l'appendice A (bibliographie sélectionnée). De plus, les enseignants.es peuvent devenir membres du forum de discussion Queatre, Queatre@uqam.ca, où ils peuvent adresser leurs questions, leurs commentaires, et cetera.

Références

Byrnes, H. (1991). Reflections on the development of cross-cultural communicative competence in the foreign language classroom. Dans B. Freed (Réd.), *Foreign language acquisition research and the classroom* (pp. 205–218). Lexington (MA): D.C. Heath.

Calbris, G. (1990). *The semiotics of French gestures.* Bloomington (IN): Indiana University Press.

Eckman, P. (1980). Three classes of nonverbal behaviour. Dans W. Von Raffler-Engel (Réd.), *Aspects of nonverbal communication* (pp. 89–109). Lisse (Pays-Bas): Swets and Zeitlinger.

Fancy, A. (1991). Didactique du français langue seconde, dramatisation et théâtre. *La Revue canadienne des langues vivantes, 47,* 342–350.

Hammerly. H. (1991). *Fluency and accuracy.* Clevedon (R.-U.): Multilingual Matters.

Heathcote, D. (1972). Training needs for the future. Dans J. Hodgson et M. Banham (Réds.), *Education I : The annual survey.* London: Hutchinson.

McNeill, D. (1970). *The acquisition of language: The study of developmental psycholinguistics*. New York: Harper and Row.

Stern, S. (1980). Drama in second language learning from a psycholinguistic perspective. *Language Learning, 30*, 77–97.

Via, R. (1976). *English in three acts*. Honolulu (HI): University Press of Hawaii.

Via, R. (1987). 'The magic if' of theater : Enhancing language learning through drama. Dans W.M. Rivers (Réd.), *Interactive language learning* (pp. 110–123). Cambridge : Cambridge University Press.

White, J. (1984). Drama, communicative competence and language teaching : An overview. *The Canadian Modern Language Review, 40*, 595–599.

Wessels, C. (1987). *Drama*. Oxford : Oxford University Press.

Appendice A

Bibliographie sélectionnée

Bausson, G., et Lavallée, M. (1997). *Guide d'interprétation théâtrale*. Collection Théâtre Essai. Montréal : Leméac.

Bergfelder-Boos, G., et Melde. W. (1993). Apprendre sur scène. *Le français dans le monde, 276*, 47–54.

Calbris, G. (1990). *The semiotics of French gestures*. Bloomington (IN) : Indiana University Press.

Calbris, G., et Montredon, J. (1986). *Des gestes et des mots pour le dire*. Paris : CLE.

Crinson, J., et Westgate, D. (1986). Drama techniques in modern language teaching. *British Journal of Language Teaching, 24*, 24–33.

Fancy, A. (1985). La dramatisation et l'enseignement du français langue seconde : Le problème des textes. *Bulletin de l'Association Canadienne de Linguistique Appliquée, 7*(2), 91–101.

Fancy, A. (1991). Didactique du français langue seconde, dramatisation et théâtre. *La Revue canadienne des langues vivantes, 47*, 342–350.

Molcho, S. (1997). *Le langage du corps : ces gestes qui nous révèlent*. Paris: Éditions Solar.

Via, R. (1976). *English in three acts*. Honolulu (HI): University Press of Hawaii.

Via, R. (1987). `The magic if' of theater : Enhancing language learning through drama. Dans W.M. Rivers (Réd.), *Interactive language learning* (pp. 110–123). Cambridge : Cambridge University Press.

Von Raffler-Engel, W. (1980). Developmental kinesics : The acquisition of conversational non-verbal behaviour. Dans W. Von Raffler-Engel (Réd.), *Aspects of non-verbal communications* (pp. 133–156). Lisse (Pays-Bas) : Swets and Zeitlinger.

Wessels, C. (1987). *Drama*. Oxford : Oxford University Press.

Adaptation One: Sound off, sound on

	Speaking	Writing	Listening	Reading	Language & Learning Awareness
Communicative & Experiential	○		●		●
Language					
Culture					●

Notes

Grade levels and programs: Core French, immersion, ESL, all grades
Grouping strategy: Large or small groups
Equipment required: Videotape
Preparation required: Taping of a target language film or TV program

Using an age appropriate target language film or television program such as a situation comedy (either taped from television or a previously recorded film), the teacher first shows the tape/film with the sound turned off. In a large group, students try to predict meaning from the action and from gestures and body language. Later they watch the same tape with the sound turned on and comment on what additional meaning the sound provides. This can be either a large or a small group activity, and students can produce oral or written reports. To vary this activity, after the class has watched the film/program with the sound turned off, the teacher asks each group to speculate on what they think happened. They write down their opinions. Then they watch the program with the sound turned on, and report orally to the class on the accuracy of their predictions.

A further dimension can be added by taping other target language programs such as a news broadcast incorporating video clips, a weather forecast, cooking show, documentary, children's show, etc., and following the above procedure.

Adaptation Two: Body language and listening skills

	Speaking	Writing	Listening	Reading	Language & Learning Awareness
Communicative & Experiential	○		●		
Language					
Culture					●

Notes

Grade levels and programs: 7 to 12, all programs
Grouping strategy: Large or small groups

For an activity that emphasizes patterns of language interaction, physical stance, and gesture, the instructor asks ESL students either individually or in pairs to go to a place where people are meeting and talking (e.g., a restaurant, a bus stop), and write their observations in their notebooks about the gestures and body language used. They either write their observations while they are watching the people or later on.

While best suited for ESL students in an English-speaking environment or FSL students in a francophone environment, other language learners in a non-target language environment can watch speakers of any other language and report back to the class on the gestures and body language that they observed. Student observations are reported to the class, and students describe in writing the most common or interesting observations that occurred. The objective is to raise awareness of real life use of body language as opposed to the exaggerated or standardized gestures seen in dramatic performances. Other non-verbal points to be observed and discussed may include the distance between people, who touches whom, who shakes hands with whom and when, etc. Besides strengthening students' listening skills, this activity has a strong Language & Learning Awareness value in the Cultural cell.

Creative Skit Activity in the Japanese Language Classroom

Yasuko Makita-Discekici

	Speaking	Writing	Listening	Reading	Language & Learning Awareness
Communicative & Experiential	○				
Language	●	●			○
Culture					○

Notes

Grade levels and programs: All, including beginners
Grouping strategy: Small groups of four or five

Editors' Introduction

Makita-Discekici has found that the students in her beginning Japanese classes enjoy creating skits and that these short dramas on a variety of topics (often related to aspects of Japanese culture such as food and the traditional theatre) improve their speaking and writing skills. She sets parameters for the student-created skits: the lines must be written in Japanese and certain grammatical elements must be present. Through repeated revisions of the scripts and rehearsal of their lines, the students' writing and speaking skills in the Language component, as indicated in the chart above, are enhanced. Since the skits are often on a Japanese theme, a subsidiary cultural value is also present.

Foreign language instruction is more effective, according to Klippel (1984), if students actively participate in the process of learning. Today, learners are often expected to be active and to use the target language before they have mastered it (Taylor, 1980). The second language teacher's main role is to facilitate the development of students' language and communication skills by providing as many enjoyable learning experiences as possible according to their needs and interests.

Role playing or dramatic activity is a valuable classroom technique that enables teachers of any language to create realistic situations in which students learn how to function in a different culture as well as how to use its language in context. Stern (1983) claims that dramatic activity increases self-confidence by demonstrating to learners that they are indeed capable of expressing themselves in the target language in real-life settings. Stern also emphasizes that drama creates low-anxiety situations, since it requires a group effort and students feel less anxious through their cooperative work.

Preparation for creative skits in the classroom

For the last four years I have used creative skits in my beginning Japanese classes, and I have found that college students really enjoy them. Through skits, students can practise the target language in meaningful contexts and in a low-anxiety classroom environment. They are given an opportunity for working together and helping each other to achieve their shared goal; they may learn interpersonal skills through the activity. The students are assigned one mid-term and one final creative skit project per semester (16 weeks). The class is divided into small groups of four or five, each creating its own script. Students decide on a setting (i.e., where and when events take place), their roles, and expressions and sentences that might be used in the chosen setting. The content of their skit has something to do with the students' real-life situations.

Details of skit activity

Usually, five days are spent on the preparation of one drama activity, and the sixth day is for performance. On the first day of the preparation period, I explain the purpose of and details about the activity, including how each student's performance is evaluated. In order to provide students with a better idea of a creative skit in general, I show some good presentations videotaped in previous semesters (I videotape all the presentations for accurate evaluation every semester). By the end of the first preparation day, each group is encouraged to decide on a setting.

There are several requirements for students to complete in the process of creating a skit. First, they need to include certain elements, which I specify, in their skit text. For example, in their mid-term skit project they are asked to include the following elements: (1) at least 10 different verbs – both affirmative and negative – in the present or future tense and in the past tense (-*mashita*/-*masendashita*); (2) adjectives in both affirmative and negative forms; (3) expressions about how to locate things and people (e.g., *Where is the hospital? It's in front of the station.*); and (4) numbers (e.g., time, prices, and the days of the month). These elements are chosen from what students have previously been taught in class. The main reason for this requirement is to provide students with opportunities to practise what they have learned in meaningful contexts.

Second, each student should have at least five lines to speak; the minimum length of a skit is 20 lines if there are four people in the group. This requirement ensures that all students have an opportunity to talk in the skit.

Third, each student is required to write out his or her group's script in *hiragana* (one of the Japanese syllabic alphabets) and in Chinese characters called *kanji* for the evaluation of individual written performance. This task provides learners with a literacy experience in the target language, as well as encouraging the students to appreciate their own contribution to the completed script.

Lastly, I ask students to use props to make the situation more real and to create an enjoyable theatre atmosphere for their presentation. Each group decides on what real objects are to be used. For example, if a group has a Japanese restaurant setting, they may eat *sushi* with chopsticks and drink Japanese tea while having a conversation in Japanese. They can use all kinds of things, such as food and household items.

Use of props helps create setting in various ways. For example, a restaurant situation can be either a very poor eating place or an expensive one; if students use a dirty table cloth and a small toy spider instead of fancy decorations and flowers, the setting can become an unpleasant place. One group, for instance, created a disco situation very effectively with music and colourful lights. Another group imitated a famous American news show by using a TV monitor, a video camera, and a microphone. Props help the audience visualize created situations and understand skit contents better, while performers are able to get into their own created situation without much difficulty. Thus, students enjoy acting with props in spite of the time and effort required to bring real objects to class for their performance.

On the second, third, and fourth days, students decide on their roles and create their own script in groups. I walk around the classroom, help students find appropriate expressions and sentences, and give them advice or suggestions while they create their script and rehearse in the classroom. Every semester I try to find a helper who can assist me in these tasks because I have found that it is not easy for me to provide all the groups (i.e., four groups of five or five groups of four students) with enough suggestions and advice during our limited time in the classroom. For the last three years I have asked for help either from some of my Japanese friends in the community or from more advanced students interested in receiving extra credit for assisting.

By the end of the fourth day, each group is asked to turn in a draft of its skit. Created skit texts are scanned and critiqued by instructors for improvement. Sometimes students are so creative that their script in Japanese may not be readily understood because they tend to invent phrases and sentences that are ungrammatical.

I usually edit the skit text, either in the classroom or in my office, together with group members. The purpose of this editing is to make sure that words, phrases, and sentences in the skit text are appropriately used in terms of context and grammar. When I do not understand something written in the script, I ask the students what they intend to say in the particular situation. I also ask them to look for the right words or phrases in the textbook or in a dictionary. Authentic language, that is, the perfect use of formal and informal Japanese, is not strictly sought at the beginning level because it requires students to learn various forms (e.g., the honorific and humble forms, the plain form) and to understand Japanese social hierarchical relationships.

The fifth day is used for rehearsal. I help students practise pronouncing their lines correctly, help them find the right *kanji* for certain words, give suggestions about what props can be used, and provide other guidance.

Evaluation

I evaluate students' performance in terms of group cooperation and of individual oral and written language skills. That is, all the members in a group receive the same points on four categories (required elements, content, length, creativity), while the rest of the categories (pronunciation and intonation, memorization, clarity, fluency, and written text) are graded individually.

First, all the required elements that I specify must be included in the skit text. Evaluation for this category is usually given based on the students' written text. Second, the content of each skit should have something to do with real life. Third, I make sure that each group member speaks at least five lines in the skit. Fourth, the skit should be original, not a copy of an existing story. Use of props is also evaluated under this category. The rating scale ranges from one (very poor) to ten (excellent) for each component. If a student's pronunciation and intonation are near-native quality, ten points are given on the pronunciation and intonation category. The performers are supposed to memorize their lines completely and speak clearly so that they can be understood well.

Memorization is encouraged for several reasons. First, I find that the effort to memorize lines helps second language learners (especially at the beginner and lower-intermediate levels) to internalize Japanese language patterns, which are quite different from English ones. Through repeated practise of memorized lines, it is hoped that learners will transfer such patterns from short-term to longer-term memory, leading to relatively permanent storage of truly internalized language patterns (J.D. Quisenberry, personal communication, March 27, 1998). Second, reading lines, or creating silence through incomplete memorization, will spoil the dramatic performance itself. It is assumed that beginners will have difficulty making an impromptu speech when they do not know what to say during performance. Upper-intermediate or advanced learners, however, can be graded on this category more leniently as long as they can improvise with appropriate expressions.

Clarity is the third category to be evaluated individually. It is important that performers utter their speeches clearly, with enough volume to be heard and understood. Japanese words consist of distinct syllables of the same duration; each syllable must be pronounced with even length and stress. This is quite different from the way in which English is spoken, with only one syllable in each word given primary stress. Therefore, I encourage my beginning students to pay attention to the syllabic nature of the scripts and to pronounce words and phrases clearly enough to ensure comprehension.

`Fluency,' that is, `smoothness' in speech, is not included in the evaluation for the mid-term skit activity given in the eighth week because fluency cannot be expected unless students are given time to get used to the target language and feel comfortable with it. Some degree of smoothness in speech, however, may be expected at the end of the semester, that is, after 80 hours of instruction in the 16th week.

I require each student to write the mid-term skit text in *hiragana* only, not in *roma-ji* (i.e., the transcription of Japanese using Roman letters). The final skit should be written both in *hiragana* and in some *kanji*. The more *kanji* are used in the text, the more points are given on the written performance category.

On performance day, each skit presentation is videotaped so that it can be watched more than once for accurate evaluation. I have found that it is too difficult to appropriately evaluate four or five students' performance at the same time during a group presentation. Videotaping also allows me to give students positive feedback for improvement. I show the skits in class later and ask students to find one good point and one point to be improved in each presentation, hoping that the students will realize that `sharing resources, supporting, encouraging, and praising each other's efforts' (Johnson, Johnson, & Holubec, 1994, p. 10) are important in completing the assigned group task.

Difficulties with the activity and suggested solutions

Most students enjoy this skit project because they are creative, imaginative, and enthusiastic about creating mini dramatic performances. In addition, in a group setting, those who know Japanese better or who are faster learners can help slower learners. That is, students who are more motivated to learn Japanese are given an opportunity to learn more by participating actively in the learning process, while slower learners may be encouraged to learn Japanese by receiving assistance from their classmates.

This activity, however, has some special requirements. Instructors need to exert great effort to make group work effective, since not all groups are cooperative; that is, not all students have the necessary social skills to function effectively as group members (Johnson et al., 1994). There may be some students who do not feel responsible for their group work or who do not cooperate with their group members for some reason. I have observed that some students do not come frequently to class during a skit preparation period and that diligent students experience inconvenience because of the irresponsible students in their group. Therefore, instructors must carefully monitor how students are working on their group project and sometimes spend extra time giving advice or encouraging those who are not cooperative to exercise the necessary social skills. It is important for instructors to ensure the active involvement of all the students in the class.

According to Johnson et al. (1994), 'positive interdependence' and 'individual and group accountability' are essential elements of successful cooperative learning in the classroom. `Positive interdependence' means that the individual efforts of each member benefit all other group members as well as that individual, while `individual and group accountability' exists when the instructor provides clear criteria for assessing both individual and group performance.

One way to make students feel more responsible for their group work is for the instructor to explain how each individual and the group are graded in detail. Another suggestion is to emphasize the importance of each person's accountability for the skit activity. It is also a good idea to inform students that extra points will be given to any group demonstrating great cooperation during the skit activity. I provide these explanations on the very first day of the preparation period (see above). Actually, if all the group members are responsible for and participate actively in the activity, their performance usually turns out to be very good.

In addition, my course syllabus indicates the following attendance rule:

> An excused absence must be given before the absence occurs. More than one unexplained absence during pair/group activities will lower one's grade by one letter (e.g., a 'B' becomes a 'C').

The main purpose of this rule is to draw students' attention to the importance of their responsible attitude towards group work in the classroom. I have observed that the number of irresponsible students has decreased since this rule was added to the course syllabus. Another difficulty with this activity is that one instructor may not be enough to help students prepare for their own skit in the classroom within a limited preparation period. Created skit texts need to be reviewed so that instructors can suggest improvements, since students may create incorrect or inappropriate Japanese sentences. This task is easier, and students get more attention during their preparation, if the instructor has an assistant or someone else in class with her or him. If the instructor cannot find a helper for this activity, I would suggest that the preparation period for the activity be one or two days longer so that all the groups can receive the feedback and assistance they need from the instructor.

In my first year of teaching I had a teaching assistant. For the last three years, as I mentioned before, I have found helpers either from the community or from more advanced classes. Networking with the local community is one good way to find a helper for the skit activity, especially if there are no advanced students available.

Possible adaptations to other contexts

This creative skit activity can be used at any level of language instruction: beginning, intermediate, advanced, or business Japanese classes. The instructor decides on required elements according to what he or she emphasizes or what expressions or sentence patterns he or she wants to teach. For example, I asked my upper-elementary and intermediate students to include a cultural theme in the context of their skit. The setting for one group was a restaurant, where a Japanese student slurped while eating noodles and her American classmates were annoyed by her eating style. In the Japanese culture, slurping noodles means that the food is very delicious and is not rude at all, but such is not the case in American culture. Thus a creative skit can be very useful for teaching culture in the language classroom.

The evaluation components and the rating scale can vary depending upon the goals and nature of language course. A course that emphasizes conversation skills does not have to require written performance. If intermediate or advanced learners are expected to demonstrate native-like pronunciation and fluency, the points should be increased on these evaluation categories. I also suggest that the length of a required skit be longer than 20 lines because these students have a better command of the language and may want to talk more.

In business Japanese classes, which focus on business-related communication modes, non-verbal communication skills such as how to bow or how to exchange name cards may be included as an additional evaluation category. Nakayama, Oda, Urabe, and Ley (1994) report that their simulation approach was successful in teaching business Japanese to beginners at the university level. At the beginning of the course, a company setting was created, and the students also decided on their positions within the setting. Various events which might occur in a Japanese company were provided, along with cultural information and a variety of learning tasks. The researchers found that students not only performed very well on the listening comprehension section on both the mid-term and final exams, but also developed some language learning strategies such as `risk-taking, self-confidence, cooperative learning, and problem-solving' (p. 210). The researchers noted that students were motivated to participate actively in their learning and to practise Japanese without fear of making mistakes because the teachers encouraged them to learn how to communicate meaning in meaningful contexts, rather than how to acquire grammatical accuracy and correct pronunciation.

In other language courses, such as ESL classes, students could dramatize some cross-cultural incidents in groups. For example, small groups of students could discuss cross-cultural misunderstandings or incidents in which they had been involved, write a skit text, and act it out in front of the class. The other students could try to guess what was happening in the play, and then the whole class could discuss its cross-cultural implications (Tomalin & Stempleski, 1993). If the instructor wished to teach language patterns through the skit, she could ask students to include specific sentence patterns or phrases according to the level of the course and learners.

While creative skit activity does not have to be language driven, teaching appropriate language usage must be one of the primary goals of the language class. This does not mean that realistic situations should be sacrificed because of certain linguistic elements. It is important that the instructor decide on clear objectives and learning activities for achieving these objectives. It is also important to consider what learning outcomes can be expected and select criteria for evaluating student performance accordingly.

As a language teacher, I highly recommend creative skit activity to any language teacher because it is enjoyable for both teachers and students, in spite of its few disadvantages. It should be emphasized that the teacher's continual encouragement, warm support, and careful monitoring are necessary for students to participate actively in this learning activity.

Note

1   I thank Dr. James D. Quisenberry, Emeritus Director of International Programs and Services at Southern Illinois University, for his valuable comments and suggestions in preparing this manuscript.

References

Austin, T., Nakayama, C., Oda, A., Urabe, S., & Ley, Y. (1994). A yen for business: Language learning for specific purposes – a Japanese example. *Foreign Language Annals, 27*(2), 196–219.

Johnson, D.W., Johnson, T.J., & Holubec, E.J. (1994). *Cooperative learning in the classroom.* Alexandria, VA: Association for Supervision and Curriculum Development.

Klippel, F. (1984). *Keep talking: Communicative fluency activities for language teaching.* New York: Cambridge University Press.

Stern, S.L. (1983). Why drama works: A psycholinguistic perspective. In J.W. Oller & P.A. Richard-Amato (Eds.), *Methods that work: A smorgasbord of ideas for language teachers* (pp. 207–225). Rowley, MA: Newbury House Publishers.

Taylor, B.P. (1980). Adult language learning strategies and their pedagogical implications. In K. Croft (Ed.), *Readings on English as a second language* (pp. 144–152). Cambridge: Winthrop Publishers, Inc.

Tomalin, B., & Stempleski, S. (1993). *Cultural Awareness.* Oxford: Oxford University Press.

Adaptation One: Creating and recording a drama

	Speaking	Writing	Listening	Reading	Language & Learning Awareness
Communicative & Experiential	●		○		
Language	○	○			
Culture					

Notes

Grade levels and programs:	All
Grouping strategy:	Employs a range of grouping strategies
Equipment required:	Camera, videotape, optional computer, optional camcorder

In this activity, the students create a drama that is photographed and made into a permanent record that could be shown to students in other classrooms or in subsequent years. In groups or as a class, students brainstorm to create an idea that they could expand into a written script for a skit or drama. An adult group might develop a story about an out-of-school event, e.g., taking a sick person to the emergency department at a local hospital or buying a used car. Younger students might develop a script, for example, about bullying in the schoolyard. Alternatively, after groups have brainstormed for an idea and developed a plot outline, instead of writing a script, more advanced learners could improvise what they are going to say while presenting the skit. Encouraging students to self-assess and provide feedback on their peers' performance can promote self- and language-awareness, while maintaining student interest.

Group members share the responsibilities for solving logistical problems (props, costumes, etc.) and assign someone to be the photographer or technician. If the appropriate computer equipment is available, digital images can be downloaded or regular photos could be scanned into a computer presentation program such as Power Point. Videotaping a performance is also a possibility if a camcorder is available.

Adaptation Two: Using drama to illustrate a variety of themes

	Speaking	Writing	Listening	Reading	Language & Learning Awareness
Communicative & Experiential	●	●	●		
Language					
Culture					●

Notes

Grade levels and programs: 11 and 12, post-secondary, adult, all programs
Grouping strategy: Employs a range of grouping strategies

Another possibility for high intermediate or advanced learners in a variety of language programs is to introduce cross-curricular topics by generating skits or role-plays (improvised or written) in the target language to illustrate cross-cultural, anti-racist, or anti-homophobic themes using sensitive case studies. Depending on the situation in the class, one example that students could use would involve a group of three students that sees a student from another culture being harassed by a group shouting 'terrorist' at him. What should the three students do? Their discussion and the actions (if any) that they take form the basis of the role-play. Situations identified in newspapers or on television are also possible sources for ideas that students can expand into role-plays. Controversial situations can give rise, not only to opportunities for role-playing, but also for class discussion, a formal debate or written response pieces.

NB – Teachers should be conscious of the danger that role-plays may appear to target individual students. It is preferable that students create the role-play scenarios, however, the teacher could have a few examples of case studies available if the students are unable to think of a suitable topic.

Student Investigations of Cultural Identity in the Foreign Language Classroom

David J. Shook

	Speaking	Writing	Listening	Reading	Language & Learning Awareness
Communicative & Experiential		●		●	
Language					
Culture					●

Notes

Grade levels and programs:	10 to 12, immersion and core French, post secondary, adult
Grouping strategy:	Groups or individuals
Equipment required:	Optional computer with Internet connection

Editors' Introduction

Shook has found that second language students who are far removed from the cultures whose languages they are studying often have stereotypic or 'culturally incorrect' insights into these cultures. He proposes ways that students can investigate various Spanish-speaking cultures by examining three components identified as being related to Hispanic cultures: language, religious traditions, and heritage (i.e., socio-economic identity and geographical ties). While these three cultural markers are valid for Spanish-speaking cultures, the same markers (language, religious traditions, and allegiance/heritage/roots) may not apply to other cultures. Instructors need to brainstorm with students as to the foci to be investigated in the language and culture that they are studying. Student investigations through international resources in their communities or through the Internet can help eliminate erroneous perceptions about the target culture. In addition, students will acquire the tools to begin an examination of their own cultural values, hence the solid bullet in the Culture/Language & Learning Awareness cell.

As many foreign language (FL) instructors would agree, 'Language without culture can degenerate into a study of forms and vocabulary; [...] culture instruction is what brings life to language learning' (Scarcella & Oxford, 1992, p. 184). However, one problem of culture instruction is exemplified in the case of many North American students who study Spanish. Often the students are far removed, either in terms of distance or in terms of social interaction, from the Hispanic cultures who speak the language the students are studying. Thus, the FL students often possess stereotypic or 'culturally incorrect' insights into and information regarding the various Hispanic cultures, problems which the instructor needs to overcome. The FL classroom, by the very nature of its language and culture content, is the perfect place to help FL learners come to a better understanding of the *cultural identities* present in the various Hispanic cultures, thereby short-cutting any possible stereotypes. In fact, as Morain (1995, p.44) states, 'suspicion of generalizations and stereotypes is indeed one of the gifts (students) can receive in foreign language class that will serve them well across the curriculum.'

This paper presents a novel approach towards language and culture instruction for North American students of Spanish that centres on student-led investigations of cultural identity in the Americas. Such investigations are designed to allow students to overcome possible stereotypes and generalizations they might hold regarding the FL culture(s). In addition, in order for FL students in North America to fully appreciate the complicated issue of cultural identity in many FL cultures, it might be helpful to them to investigate this issue alongside an examination of their own cultural identity, that is: How is cultural identity defined in Canada or the United States? A number of positive outcomes from this type of study may manifest themselves:

> There is every reason to believe that while students are learning about the culture of the people whose language we are teaching, they can also be learning about their own culture and its relationship to other cultures in the school.... They can carry away from our classes not only the ability to communicate with those who speak a *foreign* language, but an enhanced ability to communicate more sensitively with those who speak their *own* language (Morain, 1995, p. 44).

Therefore, a second positive outcome of the language and culture instructional approach described here is that it allows FL students *to learn and appreciate more about their own culture(s) at the same time as learning about the FL culture(s)*. This approach might be self-inclusive or might complement an existing methodology, as can be seen by the description below. In addition, although the examples presented here are related to the study of Spanish and the Hispanic cultures, the study of other languages and cultures might benefit from the approach described.

Approach

Pre-investigation
Any approach towards orienting FL students to investigate cultural identity first must assure that the curriculum recognizes any decisive components in the search

for cultural identity pertinent to the discussion. For example, Carlos Pesado Palmieri, a noted Argentine historian, identifies three such decisive components related to the Hispanic cultures of our world (1995). The first is *la lengua*, language. The second component is *la fe*, the faith life or religious tradition(s) of the culture. The third component is *sangre y tierra*; in other words, allegiance, heritage, roots. *Sangre y tierra* comprises much more than just ethnicity; it also takes into account one's socio-economic identity and geographical ties.

Therefore, Spanish-language instructors need to review their instructional materials in order to assure themselves that the materials do indeed emphasize linguistic and cultural information related to the three components of *lengua, fe,* and *sangre y tierra.* Common 'adjustments' might include providing more regional varieties in vocabulary lists and pointing out Spanish vocabulary originating from other cultures; recognizing in the class calendar the various religious and secular holidays present in the Hispanic cultures; providing listening activities in which students hear regional pronunciation differences; and so forth.

Student Investigations

Prior to investigation, the students need to know how to carry out their investigations. Therefore, classroom activities need to be designed to help students learn/review/practise proper interview protocols in Spanish (for example, the use of *tú/Ud.*, question posing, small-talk etiquette); use Spanish characters while typing on the computer; and utilize circumlocution and other repair strategies for communication breakdowns, and so on.

The students now should be ready to embark on the actual investigations. Formally or informally, instructors need to make checks that the students recognize/recall the three components of cultural identity: *lengua, fe,* and *sangre y tierra.* The students then are presented with the task at hand, addressing the research questions regarding cultural identity found in Table 1, or others determined more relevant by the instructor(s).

The investigations might be done by individual students, dyads, or small teams of students; in addition, each individual or group may research either the Hispanic or the North American side, or do a parallel investigation of both cultures at once. Prior to beginning the investigations, the instructor should help the students identify the possible informational sources available in their community, including the identification of Hispanic and Canadian/US resources (embassies, consulates, trade groups, civic organizations, etc.); Internet resources such as World Wide Web pages and the *soc.culture.X* news groups; and so on. It is highly recommended that the students prepare a plan for investigation, detailing who?, why?, where?, and how? so that reasonable goals are made and achieved.

Post-investigations

The final step in this approach of investigating cultural identity in the Americas is the presentation of the investigation results. Written, oral, and even multimedia presentations are all possible, but the students need to be made responsible for accurate cultural information and language use: therefore, it is of utmost importance that such presentations are evaluated by the language instructor in some formal way.

Table 1. Sample research questions for investigating cultural identity

Hispanic Cultural Identity	Canadian Cultural Identity	US Cultural Identity
1. What is the status of Spanish as a unifying marker of cultural identity in _____ ?	1. What is the status of English/ French as a unifying marker of cultural identity in Canada?	1. What is the status of English as a unifying marker of cultural identity in the US?
2. Is the Roman Catholic faith a unifying marker of cultural identity in _____ ?	2. Is Protestantism/ Catholicism a unifying marker of cultural identity in Canada?	2. Is Protestantism a unifying marker of cultural identity in the US?
3. What are the ethnic and socio-economic unifying markers of cultural identity in _____ ?	3. What are the ethnic and socio-economic unifying markers of cultural identity in Canada?	3. What are the ethnic and socio-economic unifying markers of cultural identity in the US?

Some presentation methods include poster sessions (in Spanish) by the various investigating groups in class; setting up a WWW home page with the results to be updated by different classes year after year (in Spanish or bilingual); a class presentation during 'Foreign Language Week' or a 'Parents' Night' at the school, and so on.

Such an approach to language and culture instruction can be adapted as teachers see fit for their students in terms of language experience and cultural backgrounds, as well as for their curriculum (studying one Hispanic country per unit in a beginning course, for example, or making 'the search for cultural identity' the basis for an advanced course). In addition, instructors will need to determine the necessity of spending class time for *language* review for each stage of the approach (pre-, during, or post-investigation) for their particular students: working with numbers/percentages; geographical terms; the differences between written and oral language, for example.

In sum, incorporating this approach towards language and culture instruction in the FL classroom can result in students overcoming possible stereotypes of the various Hispanic cultures and, at the same time, coming to a better understanding of their own cultural identity.

References

Morain, G. (1995). Teaching for cultural diversity. In V. Galloway & C. Herron (Eds.), *Research Within Reach II* (pp. 43–60). Valdosta, GA: Southern Conference on Language Teaching.

Pesado Palmieri, C. (1995, August). *Hitos clásicos de la identidad cultural hispanoamericana y argentina*. Buenos Aires: Faculty Development Program in Argentina, University System of Georgia.

Scarcella, R.C., & Oxford, R.L. (1992). *The tapestry of language learning*. Boston: Heinle and Heinle.

Adaptation One: Stereotypes

	Speaking	Writing	Listening	Reading	Language & Learning Awareness
Communicative & Experiential					
Language					
Culture	●		○		●

Notes

Grade levels and programs: 10 to 12, immersion and core French, postsecondary, ESL

Grouping strategy: Groups or individuals

A popular television game show, Family Feud, provides a format that can be used at a fairly mature level for asking less fluent students to confront their stereotypes about other cultures. For this adaptation, students do a survey of class attitudes to other cultures, then try, in teams, to guess what the likely results of the survey would be.

Ask a group of students who are to be the contestants to leave the room. The instructor asks the remainder of the students to give the first three words or phrases that come to mind when given the name of each of a number of cultural groups. Responses to the word 'British' might include 'stiff upper lip,' 'soccer hooligans,' and 'Shakespeare,' for example. If the teacher wishes to focus on a particular target culture, the questions might be more specific, so that students are asked about Italian food, Italian music, Italian temperament and so on. After the results of the survey have been collated, either by the teacher or by a small group of the students, the responses are ranked in order of frequency. The students who are the contestants are put into teams, return to the room, and are asked the same question. The team that is able to guess the three most frequent responses given by the balance of the class to the question is awarded points and wins the game.

Following the competition, there should be a class discussion as to the source and accuracy of the student perceptions. Do they really think all British people are soccer hooligans? Where do they think such an idea came from? How could they check the accuracy of the suggestion? Students who have visited or lived in the countries in question should be particularly encouraged to share their

131

observations to ensure that the discussion is well informed. Follow-up research should be encouraged to explore the accuracy of class assumptions.

Adaptation Two: Identifying cultural patterns

	Speaking	Writing	Listening	Reading	Language & Learning Awareness
Communicative & Experiential					
Language			●		●
Culture					●

Notes

Grade levels and programs: 10 to 12 immersion and core French, post-secondary, adult ESL

Grouping strategy: Groups or individuals

As an extension of the ethnographic research suggested in Shook's article that would reinforce the awareness of their own cultural patterns, students are asked to note the speech patterns at their family dinner table or among their circle of friends over the course of a week. To encourage students to become conscious of cultural patterns in the target language, it is useful to ask students to reflect explicitly on their own culture and then subsequently make comparisons with the target culture. When observing their own family or friends, students focus on some of the following elements: selection of topics, kind of topics, turn taking, interruptions, register, and other discourse analysis features. The teacher then asks the students to identify cultural patterns. For example, questions to be examined could include: Are young children allowed to talk? Does one person tend to dominate the conversation and why? What is the tone of the conversation? Students will recognize that speech patterns are not always the same for all speakers and that speech patterns differ due to gender, class, and other factors.

In Part 2 of this activity, the students draw on their observations from their own language and culture to examine interactions in the target language by watching a television program such as a sit-com or by observing native speakers should this be possible. This adaptation is essentially a listening activity to encourage cultural awareness (Culture/Language & Learning Awareness) and language and learning awareness (Language/Listening and Language & Learning Awareness).

Error Correction in the L2 Classroom

Maria Mantello

	Speaking	Writing	Listening	Reading	Language & Learning Awareness
Communicative & Experiential					
Language		●			○
Culture					

Notes

Grade levels and programs: 4 to 12, all programs, including post-secondary, adult
Grouping strategy: Individual activity

Editors' Introduction

As teachers, we all grapple with the question of how to correct target language errors in students' writing: what to correct, how effective our error correction practices are, how our students will react to the error correction strategies we adopt, and so forth. In this article describing an example of teacher research, Mantello tries two different methods of selective error correction in her Grade 8 extended French class: coded feedback and reformulation. In this case, she targets errors in the use of the passé composé. Coded feedback shows the students both the location and the nature of the error. Reformulation requires a rewriting of the student composition so that it sounds more 'native-like.'

The principal focus of this article is on Language/Writing and we have indicated a subsidiary focus on Language/Language & Learning Awareness because of the analytic attention to one tense (passé composé). Mantello's findings have implications for a range of teaching contexts where students have attained intermediate levels of proficiency, and where, as in all classes, proficiency levels vary from student to student.

Introduction and rationale

One of the most frustrating tasks of any L2 teacher is correcting errors and then seeing them recur in student writing. A great proportion of our time is consumed in correcting errors, but there is often a nagging feeling that we are correcting the same errors over and over again. It is natural, then, to wonder whether the time and effort spent addressing student errors is time well spent. In other words, do our efforts in error correction actually translate into student learning?

Researchers in the field of second language acquisition share similar concerns. For example, in their article 'French Immersion Research Agenda for the 90s' Lapkin and Swain state that 'it is perhaps surprising given the frequency of errors in language learning, and of error correction in second language, that so little is known about the effects of error correction' (1990, p. 655). In her study of ESL teacher responses to student writing, Zamel concludes that, generally speaking, our teachers' error correction practices tend to be random and arbitrary instead of being based on a clear and focused strategy (1985, p. 88). Two other researchers, Cardelle and Corno, believe that the type of error correction used by L2 educators is rarely chosen based on cognitive psychological theory (1981, p. 252). There seems to be a general lack of knowledge as far as error correction approaches and strategies are concerned.

Typically we use an error correction method until we encounter problems, and then attempt to modify our techniques. What tends to remain a constant in these experiments, however, is the notion that we must address all errors that appear in student writing. That is to say, we correct errors comprehensively, addressing all errors. There may be a number of reasons for this. Perhaps we feel that we owe it to the students, or that we aren't doing our jobs if we don't correct every error. On the other hand, what is the true objective of teaching: addressing all errors or ensuring that the students learn? It is customary for L2 teachers to ask students to write out a 'good copy' which is an accurate, error-free copy. This seems to address student expectations. In fact, according to Leki's study on the preferences of ESL students for correction, L2 students are concerned about the errors they make and want their teachers to correct all of their errors (1991, p. 206).

Leki states, however, that many studies point to the ineffectiveness of error correction. For example she refers to Knoblauch and Brannon's literature review on native speakers in which they conclude that 'marking errors on students' papers does not help them improve their writing nor eliminate their errors' (1991, p. 204). Similarly, studies dealing with L2 writing are not supportive of comprehensive error correction techniques (Hendrickson, 1978; Robb, Ross, & Shortreed, 1986; Semke, 1984; Goring Kepner, 1986).

Why is it then that teachers continue to correct errors comprehensively? This certainly isn't the case in skill areas other than SLA; in sports for example, learners work on a few skills at a time. Correction by the teacher or coach is not general but particular, directing the learner's attention to one specific movement of a process. Similarly, in L1 English classes, teachers might subordinate the correction of surface-level errors in order to respond to the ideas in a written text. Ideas, therefore, take precedence over form.

A Study in my Classroom

With this in mind I recently conducted a study on error correction with my Grade 8 Extended French students as part of the requirements of the Master of Arts program. Given the results of previous studies dealing with comprehensive error correction as well as my own experience with comprehensive error correction, I decided to correct errors selectively rather than comprehensively. Selective error correction involves correcting a limited number of language structures consistently and persistently over a period of time.

I chose to address only one structure during the error correction phase of the writing process. I limited the amount of corrective feedback because of the beginner level proficiency of the students in my class. Most of the students in my classes had been enrolled in core French in Grades 4, 5, and 6 and had spent only one year in the Extended French program. I targeted the *passé composé* structure, since, in my experience, students usually find this a complex structure, yet it is an important learning component in their program.

As I had two Grade 8 classes, I took the opportunity to experiment with two error correction methods: coded feedback and reformulation. Coded feedback shows the students both the location and the nature of the error; for this group I underlined all errors involving the *passé composé* .

The other method I used, reformulation, was developed by Levenston in response to his concerns that standard methods of feedback were providing students with only partial or limited feedback. Reformulation entails having a native writer of the target language rewrite a learner's composition so that surface errors such as grammar and vocabulary are addressed, and so that it sounds more 'native like.' The L2 learner then compares his text with the reformulated version and notes differences in specific categories provided by the instructor (this is described in Cohen, 1990, pp. 115-121).

The students in both classes wrote two pre-tests and post-tests which consisted of multiple choice tests and free-writing samples. These tests allowed me to gauge the proficiency level of the students with regards to the *passé composé* structure. Students also completed seven in-class written assignments over a period of about four months.

Students were asked to correct their own errors involving the *passé composé* and to submit them to me for further feedback. So far, everything for the two classes has been identical, but at this point students received one of the treatments described above depending on which class they were in. In other words, one group received coded feedback and the other received reformulation.

Results

The data collected in the study reveal that by the end of the study both groups of students significantly improved their ability to identify and to produce the *passé composé* structure correctly. While the reformulation group took a little longer to respond to the treatment, by the end of the study one group did not outperform the other group on the tests. It was interesting for me, as a teacher, to see how each method affected both strong and weak students. To indicate these differences, it may help to focus in on the individual responses of a typical 'strong' student and a 'weak' student.

The reformulation technique worked especially well with a strong student (Annie) who found it both challenging and stimulating. Not only did Annie's proficiency with the *passé composé* improve but so did her writing as a whole. For example, she began to pay close attention to her writing style, various organizational features, and basic mechanics. She attempted to vary her sentence structure. In addition, unlike the strong student in the coded feedback group, Annie began to use verbs in the imperfect tense even though this tense was not targeted during the study. It is likely that she became aware of this structure during the comparison activity.

In fact Cohen (1990) states that the success of the reformulation technique is largely due to the student's ability to reflect on the differences between the two versions of the text. Annie made some astute observations as to the differences between the two texts and her writing improved in exactly those areas where she was able to make observations. This suggests that she reflected on the differences and attempted to incorporate her observations into subsequent written assignments. The weak student in this group (Corinna), on the other hand, was overwhelmed by the comparison activity. She was not able to articulate the differences between the two texts and her comments were largely limited to stating that the reformulated text was 'better.' She clearly required assistance with this analytic task. While she did improve her proficiency level with the *passé composé*, she did not improve to quite the same extent as the weak student in the other group (Leanne). It seems that weaker students, in general, benefit from an error correction technique that makes corrections more explicit.

The coded feedback method worked particularly well with the weaker L2 student who seemed to benefit from the explicit nature of coded feedback. Coded feedback helped the strong L2 student (Lee) only initially, suggesting that this technique should be used sparingly with stronger L2 students. These observations also suggest that error correction strategies need to be tailored to the linguistic ability of the individual student.

One element common to both reformulation and feedback is the fact that they both incorporate problem-solving. In choosing an error correction strategy, it seems reasonable to choose a method that engages students in the error correction process rather than providing corrections for them.

Error correction in your classrooms

It is important that as L2 teachers we reflect on why it is that we correct errors in the first place. We should constantly keep before us that the only true objective in error correction is student learning. In choosing an error correction strategy we might consider incorporating some of the following elements:

- problem-solving;
- individualized feedback based on L2 proficiency levels;
- explicit feedback for weaker students;
- using a variety of methods, especially for stronger students;
- focusing on a limited number of significant structures.

References

Cardelle, M., & Corno, L. (1981). Effects on second language learning variations in written feedback on homework assignments. *TESOL Quarterly, 15*, 251–261.

Cohen, A.C. (1990). Writing as process and product. *Language learning insights for learners, teachers, and researchers*, 103–131. New York: Newbury House.

Goring Kepner, C. (1991). An experiment in the relationship of types of written feedback to the development of second language writing skills. *Modern Language Journal, 61*, 305–313.

Hendrickson, J.M. (1978). Error correction in foreign language teaching: Recent theory, research and practice. *Modern Language Journal, 26*, 387–398.

Leki, I. (1991). The preferences of ESL students for error correction in college-level writing classes. *Foreign Language Annals, 24*, 203–211.

Lapkin, S., & Swain, M. (1990). French immersion research agenda for the 90s. *Canadian Modern Language Review, 46*, 638–669.

Robb, T., Ross, S., & Shortreed, I. (1986). Salience of feedback on error and its effect on EFL writing Quality. *TESOL Quarterly, 20*, 53–63.

Semke, H.D. (1984). Effects of the red pen. *Foreign Language Annals, 17*, 195–202.

Zamel, V. (1985). Responding to student writing. *TESOL Quarterly, 19*, 79–101.

Adaptation One: Before and after compositions

	Speaking	Writing	Listening	Reading	Language & Learning Awareness
Communicative & Experiential	○				
Language		●		●	●
Culture					

Notes

Grade levels and programs: 7 to 12 immersion, 10 to 12 core French, post-secondary, adult

Grouping strategy: Whole class

As a whole class variation on the reformulation activity described in the Mantello article, we suggest that the teacher select a piece of student writing that an individual student, two students working together, or a larger group has created. The teacher then reformulates part of or the entire piece and puts the reformulation and the original on overhead transparencies. It would be helpful if the teacher provided in advance some guidelines as to what students are to look for (e.g., a language convention such as capitalization or discourse organization). The teacher then asks the class to observe the differences between the two versions of the text, and elicits student views on why the changes were made, how they serve to correct or improve the original text, and so forth. This procedure permits a wide-ranging discussion, not only of the target structure (if there is one), but also of other grammatical or discourse features of the text. For this reason, a principal rather than a subsidiary emphasis has been placed in the Language/Language & Learning Awareness cell. The reading and writing cells in the Language component also have a principal focus.

Adaptation Two: Practising second language pronunciation

	Speaking	Writing	Listening	Reading	Language & Learning Awareness
Communicative & Experiential				○	
Language	●		●	○	●
Culture					

Notes

Grade levels and programs: 4 to 12 immersion, 7 to 12 core French, post-secondary, adult

Grouping strategy: Pairs

Equipment required: Audiotape recorders

Preparation required: Tape recording of native speaker

Teachers often confront the need to correct oral as well as written work on a daily basis. In this adaptation, we examine the issue of the limited time available to correct spoken discourse and to work on pronunciation and other aspects of speaking skills.

Ideally, the teacher will try to arrange a quiet spot (a corner of the classroom, a learning centre, the corridor) for one pair of students at a time. Students listen to and agree on the meaning of a short text, preferably from a play or skit that the students will perform, or perhaps a school announcement for the loudspeaker system. They then read the text into a tape recorder. The same text has been recorded by a native speaker and is available on a second tape recorder. Working with the two tape recorders, students listen to the two examples of the recorded texts in segments, compare them, and work on improving their pronunciation, diction and/or intonation. Finally, they record their text a second time and incorporate what they have learned, and then identify the areas of improvement.

Handcrafted Books: Check this out!

Beatrice Dupuy and Jeff McQuillan

	Speaking	Writing	Listening	Reading	Language & Learning Awareness
Communicative & Experiential		●			
Language		●			○
Culture					

Notes

Grade levels and programs:	7 to10, immersion, core French, ESL
Grouping strategy:	A range of grouping strategies
Equipment required:	Word processing, if desired

Editors' Introduction

Dupuy and McQuillan suggest that intermediate level learners of French create their own storybooks for use by younger learners. Students write original or retellings of familiar stories, illustrate them, and then donate them to school libraries in local communities. The sharing of the students' stories gives this activity a Communicative & Experiential/Writing focus, hence the principal emphasis in this cell on the chart. The authors also suggest that students, with their teacher's help, engage in an editing process of their written work to clarify and correct content and style and to achieve coherence. This procedure also assures grammatical and lexical accuracy and provides a principal focus on Language/Writing. The reflection required in the editing process involves a subsidiary focus on Language/Language & Learning Awareness.

There is strong evidence that reading, particularly self-selected or 'free voluntary' reading (FVR) is a major contribution to both first and second/foreign language development and literacy (Krashen, 1993; Elley, 1991; Elley & Manghubai, 1983). FVR has also been found to be more motivating than traditional form-focused instruction, therefore resulting in more positive attitudes toward reading and greater frequency of out-of-school reading (Greaney & Clarke, 1973; Cho & Krashen, 1994, 1995; Constantino, 1994, 1995; McQuillan, 1994, 1995; Tse & McQuillan, in press). However, despite these advantages, FVR is seldom a significant part of beginning and intermediate second/foreign language curricula (Huber, 1993), and many second/foreign language students report doing little reading for pleasure in the language they study (McQuillan, 1995; Dupuy, in preparation).

One reason for the lack of FVR in second/foreign language programs is the difficulty of finding texts that beginning and intermediate adult students find both interesting and comprehensible. Simple children's stories, for example, may be comprehensible but not very interesting; conversely, novels, magazines or newspapers may be interesting, but unlikely within the linguistic reach of beginning/intermediate students. There is also the matter of cost and availability: imported foreign language texts are often very costly, and not readily available in many areas.

One solution to this problem is to have second/foreign language students create their own texts for their fellow students at a similar or lower level of competence. These handcrafted books can provide students with comprehensible texts on topics of interest to students at low cost. Producing such books in a second/foreign language context also gives intermediate students an authentic task and useful purpose in composing (Johns, 1990).

What was tried?
At the beginning of the semester, intermediate semester (3rd semester) French as a Foreign Language students were invited to participate in building a reading collection for lower level students of French. They were told that their stories could be original or retellings of familiar, not-so-familiar tales from their culture – anything from children's stories to classic novels (Appendix). They were told that whatever was of interest to them was fine. Students were also advised to write without the use of the dictionary, since it was important to ensure that these texts remained at a level appropriate for beginners and intermediates. If students with an extra year of exposure to French did not know a word or expression, chances were that their fellow students at the lower level would not either. Interest and comprehensibility were the key factors to be considered.

Students were also advised to illustrate their story. Not only would the illustrations make their story more appealing to read, it would also enhance their comprehensibility. Some students drew their own illustrations, while others chose to cut out pictures in magazines or have friends help them. Another way to approach illustrations would be to have intermediate and beginning students collaborate, where intermediates would write the stories and beginners illustrate them.

Handcrafted books were part of the writing component of the intermediate course. Students participated in writing with a real purpose – texts that would be part of the foreign language library of the school, read by peers and future students. The types of texts that students produced were varied: children's stories, both original (L'Étrange Boucle d'oreille noire, Le Mauvais Noël de Françoise Frisée, etc.) and retellings (La Chenille qui avait très, très faim, Boucles d'Or et les trois ours, La Petite Poule rousse, etc.); fables (Crapaud apprend une leçon: Ne jamais remettre à demain ce qu'on peut faire aujourd'hui); limericks (Un amour de Fromage); travel reports (Chicago, Okinawa, La Nouvelle-Orléans, etc.); and comics (Le NoneSuch). Other types of texts such as magazines/ newspaper articles, collections of poems around a theme or short stories could also be produced by students. Teachers helped students in the editing of their texts. On the first draft, teachers restricted their comments to the content of the story. Recommendations regarding the development and coherence of the story, the sequence of events or the characters were made when necessary. On the second draft, students and teachers worked collaboratively on improving the style and accuracy of their text. Interest and comprehensibility were the main criteria for assessment. Teachers graded the handcrafted books on a Pass (HP, P, LP)/Fail basis; only students who did not turn in a handcrafted bok received a failing grade for the project.

What was accomplished?

About four hundred handcrafted books, ranging from handwritten, stapled texts with no illustrations, to word-processed, desk-top publishing quality documents with computer graphics, have been produced in the course of a semester. A home-made library, where handcrafted books will be kept for other classes and future students, has also been opened.

Another major accomplishment was that after participating in this project, students viewed themselves in a different light. They were happy to be able to show friends and parents what they had created, and proud to know that their work would be part of a library. They enjoyed the fun and creative aspect of the project. Students experienced the pride of authorship. They had become more than writers. They had become authors.

What will be done next?

In the hope of expanding the use of this library, the books will be placed on the Internet. It will provide maximum latitude to the user in downloading and reproducing these handcrafted books, as well as an opportunity for students to share their creations with a much wider audience. Students and teachers will have a source of easy and interesting reading materials.

References

Cho, K., & Krashen, S. (1994). Acquisition from Sweet Valley High series: Adult ESL acquisition. *Journal of Reading, 37*, 654–662.

Cho, K., & Krashen, S. (1995). From Sweet Valley Kids to Harlequins in one year: A case study of an adult second language acquirer. *California English, 1*, 18–19.

Constantino, R. (1994). Pleasure reading helps, even if readers don't believe it. *Journal of Reading, 37*, 504–505.

Constantino, R. (1995). The effects of pleasure reading. *Mosaic, 3*, 15–17.

Dupuy, B. (in preparation). Voices from the classroom: Students favor extensive reading over grammar instruction and give their reasons.

Elley, W. (1991). Acquiring literacy in a second language: The effect of a book based program. *Language Learning, 41*, 375–411.

Elley, W., & Manghubai, F. (1983). The impact of reading on a second language learning. *Reading Research Quarterly, 19*, 53–67.

Greaney, V., & Clarke, M. (1973). A longitudinal study of the effects of two reading methods on leisure-time reading habits. In D. Moylle (Ed.), *Reading: What of the future?* (pp. 107–114). London: United Kingdom Reading Association.

Huber, B. (1993). Characteristics of college and university foreign language curricula: Findings of the MLA's 1987–1988 survey. *ADFL Bulletin, 24*, 6–21.

Johns, A. (1990). L1 composition theories: Implications for developing theories of L2 composition. In B. Kroll (Ed.), *Second language writing* (pp. 24–36). Cambridge: Cambridge University Press.

Krashen, S. (1993). *The power of reading*. Englewood, CO: Libraries Unlimited.

McQuillan, J. (1994). Reading versus grammar: What students think is pleasurable for language acquisition. *Applied Language Learning, 5*, 95–100.

McQuillan, J. (1995). How should heritage languages be taught? The effects of a free voluntary reading program. *Foreign Language Annals, 29*, 56–72.

Tse, L., & McQuillan, J. (in press). Changing reading attitudes: The power of bringing books into the classroom. In R. Constantino (ed.), *Linguistic minorities and literacy: Access and opportunity*. Englewood, CO: Libraries Unlimited.

145

Pauvre Raoul!

Shelby E. Stover

Quand Raoul s'est levé ce matin, il a eu un petit accident. Il a marché sur un des patins à roulettes de sa soeur Claire. Il est tombé par terre, et s'est blessé le coude. Mais heureusement, son coude n'était pas cassé.

Pour le petit-déjeuner, la mère de Raoul avait préparé des tartines et des céréales. Quand Raoul s'est assis, sa serviette est tombée par terre, il l'a ramassée, mais quand il s'est relevé, son chien avait mangé son petit déjeuner!

Tous les matins, Raoul et son voisin vont à l'école à pied. Mais ce matin là, il faisait mauvais temps, bien sûr! Sur la route de l'école, il pleuvait beaucoup, et les deux jeunes gens n'avaient pas de parapluie!

Dans sa classe d'histoire, le professeur a rendu l'examen aux étudiants. À sa surprise, Raoul a reçu un "D". Quel dommage!

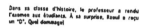

Pour le déjeuner, à la cafétéria, il y avait des haricots verts, du poulet délicieux, et des petits pains. Raoul avait très faim. Malheureusement, il avait oublié son argent. Raoul n'a pas déjeuné ce jour-là.

Quand Raoul est rentré chez lui, sa mère voulait l'emmener dans les magasins pour acheter de nouveaux vêtements. Raoul était triste, parce qu'il désirait jouer avec ses amis. Pauvre Raoul!

À huit heures du soir, le père de Raoul a dit que Raoul était fatigué, mais Raoul a dit que non. Mais comme son père est le chef de famille, Raoul s'est couché à huit heures. Il espérait que tout irait mieux demain.

used with permission

Adaptation One: Creating books for younger readers

	Speaking	Writing	Listening	Reading	Language & Learning Awareness
Communicative & Experiential	●			●	
Language	○	●			
Culture					

Notes

Grade levels and programs:	7 to 12 immersion, 10 to 12 core French, adult
Grouping strategy:	A variety of groupings
Equipment:	Optional word processing and graphics
Preparation required:	11" x 17" sheets of cardboard or Bristol board; arrangement to collaborate with a beginning target language class

This adaptation is similar to the activity described in the article, but involves a buddy system with more advanced students reading with beginners. The principal focus now moves to the Communicative & Experiential/Speaking and Reading cells. The buddy system provides an ideal activity for intermediate or secondary French immersion or ESL classes and for senior secondary core French. The more advanced students create children's storybooks, in big book format, and then actually visit primary or elementary second language classes to read their books aloud. Adult community-based ESL or other adult students might enjoy creating books to read to their children or grandchildren.

These big books go through an editing process similar to the one Dupuy and McQuillan describe (see page 144). It is important that the final text be error-free, hence the emphasis on Language/Writing. When the final version is ready, students receive 11" x 17" sheets of Bristol or cardboard on which to produce their books. Each page contains a small amount of text written large enough so that the younger students can see and follow along with the person who is reading aloud. This allows students to develop their listening skills, but also their reading decoding skills because the large print allows them to make sound-text connections as they follow along with the person reading the book. Each page should also be illustrated to help the younger learners better understand the story.

Artistically inclined students may draw their pictures, while others might use computer-generated illustrations (e.g., clip art), or trace or cut out pictures to illustrate the books.

Rehearsal for reading aloud is also necessary. Here the teacher and students provide feedback to the reader on his/her pronunciation, diction, volume, enthusiasm, and body language. Advanced students could also work on engaging younger students in a dialogue while they read the book by asking questions about the pictures or new vocabulary and asking them to predict what will happen next.

Adaptation Two: Re-telling familiar stories

	Speaking	Writing	Listening	Reading	Language & Learning Awareness
Communicative & Experiential	●	●	●	●	
Language					
Culture					

Notes

Grade levels and programs: 11 and 12 core French and immersion, post secondary, adult ESL

Grouping strategy: Small groups and whole class

Preparation required: Choice of book

The teacher reads aloud to the class a version of a well-known story in the target language, such as *Cinderella* or another story that has appeared in many cultures, for example, La Fontaine's *Fables*, *Little Red Riding Hood*, etc. After the teacher has read his/her version of the story, a large-group discussion follows to check the students' comprehension and to see if the students have ever heard a similar story in their first language. If all students indicate that a version of the selected story exists in their culture, the activity can proceed to a writing stage. In class or for homework, students write a target language version of the story as it is told in their culture. When finished, the teacher then arranges the students in groups of three or four (culturally mixed, in the case of ESL students) to tell their versions of the story to their peers (oral sharing). A whole class follow-up discussion would then focus on the differences that existed and the possible meanings of these differences.

If all students do not appear to know a version of the chosen story, then this activity will work best as a group activity focused on speaking and listening only. The teacher chooses groups of three or four students, and ensures that at least one student knows a version of the selected story. That student then shares his/her version of the story in the target language with the others and their collective task includes identifying the differences between the teacher's and the students' versions. A whole-class, follow-up discussion, similar to the one described as the ending of the writing-focused version of this adaptation, would provide further language practice.

149

Cooperative Learning in Second Language Classes: Two Techniques to Consider

Miles Turnbull

	Speaking	Writing	Listening	Reading	Language & Learning Awareness
Communicative & Experiential	●		●		
Language					
Culture					

Notes

Grade levels and programs: All

Grouping strategy: Groups, pairs

Editors' Introduction

Turnbull describes two cooperative learning techniques, 'timed pair-share' and 'round robin.' He presents both sides of the pedagogical and theoretical arguments concerning the use of cooperative learning for teaching a second language. It would appear from the literature that cooperative learning, in its classic form, is most successful in the heterogeneous classroom where students are obliged to use the target language to communicate with their peers. This approach could also be successful in second language classes where students are reasonably proficient in the second language and highly motivated to improve their second language competencies, especially their speaking and listening skills. Motivated students working in small groups or pairs have more opportunities for speaking and listening in the target language than in a teacher-led discussion. If the teacher is able to provide activities that require real communication, such as information gap activities, students are required to make an effort to broaden their vocabulary and syntax, and the conversation is less likely to drift into the first language or into artificial communication.

Cooperative learning: A working definition

Cooperative learning is designed to engage students actively in the learning process through carefully structured group work (pairs or small groups) such that learners interact, exchange specific information and are held accountable for their learning. Let's examine a couple of examples.

Timed pair-share and round-robins: Two examples

Recently, I attended a session by Dr. Spencer Kagan (renowned author and researcher on cooperative learning) at the annual conference of *La Société pour la promotion de l'enseignement de l'anglais au Québec*. I was rather taken, to say the least, when he very successfully organized a room of about 800 teachers into groups of two, then four, in order to demonstrate his timed pair-share and round-robin ideas for second/foreign language classroom teaching.

Kagan's objective was to demonstrate cooperative learning techniques that are easy to incorporate into everyday teaching routines without a great deal of planning or agonizing (unlike STAD, Jigsaw, etc.). Timed pair-share and round-robin require little prior planning and can even be used spontaneously if this becomes appropriate. Both techniques are designed to encourage equal participation and listening.

In timed pair-share, students first think to themselves on a topic given to them by the teacher. Next, they are paired with another student. The teacher clearly indicates that each person will have a specific amount of time to speak. Only one student speaks at a time, while the other *must* listen (after all, encouraging listening is important!). After the specific time, the teacher uses a predetermined signal (such as a whistle, hand raising, a funny sound-maker) and the second student speaks. This can be followed by a sharing with the class, if desired.

In a round-robin, students are organized into groups of three or four. Each student in turn shares something with his or her teammates. Only one student speaks at a time, and again, the others listen. This technique can be adapted as a round-table where each student in turn writes one comment or answer as a paper and pencil are passed around the group. The round-robin and round-table techniques could be interesting ways for groups of students to create stories cooperatively.

I have been experimenting with these techniques in a university-level course on second language acquisition theory. I have found it quite easy to organize 40 students into groups without much planning. The students agree that these techniques allow for more equal participating (for example, students who have a tendency to listen and not speak in more loosely structured group activities get more opportunity to talk). However, the students and I have found these techniques highly structured and even regimented. I recommend that one use these techniques judiciously, especially with adult learners.

Now let's consider some of the pedagogical and theoretical arguments in favour of cooperative learning.

Pedagogical arguments

Long and Porter (1985) highlight five important pedagogical arguments for the use of collaborative learning in SL classes.

- Group work has the potential for increasing the quantity of language practice opportunities, and this enhances fluency in the SL/FL. Grouping strategies provide about 500 percent more opportunities for learners to talk than do teacher-fronted classes.

- The quality of student talk can be enhanced through cooperative groupings. Student groups are natural settings for authentic conversation which prepares learners for the demands of real-life communicative situations.

- Group work can be an effective teaching technique for individualization of instruction. Students with particular needs or strengths and weaknesses can work on these collectively while supporting and helping each other in the process.

- A positive affective climate can be created by cooperative learning. Students feel less pressure to speak and may be less fearful of a teacher scrutinizing their language production. Moreover, group work can allow for more personalized and creative work to occur than is possible in large groups.

- Cooperative learning is motivating because of the aforementioned reasons and because it allows for greater instructional variety in the SL classroom.

Theoretical arguments

Cooperative learning allows for greater comprehension of the input SL/FL learners receive and provides more opportunities to talk (i.e., output). Furthermore, it is suggested that learning first occurs when learners interact with others (especially others who are more advanced). Let's examine each of these in a bit more detail.

- It has been claimed that comprehensible or understandable input is crucial in second and foreign language acquisition. In cooperative learning, students hear more language that the learner understands and which contains vocabulary and structures that are 'a little beyond' their ability level. It is also argued that collaborative groupings are superior to individualistic learning structures because they provide students with important redundant input. For more information, see Krashen's Input Model (Krashen, 1981, 1982); McGroarty (1993); and Holt (1993).

- Besides greater opportunity to hear more language at an appropriate and understandable level, well-thought-out pairing and grouping strategies allow learners to talk or output more. It is argued that simply understanding what one hears or reads is not enough for learners to produce the SL/FL with accuracy and fluency. Producing language allows students to move beyond their present level of SL/FL development. For example, research has shown that collaborative learning helps French immersion students improve the accuracy of their oral and written production. For more information, see Swain (1985, 1993, 1995, in press); Swain and Lapkin (1995a, 1995b); Kowal and Swain (1994, in press).

- It is also suggested that knowledge is first constructed between learners engaged in social interaction. Subsequently, learners can then internalize

152

what they have learned through this social dialogue. For more information, see Vygotsky (1987); Donato & Adair-Hauck (1992); Adair-Hauck & Donato (1994); Donato (1994); Swain (1995, in press).

What about the difficulties and weaknesses of cooperative learning?

Counter-arguments

The principles of cooperative learning are based on a number of assumptions, some of the most problematic of which are as follows:

- Learners are strongly motivated to learn the target language.
- Learners will recognize the value of cooperative activities.
- All output opportunities develop competence.

Clearly, each of these assumptions is open to challenge. Not all learners are highly motivated to learn the language; indeed, one might argue that most school-based language classrooms include at least some learners who are present under protest. Many younger learners, freed from direct teacher supervision, cannot resist the opportunity to chat quietly to a peer in the mother tongue. Peer pressure may even suggest that making a genuine effort to converse in the target language is 'uncool' behaviour.

Not all learners will recognize the value of cooperative activities. Culturally based expectations of educational approaches may lead learners to dismiss such interaction as worthless, because there is no apparent source of expertise on which to draw. Some learners perceive teachers as failing to do their job when they apparently resign control of the class to allow 'chatter.'

It is also arguable whether all output opportunities develop competence. In many cooperative learning situations, such as the ones described earlier in this article, there may be no feedback to the speaker to indicate whether the communication has been successful. When there is no real information to communicate, merely a requirement to use language, learners have little incentive to stretch their expertise. They will tend therefore to restrict themselves to long familiar syntax and lexis and consequently gain little from the opportunity to speak.

It is of course possible to design activities that increase the likelihood of real communication. Information gap activities, which rely on one partner's having information that the other needs in order to perform a task, often provide an incentive to struggle with the language. Obviously, if the partners come from different language backgrounds and the target language is the only possible medium of communication, the cooperative activities will be more successful. Too often, however, cooperative learning sees learners who share a common language base produce a perfunctory performance in highly artificial activities that do not honour the conventions of real communication.

References

Adair-Hauck, B., & Donato, R. (1994). Foreign language explanation within the zone of proximal development. *The Canadian Modern Language Review/La Revue canadienne des langues vivantes, 50*(3), 532–557.

Donato, R. (1994). Collective scaffolding in second language learning. In J.P. Lantolf & G. Appel (Eds.), *Vygotskian perspectives to second language research* (pp. 33–56). Norwood, NJ: Ablex Publishing.

Donato, R., & Adair-Hauck, B. (1992). Discourse perspectives on formal instruction. *Language Awareness, 1*(2), 73–89.

Holt, D. (Ed.) (1993). *Cooperative learning: A response to linguistic and cultural diversity.* Washington, DC: Centre for Applied Linguistics.

Kowal, M., & Swain, M. (1994). Using collaborative language production tasks to promote students' language awareness. *Language Awareness, 3*(1), 1–21.

Kowal, M., & Swain, M. (in press). From semantic to syntactic processing: How can we promote it in the immersion classroom? In R.K. Johnson & M. Swain (Eds.), *Immersion education: International perspectives.* Cambridge: Cambridge University Press.

Krashen, S. (1981). *Second language acquisition and second language learning.* New York: Pergamon Press.

Krashen, S. (1982). *Principles and practice in second language acquisition.* New York: Pergamon Press.

Long, M.H., & Porter, P.A. (1985). Group work, interlanguage talk and second language acquisition. *TESOL Quarterly 19*(2), 207–228.

McGroarty, M. (1993). Cooperative learning and second language acquisition. In D. Holt (Ed.), *Cooperative learning: A response to linguistic and cultural diversity* (pp. 19–46). Washington, DC: Centre for Applied Linguistics.

Swain, M. (1985). Communicative competence: Some roles of comprehensible input and comprehensible output in its development. In S.M. Gass & C.G. Madden (Eds.), *Input in second language acquisition* (pp. 235–254). Rowley, MA: Newbury House.

Swain, M. (1993). The output hypothesis: Just reading and writing aren't enough. *The Canadian Modern Language Review/La Revue canadienne des langues vivantes, 50*(1), 158–164.

Swain, M. (1995). Three functions of output in second language learning. In G. Cook & B. Seidhofer (Eds.), *Principles and practice in the study of language.* Oxford: Oxford University Press.

Swain, M. (in press). Collaborative dialogue: Its contribution to L2 learning. *Revista Canaria de Estudios Ingleses, 33.*

Swain, M., & Lapkin, S. (1995a). Problems in output and the cognitive processes they generate: A step towards second language learning. *Applied Linguistics, 16*, 1–32.

Swain, M., & Lapkin, S. (1995b). Peer interaction and second language learning: Focus on meaning versus focus on form in meaningful contexts. Paper presented in Second Language Classroom Research, November 6, 1995.

Vygotsky, L.S. (1987). Thinking and speech. In R.W. Rieber & A.S. Carton (Eds.), *The collected works of L.S. Vygotsky, Vol. 1.* New York: Plenum.

Adaptation One: A round-table writing activity

	Speaking	Writing	Listening	Reading	Language & Learning Awareness
Communicative & Experiential	○	●		○	
Language					
Culture					

Notes
Grade levels and programs: 4 to 6 immersion, 7 to 9 core French, adult ESL community
Grouping strategy: Small groups

In this adaptation, the round robin technique becomes a round-table activity to provide a principal focus on Communicative & Experiential/Writing. The instructor divides the class into groups of about four, has sufficient sheets of paper available (one for each student) with one sentence written on each sheet. As many different sentences as possible should be used, or the teacher may put the same sentence on each sheet to see how many different stories the students generate. Each sentence is a potential story starter, for example: 'I was carrying my tray into the school cafeteria looking around for a seat ...' Each student adds one sentence to the story, or if the class is fairly fluent, each may write for several minutes. When the time is up, each student passes his/her sheet to the right and, in turn, receives another sheet. The receiving student reads what the previous students have written and adds his/her own contribution to the story. The procedure continues until the story is returned to the first writer. This activity often generates considerable amusement and a relaxed atmosphere for writing. Students may even begin to edit each other's work, and they may wish to vote on which story is the best, and explain their rationale. Advanced students could discuss the stories in terms of discourse features, i.e., degree of cohesiveness and coherence.

Adaptation Two: A get acquainted activity

	Speaking	Writing	Listening	Reading	Language & Learning Awareness
Communicative & Experiential	●	●	●		
Language					
Culture					

Notes

Grade levels and programs:	Core French, ESL
Grouping strategy:	Groups of four or five
Preparation required:	Preparation of grid

A 'get acquainted' activity for the beginning of the year is a variation on the think-pair-share concept. Individual students first think about what they would like to know about their peers. (Beginners are likely to ask questions such as 'Do you have any brothers?' 'where do you come from?' whereas more advanced learners might ask their peers to describe their most embarrassing moments or favourite pastime.) Next, students divide into groups of four or five. The teacher gives each student a grid, to be completed as in the following diagram with names and questions. Individual students write the questions they generated on the horizontal rows on the left side of the grid.

In turn, each student asks one of his or her questions and the other students respond. Students take turns asking one question at a time so that all students have an equal opportunity to ask at least some questions in the time provided.

This initial interviewing stage could be followed by a larger group activity, allowing others to learn about the students from each small group. This could be achieved by organizing the class into two circles in the middle of the class, one inside the other.

Students start by summarizing the answers to one of their questions to the student in front of them. The teacher then asks both circles to rotate in a clockwise direction four paces. Students then summarize their answers to a second question for a new student.

Alternatively, the teacher could do a large group sharing of the interview information by calling on various students to share what they learned during the interviewing. The teacher could also ask students to write about what they learned about one or more students and post this information on a notice board or email conference for others to read.

This activity could be preceded by a mini-lesson on question formation. In this case, students would apply what they learned from the mini grammar lesson while creating their questions. Students could also engage in a self- or peer-correction stage before beginning the interviewing.

Your Questions	Sharon	Miles	Jill
Do you have any brothers? Where do you come from?	No	yes	No

Love, Sex, and Union: A Multidimensional Module

Miles Turnbull

	Speaking	Writing	Listening	Reading	Language & Learning Awareness
Communicative & Experiential	●	●	●	○	
Language	○	○			○
Culture					○

Notes

Grade levels and programs: 10 to 12 immersion, post-secondary, adult ESL
Grouping strategy: groupings
Equipment required: Computer with e-mail access, videoconferencing (optional)
Preparation required: None, unless technology is used

Editors' Introduction

In this article, Turnbull describes the way in which he and his senior secondary and post-secondary-level students developed a multidimensional module relevant to their lives and interests. Although the topic of love, sex, and union appealed to this particular group of students, students may decide upon any topic of interest to them. For example, younger students may want to do a survey on, for example, what is in their lunch boxes, their favourite television program or sport or food. The core activity is the development of a survey questionnaire and its administration (in person, by e-mail, through videoconferencing) with a number of target language speakers, and the subsequent analysis of the data. The development, application, and analysis of the survey provide opportunities for grammatical instruction as the students develop the questions and interpret the answers, engage in cultural discussions with the survey respondent and with classmates, and real life interaction with target language speakers as shown by the emphases in the Communicative & Experiential/Speaking, Writing, and Listening cells above.

Union? Not marriage?!

Some would suggest that the title of the multidimensional module that I describe below is politically correct, trendy, and racy, but also reflective of societal reality, respectful of diversity, and even forward-thinking! In fact, I believe that this module has all of these qualities, in one way or another. I have gradually developed it over the past seven years in my FSL classes at the university and senior secondary levels. I have also, most recently, adapted it for ESL in a summer language bursary program. The theme has been of particular interest to almost all my students (I wonder why?). Motivation and interest have never been a problem. I admit that I have been fortunate to have worked at the university level, where the students are able to decide if the subject matter is appropriate for them. Moreover, the senior secondary context in which I worked was quite progressive and did not have to contend with curriculum censure by parental groups.

My intention here is to present the module that I have developed as an example to suggest how teachers could create their own (especially in the absence of published material that reflects this approach for the university level) in order to address the specific ages, needs, and interests of their students. However, the key principles presented here can easily be transferred to the creation of a multidimensional module for any language at any level. First, let's examine the theoretical framework upon which this multidimensional teaching approach is based.

The multidimensional approach for second language (L2) teaching was first proposed by Stern (1982, 1983). He referred to a near-consensus about the inadequacy of grammar-based L2 curricula (involving the presentation and practice of linguistic elements in artificial, non-communicative contexts) for developing communication skills and cultural knowledge and empathy. He suggested that an L2 curriculum should integrate four syllabuses: communication, language, culture, and general language education. In his view, this multiple approach is more theoretically defensible than a grammar-based approach and is more educationally desirable because it reflects the social and cultural nature of languages. Stern's ideas have been adopted most enthusiastically by the Canadian Association of Second Language Teachers, which published the *National Core French Study – NCFS* (Leblanc, 1990), recommending a curriculum model for core French delivery in Canada integrating Stern's four syllabuses. Although Stern suggested that any of the syllabuses could be the starting point for the organization of the curriculum, the NCFS recommends that the communicative-experiential syllabus be the basis of most teaching units, culminating in an educational project. The teaching module described here reflects the latter view.

For those who might be concerned that such an approach is not 'academic' enough for university, I would argue that a multidimensional approach can be just as rigorous and scholarly as a grammar-based approach. Moreover, I am convinced that students can learn to apply the grammar they already know in authentic and interesting communicative contexts. Those who suggest that students who come from high school know nothing, need only examine the textbooks that have been used in these contexts in the past. Many of them are almost as exclusively grammar-based as most of the existing university texts and present more or less the same linguistic structures, with less detailed rules.

Fortunately, core French programs are in the process of changing to reflect a multidimensional approach. I anticipate that future French students (from core French, at least) who arrive at university will have much greater overall proficiency in their second language. In the meantime, however, these students need an opportunity to use their knowledge, test some hypotheses, and notice the gaps in their present L2 knowledge, as Swain (1995, in press) has suggested. The module described here provides such an opportunity.

The key to creating a successful multidimensional module is the selection of an appropriate topic. The authors of the communicative-experiential syllabus of the NCFS (Tremblay, Duplantie, & Huot, 1990) suggest that the content of the multidimensional curriculum, which they call 'fields of experience,' must consider the life experiences of the learners, their intellectual development, interests, and needs. In my case, the Love, Sex, and Union 'field of experience' does just that.

My description of the Love, Sex and Union teaching module will include an overview of the objectives of each syllabus, followed by a list of suggested steps to achieve these objectives. Although the 'didactique' of each step will be clearly described, I will focus on the educational project, which is reflected in the overall experiential goals listed above.

Syllabus	Objective(s)
Experiential	• conduct an attitude survey of native speakers of the target language (TL) • prepare a research report of the survey results • discuss one's feelings and attitudes about love, sex, and union
Communicative	• use all four skills in authentic and interesting contexts • interact with native speakers of the TL • view a film in the TL • negotiate meaning in communicative activities
Language	• create a vocabulary bank for the unit • negotiate form in communicative activities • convert L1–L2 cognates (morphology and phonology) • express one's opinion using appropriate verb conjugations (grammar)
Culture	• investigate the attitudes of native speakers of the TL and compare to the culture of the learners
General Language Education	• use cognates and brainstorming as language learning strategies • reflect on one's learning and knowledge

Overall Experiential Goal

Learners will work in groups of 3–4 and prepare a survey on a topic of their choice (related to Love, Sex, and Union) which they will administer (orally) to native speakers of the target language. Students will prepare a research report of their results.

Suggested steps

Step 1

• **Brainstorm** (either in small groups or collectively) to encourage students to reflect on their knowledge and experience and propose a list of possible topics related to the overall theme. (Assign a secretary so that a vocabulary list can be created and distributed.) The principal objectives here are to relate the topic to students' lives and to create a bank of vocabulary for the unit.

Step 2

- **Discuss** the experiential goal of the unit and the steps to be followed to reach this goal. This step recognizes the learner as an active participant in the creative process of learning, leading to autonomy as advocated by many L2 educators, including the Council of Europe (1981) and Dickinson (1987). As the students become aware of the objectives of the unit, they are empowered to take responsibility for their own learning. They become more engaged, and feel less that curriculum they don't like is being imposed upon them.

Step 3

- **Reflect** on the meaning of the unit's title (preferably in small groups). In order to express an opinion about the concept of union and not marriage, for example, a grammar lesson expressing one's opinion (I think, I believe, I agree/disagree, etc.) and the appropriate verb conjugation (e.g., subjunctive after Je ne pense/crois pas que vs. indicative after Je pense/crois que) is possible. Obviously, many other linguistic structures could be examined here, but the key is to exploit language syllabus content that is relevant to the context created by the communicative-experiential syllabus objectives.

Step 4

- **Develop** the survey. To prepare students for the development of their survey, I use two articles (see references below) that summarize an attitude survey relating to love, sex, and union. This step allows for a real intersection of the communicative-experiential, language, and general language education syllabuses.

First, I exploit these documents from a linguistic and general language education point of view. Given the significant number of words related to this theme that have Latin and Greek origins (e.g., sexuality, pornography, marriage, homosexuality), I use these documents to teach the written and oral recognition of cognates (see Tréville, 1993, and Turnbull, 1995, for support of the teaching of cognates as a general language education strategy and an approach for vocabulary development). Of course, one could exploit these articles with many other linguistic objectives in mind.

Second, I use a Jigsaw activity to review the content of the two articles. Expert groups ensure comprehension of one article which is then summarized in the home groups (see Holt, 1993, for support of the use of collaborative learning in L2 classes and a description of the Jigsaw activity).

The students then stay in their home groups for the survey work. The groups choose a topic related to the overall theme that interests them. The groups then develop their survey questions and refine them using available resources. A final conference with the teacher is required before conducting the survey. This conference allows the teacher to identify the students' language difficulties, and could be an excellent opportunity to offer a mini-grammar lesson related to one or more of these difficulties.

Step 5

- **Conduct** the survey with native speakers of the TL. It is best if this is done on the students' own time. I require a minimum of 30 native speakers in the ESL summer language program. However, for FSL classes in non-francophone areas, I aim for a minimum of 15 but recommend as many as possible, and 30 ideally. I give the FSL students a bank of willing participants whom I have already contacted or know personally. I also recommend that the students try the local French school, the local francophone society, and the close-by francophone region.

This step usually becomes the most authentic, exciting, and sometimes nerve-wracking for the students. Although many of them find this contact with native speakers difficult, they invariably report that it is a highlight of their course. In fact, this authentic contact with native speakers allows for a real intersection of the communicative-experiential and culture syllabuses, and really brings the language learning experience alive for the students!

Step 6

- **Prepare and present** the research report. Here, I include a lesson on the proper format of a research report, which the students find useful for other university courses. I encourage peer correction when they are preparing the written version of their report. Their presentation of this report could be oral to the rest of the class, in poster format for others to see, or for the school newspaper.

I will take the liberty here of switching to the past tense to describe some of my experiences with this part of the module. My students have created some excellent reports (and some not so excellent ones) on topics such as sex before marriage, common-law union, homosexuality, senior citizens' sex life, and more. They have often been very curious about the differences between their culture and the target community. Besides fostering cross-cultural understanding, this curiosity really engages the students. I remember specifically a discussion about homosexuality and AIDS that happened as a direct result of a student presentation. This discussion was particularly interesting and engaging because there were students from Romania, Jamaica, Uganda, Bermuda, Italy, and several Canadian provinces in my class.

Step 7

- **Listen.** As one of the final activities, I usually show a film related to the topic (I recommend *Le Déclin de l'empire américain* or *Trop belle pour toi* in French and *Muriel's Wedding* or *When Harry Met Sally* in English). The activity includes a pre-viewing discussion (which helps students prepare for a difficult listening activity), a comprehension checklist, and a follow-up discussion.

Step 8

- **Reflect** on the unit and what was learned. Students evaluate their own work and that of their peers in the survey activity. They indicate which activities they enjoyed the most and least, which one they found difficult or easy. They reflect on what they have learned about native speakers of their second language, the grammar and vocabulary learned, and whether cognates are useful for understanding written and spoken French or English. This step reflects some of the objectives of the general language education syllabus (Hébert, 1990) which values self-evaluation and reflection as important strategies for the language and personal development of the learner.

Conclusion

I have always enjoyed doing this unit with my students, and their self-assessments and course evaluations have repeatedly indicated great satisfaction and interest in it. I recommend that you give it a try!

References

*Chartrand, L. (1992, janvier). L'Avortement plus acceptable que la cigarette. *L'Actualité*.

Council of Europe (1981). *Modern languages*. Report presented by CDCC Project Group 4 with a résumé by J.L.M. Trim, Project Adviser. Strasbourg: Council for Cultural Co-operation of the Council of Europe.

Dickinson, L. (1987). *Self-instruction in language learning*. Cambridge: Cambridge University Press.

*Fennel, T. (1995, January 2). Bedtime stories. *Maclean's*, p. 27.

Hébert, Y. (1990). *Syllabus formation langagière générale*. Ottawa: Canadian Association of Second Language Teachers.

Holt, D.D. (1993). *Cooperative learning: A response to linguistic and cultural diversity*. Edited volume. McHenry, IL: Centre for Applied Linguistics and Delta Systems.

Leblanc, R. (1990). *National core French study: A synthesis*. Ottawa: Canadian Association of Second Language Teachers.

*Seymour-Smith, M. (1975). Survey of attitudes. *Sex and society* (pp. 14–15). New York: Diagram Publishing. (Translated for French classes.)

Stern, H.H. (1982). French core programs across Canada: How can we improve them? *The Canadian Modern Language Review/La Revue canadienne des langues vivantes, 39*, 34–47.

Stern, H.H. (1983). Toward a multidimensional foreign language curriculum. In R.G. Mead (Ed.), *Foreign languages: Key links in the chain of learning* (pp. 120–146). Middlebury, VT: Northeast Conference.

Swain, M. (1995). Three functions of output in second language learning. In G. Cook & B. Seidhofer (Eds.), *Principles and practice in the study of language*. Oxford: Oxford University Press.

Swain, M. (in press). Collaborative dialogue. Its contribution to L2 learning. *Revista Canaria de Estudios Ingleses, 33*.

Tremblay, R., Duplantie, M., & Huot, D. (1990). *The Communicative-Experiential Syllabus*. Ottawa: Canadian Association of Second Language Teachers.

Syllabus. Ottawa: Canadian Association of Second Language Teachers.Tréville, M.-C. (1993). *Rôle des congénères interlinguaux dans le développement du vocabulaire réceptif: Application au français langue seconde*. Québec: Centre International de Recherche en Aménagement Linguistique.

Turnbull, M. (1995). Cognates can help: Using similarities in French and English. Workshop presented at SPEAQ'95, Montreal.

*Articles used in step 4 described above.

Adaptation One: An e-mail survey

	Speaking	Writing	Listening	Reading	Language & Learning Awareness
Communicative & Experiential		●		●	
Language		○			○
Culture					○

Notes

Grade levels and programs:	4 to12 immersion, 7 to12 core French
Grouping strategy:	Small groups
Equipment required:	Computer with e-mail access
Preparation required:	Establishing contact with target language classes

If it is difficult to find enough target language speakers so that the students can do a meaningful survey, teacher might set up an electronic keypal exchange with a class in Quebec or France or in a French-language school in a different city. An immersion class, preferably in another city but possibly in the same city or school, might also be interested in participating.

After deciding on an interesting topic, groups of about four students reinforce their writing skills by creating a short questionnaire with about three questions. Each group would therefore have different questions to ask the target language speakers. The development of questionnaires provides an opportunity for the teacher to review question formation as students consider the kinds of questions they want to ask. This activity also includes cultural and language components, including the age-appropriate language to be used. For example, in some FSL classes, the question of the proper use of 'tu' or 'vous' arises.

The teacher then compiles all questions from all groups and creates one class survey containing a variety of topics. This class survey is then sent electronically to a native-speaker keypal class in Quebec or elsewhere. Each student in the keypal class then answers the survey in the target language and returns these surveys to the original class. Each group from this original class would be responsible for writing up and graphing the responses to the questions they generated.

This process would ideally be reversed so that the keypal class in Quebec would also benefit from this cultural and linguistic exchange. Students from the keypal class in Quebec would therefore create their own surveys in their second language (English in this case) and send their survey to the original class who would respond in English.

Adaptation Two: An invited guest

	Speaking	Writing	Listening	Reading	Language & Learning Awareness
Communicative & Experiential	●	●	●	○	
Language					
Culture					

Notes

Grade levels and programs:	7 to 12, post-secondary, adult
Grouping strategy:	A variety of groupings
Equipment required:	Computer with e-mail access, telephone

This adaptation maintains the contact with native speakers from Turnbull's article, however, here students write up the report of a case study focusing on one native speaker's opinions about a chosen topic. The teacher invites a native speaker he/she knows or someone recommended by a local community centre.

Before inviting the guest to their class, students choose a topic to discuss. We suggest a topic with a cultural focus: What do you think about the ways in which young francophones dress and behave in schools these days? Do you think Québec should separate from Canada? Do you think that francophones in Canada are very different from francophones in France or in francophone Africa?

After receiving confirmation of the visit, students then work in pairs or in small groups to create a list of specific questions to ask the visitor. The idea is that each student must ask at least one question during the guest's visit. We also recommend that the teacher engage students in a session to share their questions before the visit; the objective of this sharing is threefold: to ensure that the questions are non-offensive, to avoid repetition and ensure that each student has at least one distinct question, and to verify the accuracy of the students' questions. In addition, it would be interesting to have students predict how they think the visitor will respond to the questions based on background information the teacher presents about the visitor to the students (e.g., gender, age, racial background, geographical origin, employment, family characteristics, etc.).

Following the visit, students prepare a written or oral report to describe the answers given to their questions, including a reflection on the differences and similarities between what the students had predicted the visitor would say and what he/she actually did say. Students should also be encouraged to propose possible reasons why their predictions and the visitor's answers were similar or different, leading to a discussion of the difficulties and dangers of making cultural generalizations.

The Language Management System

J. Clarence LeBlanc

	Speaking	Writing	Listening	Reading	Language & Learning Awareness
Communicative & Experiential	●				●
Language				○	
Culture					

Notes
Grade levels and programs: Beginners
Grouping strategy: Whole class

Editors' Introduction

LeBlanc suggests strategies that can increase teachers' use of the target language in the classroom and encourage beginning students' listening comprehension and speaking skills by giving the students the language tools they need to more fully involve themselves in everyday classroom activities. He introduces a number of these 'Phrases de communication' or survival expressions by explaining to students that these sentences will allow them to respond to any classroom situation in French and that they are a genuine means of communication. When students have learned a number of these sentences, such as 'Qu'est-ce que vous voulez dire? (what do you mean?)' or 'Pardon, je n'écoutais pas, (sorry, I didn't hear you)' they can become active participants in their language learning, hence the principal emphases on the Communicative & Experiential/ Speaking and the Language & Learning Awareness components. In addition, teachers can respond in the target language and thus lessen the tendency to use the first language in the classroom.

The first step to oral communication in the second-language classroom

One of the most common resolutions made by FSL teachers each year is to 'speak the target language almost exclusively in class.' Assuming reasonable teacher fluency, why do so many teachers fail to maintain their resolve? Why do teachers use and tolerate so much English in their classrooms by the end of September, even while using 'communicative' or integrated methods? And why do students resist, complain, and panic when the teacher communicates in French, even though most of them would like to learn to speak French?

Analysis

If we analyze the verbal interaction in the classroom, or anywhere else for that matter, we find that when a second language is spoken, one of a definite series of mental situations is created in the listener. These are analyzed in the following table under Situations. It becomes obvious that if the student had the verbal tools to respond to the exact situation in French, the French atmosphere would be maintained and the next step would be up to the teacher. These verbal tools are in the Appendix under 'Phrases de communication.'

Please note the gradation from full understanding to none at all. One might reverse the order with exactly the same results.

Situation	
Understands question, knows answer.	Gives answer, teacher beams.
Understands but needs one French word to answer.	Comment dit-on _____ en français?
Understands but doesn't know the answer.	Je ne sais pas.
Understands but forgot the answer.	J'ai oublié.
Understands, but forgot the answer.	Qu'est-ce que vous voulez dire?
Understands, knows answer, but feels that the question is indiscreet.	Je regrette, cela me regarde.
Understands but lacks the vocabulary and structures to answer.	Je ne sais pas dire cela en français.
Did not hear the stimulus because teacher spoke too softly.	Parlez plus fort, s'il vous plaît.
Did not hear, but wasn't listening.	Pardon, je n'écoutais pas.
Feels (s)he would understand if you spoke more slowly.	Parlez plus lentement, s'il vous plaît.
Would like you to repeat.	Répétez, s'il vous plaît.
Understands all except one word.	Que veut dire le mot _____ ?
Does not understand, says so.	Je ne comprends pas.
Does not understand but says 'je ne sais pas,' etc.	Must be detected and taught to give the exact 'Phrase de communication' that conveys the degree of understanding or lack thereof.

Systematic use of 'Phrases de communication'

1. On the first day of class, do all the initial school business in English unless students already understand French. Then explain to the students that the purpose of the class is to learn to communicate in French and that, in the same way that one could not learn to play hockey without getting on the ice, one cannot learn to speak French by speaking English. Make this talk as motivating as possible.

2. Still in English, tell them that speaking French is going to be easy because you are going to give them some magic sentences that will allow them to respond to any situation in French. Do the analysis in a manner appropriate to their level and use examples to show that each 'phrase' has a precise use.

3. It is very important to convince the pupils that the phrases are part of a system that involves real communication. For example, if the teacher asks a question and they respond with an accurate use of 'Je ne sais pas' or 'Je ne comprends pas' they have communicated real information to the teacher. They also made the teacher responsible for the next step in the exchange. Dare them to find a circumstance where the system would not work.

4. At this point a spirit of determination is essential. If the teacher tolerates even one student who speaks English to disrupt, or even participate, the system will be threatened as will the purpose of the class. Cajole or discipline, but enforce the use of French. The 'phrases' thus become the means to communicate, and the more loquacious students will quickly learn to use them rather than remain silent. Often, the teacher saying 'Je ne comprends pas' to a student who speaks English is sufficient reminder.

5. Write the 'phrases' on the board or distribute the list. Explain each meaning and drill the pronunciation. Use each sentence in several meaningful contexts. (Obviously, for real novices it is advisable to teach only a few 'phrases' at a time over several days or weeks while presenting basic phonetics, vocabulary and structures – but even then the use of 'Je ne comprends pas,' 'Parlez plus fort,' etc. will enhance the teaching.)

6. The next distinctive step is to demonstrate the specific purpose of each 'phrase' and show that the correct one must be used. For example if you ask 'Où est ton coude?' the student cannot logically answer 'Je ne sais pas.' If he doesn't understand the question he can't know whether he knows the answer, and if he understands, he can't fail to know where his elbow is. Therefore, he must either say 'Je ne comprends pas' or, if he understands 'Où est,' must say 'Que veut dire le mot coude?' This same process is to be followed for each phrase. Even 'J'ai oublié' must be used scrupulously to distinguish between material already known and other.

7. Even after days of practice there can be difficulties of recall under stress. Since the important thing is that the phrases be used, there is no reason not to make them readily accessible. Teachers should insist that the students write the phrases on the first page of their scribblers. It is also helpful to write them, in French only, on posters and have them in a conspicuous place. Some teachers have hung them as mobiles.

8. To emphasize the teacher's determination to communicate in French, it is imperative that normal class business be done in French. This may require the use of 'Comment dit-on' – a whole sentence – but such sentences are likely to

be needed regularly. Similarly, in each classroom situation there will be certain additional sentences that take on the same status as the 'phrases' and may be added to the list. For example:

'Est-ce que je peux   ... sortir de la classe?'
                            ... avoir un livre?'

Or 'Venez ici, s.v.p.,' etc.

They become 'Les phrases de la classe.' Some theorize that the major success of immersion is due to the fact that everyday business of the class is done in French.

9. After a reasonable period there must be a test of the phrases themselves – orally if possible.
10. Some teachers find that an 'English break' of two minutes at the end of the class is a useful practice for questions which are beyond the pupils' vocabulary. Similarly, some teachers permit a student to say 'Est-ce-que je peux parler anglais pour une minute' in certain circumstances.
11. Because this system forces students to speak French, the teacher must realize the limitations of novice language students. They will often use defective grammar and odd circumlocutions to communicate. If they are allowed to express themselves in this way they will be more eager to correct their mistakes gradually. Halting communication in French leads to better fluency while the use of English regularly in the classroom leads to very little (as generations of frustrated students have learned while remaining unilingual).

Bonne chance!

Appendix

Phrases de communication – demander la permission:
> Est-ce que je peux aller aux toilettes, s'il te plaît?
> Est-ce que je peux aller boire?
> Est-ce que je peux tailler mon crayon?
> Est-ce que je peux ouvrir la fenêtre?
>   ... fermer la fenêtre?
> Est-ce que je peu aller à la cafétéria?
>   au bureau?
>   au gymnase?
>   à l'infirmerie?
>   à la bibliothèque?
>   au bureau du conseil étudiant?
>   au bureau de l'orienteur?
>   de l'orientrice?
>   à la salle d'ordinateurs?
>   au laboratoire?

Est-ce que je peux emprunter   une agrafeuse, s'il te plaît?

du ruban adhésif (scotch)?

du ruban-cache?

un stylo, un crayon?

du liquide correcteur?

une gomme à effacer?

une règle?

un dictionnaire?

Est-ce que je peux avoir   une punaise, s'il te plaît?

un trombone?

une feuille mobile?

un Kleenex?

Général: Je ne sais pas.

Je ne comprends pas.

Comment dit-on ___ en français?

Que veut dire ___ ?

Excusez-moi.

Pardon.

Quelle page, madame (monsieur)?

Est-ce que tu peux répéter, s'il te plaît?

And many other similar phrases and language functions that will accumulate under the heading 'phrases de la classe.'

Adaptation One: Social chit chat

	Speaking	Writing	Listening	Reading	Language & Learning Awareness
Communicative & Experiential	●		○		●
Language	○				
Culture					○

Notes

Grade levels and programs: All
Grouping strategy: Whole class

Native speakers in social situations make heavy use of 'Phrases de communication' or formulaic phrases. Greetings and preliminary small talk can therefore be taught using an approach similar to that suggested by Leblanc for classroom management.

The teacher should begin by analyzing the likely social needs of the class members. Adult ESL learners living in a target language environment will appreciate phrases that allow them to greet neighbours, and exchange pleasantries with shop assistants and other native speakers they encounter on a daily basis. Phrases such as 'It's turned cold, hasn't it?' or exchanges such as 'How's it going?' 'Not too bad, thanks' might be suitable for such adult learners. Younger students will obviously require age appropriate expressions that will allow them to interact with their peers in an appropriate way. The actual vocabulary of currently popular teenage slang will change from year to year, but the basic patterns of a greeting, a response and an initiating query about the quality of life are always going to be needed.

Students who do not live in a target language setting need regular classroom opportunities to practise these small social interactions. Classes might routinely begin with a few moments set aside for social interaction in which students greet each other and the teacher with appropriate use of formulaic phrases. As student proficiency grows, the teacher can introduce additional formulaic phrases, extending the interactions or showing students how language should be adapted to suit different audiences. For more extended practice, the class might create short skits of meetings and greetings with a variety of partners of varied age and status to help students focus on culturally appropriate uses of formulaic phrases.

Adaptation Two: What's in the box?

	Speaking	Writing	Listening	Reading	Language & Learning Awareness
Communicative & Experiential	●		●		
Language	○				
Culture					

Notes

Grade levels and programs:	1 to 8, core French, immersion, ESL
Grouping strategy:	Whole class
Preparation required:	Selection of small items, preparation of a box with a hole

Students can be encouraged to attempt a range of situations in the target language if the task is simplified via the use of formulaic phrases. In the younger grades, one such task might be the language game, 'What's in the box.' In this game, the teacher places a small item into a box which has a hole cut in one side. A student volunteer puts his or her hand through the hole, identifies the item by touch, and then challenges the other students to guess what the item is. The rules of this game can be manipulated in many ways to adjust the level of difficulty, as outlined below.

In the simplest form of this game, formulaic phrases are used to help the class members generate questions to which the volunteer has only to answer 'yes' or 'no.' Before the game begins, the teacher would introduce the class to phrases such as 'Is it red?' 'Can you eat it?' These phrases would be available on the blackboard or a question sheet for student reference. The game can be made easier in the early stages by showing the range of items to the class in advance or by selecting items from a single category such as fruits.

The game can be made more challenging if the class is divided into teams. In turn, a member of each team tries to describe the item, without using its name, for the rest of the team to guess. Here the formulaic phrases introduced might include items such as 'It feels like … ' 'You use it to … ' 'You usually find it in the … ' and so on.

Stratégies d'écoute des nouvelles radiodiffusées sur Radio-Canada

Christine Besnard

	Speaking	Writing	Listening	Reading	Language & Learning Awareness
Communicative & Experiential			●	○	
Language			●		●
Culture					

Notes

Grade levels and programs:	9 to 12, post secondary, adult, FSL, foreign language, ESL
Grouping strategy:	Individual, pairs
Equipment required:	Radio, audiotape, videotape
Preparation required:	Taping of newscasts in target language

Editors' Introduction

By asking French as a second language students to listen to brief newscasts on Radio-Canada or TFO, the teacher engages the class in a listening activity that has strong communicative elements and encourages students to recognize and learn vocabulary and expressions typically used in these communications. As a pre-listening activity to familiarize the students with the specialized vocabulary of newscasts, Besnard suggests that students read target language magazines that deal with subject matter similar to that heard on news programs. She also suggests that an advantage of taped newscasts is that they can be heard a number of times and students can make lists of unfamiliar vocabulary. In order to practise this new vocabulary and to reinforce the students' speaking skills, she further recommends class discussions about the events reported in the news bulletins.

« ...celui qui peut comprendre dans une langue étrangère les informations de la radio { ... } peut tout comprendre dans cette langue » *Louis-Jean Calvet*

Pourquoi les nouvelles ?

- Elles font partie de ce que tout(e) étudiant(e) devrait écouter tous les jours pour se tenir au courant de ce qui se passe au Canada et dans le monde.
- Elles présentent un vocabulaire extrêmement riche et varié car elles traitent d'un grand éventail de sujets tels que la politique, la santé, les sports, l'environnement, les conflits sociaux, l'éducation....
- Elles facilitent l'acquisition d'un lexique de base que tout(e) citoyen(ne) doit posséder pour pouvoir faire intégralement partie de la Cité et mieux s'y intégrer.
- Ce genre d'exploitation est facilité par le fait que les étudiant(e)s connaissent les nouvelles en anglais et peuvent s'y référer, en cas de difficulté. De plus, ce type de document sonore fait partie du vécu des apprenant(e)s, de ce qu'ils/elles connaissent (ou qu'ils/elles devraient connaître) sur le Canada et le reste du monde.

Objectifs visés

- Ce type de travail cherche à déboucher sur un enrichissement lexical ainsi que sur une réflexion morpho-syntaxique à partir d'échantillons de français oralisé.
- Cette activité de compréhension auditive vise à encourager les étudiant(e)s à écouter régulièrement les nouvelles en français afin qu'ils/elles acquièrent une certaine automomie linguistique. Elle cherche aussi à les aider à acquérir une autonomie d'apprentissage qui leur permettra de poursuivre leur formation seuls, une fois qu'ils/elles auront quitté l'université.
- La fréquence et la brièveté de ce type d'émission radiophonique permet à l'étudiant(e) de faire un travail sérieux de ré-écoute et de concentration mentale.
- Même si les nouvelles lues à la radio présentent un français oralisé qui n'est donc pas véritablement authentique, on y entend un français du Canada relativement homogène que les étudiant(e)s doivent s'entraîner à comprendre.
- En conclusion, ce genre d'exercice cherche à atteindre deux objectifs. Le premier est d'ordre linguistique puisqu'en entraînant les apprenant(es) à écouter et à comprendre les nouvelles nationales et internationales radiodiffusées, l'on vise l'enrichissement du lexique qu"ils/elles possèdent dans les domaines de l'actualité et de la vie au quotidien. Le deuxième est d'ordre pédagogique puisque l'on cherche à encourager les étudiant(e)s à prendre leur propre apprentissage en main et à acquérir, individuellement ou en groupe, une méthode de travail efficace qu'ils/elles pourront utiliser en autonomie.

Travail préalable de documentation

- Il est recommandé que les apprenant(e)s lisent, aussi souvent que possible, les journaux et les magazines de langue française tels que *Le Monde*, *Le Devoir*, *La*

Presse, L'Actualité... qui traitent des mêmes nouvelles que celles présentées à la radio.

- À partir de la lecture de ces publications, ils/elles seront en mesure de dresser la liste des mots et expressions-clés qui jalonnent ce type d'écrits et dont les journalistes se servent pour traiter de thèmes tels que la politique, le social, l'économie, l'éducation, les spectacles... Ce vocabulaire spécialisé, une fois repéré dans la presse écrite puis compris et maîtrisé, facilitera, ultérieurement, la compréhension orale des nouvelles radiodiffusées.

- Grâce à cette « recherche documentaire » préalable, les étudiant(e)s se rendront compte de la prévisibilité de ce type de lexique, de son grand rendement linguistique et donc, de l'importance de le posséder.

Stratégies d'écoute

Nous encourageons les auditeur(e)s à:

- Enregistrer le bulletin de nouvelles afin de pouvoir le ré-écouter à loisir et à leur propre rythme.

- Éviter de se précipiter sur leur dictionnaire car celui-ci ne peut, à lui seul, résoudre les problèmes de compréhension. Au contraire, nous leur suggérons d'utiliser les informations périphériques (contexte, connaissance de l'actualité en anglais...) à leur disposition pour mieux comprendre ce qu'ils/elles entendent.

- Prendre conscience de l'existence de deux types de lexique, dans ce qu'ils/elles entendent: le lexique spécialisé de la politique, de l'environnement, des conflits sociaux... et celui relevant du registre radiophonique (« Ici, Radio Canada », « notre envoyé spécial à... », « Je passe la parole à Monsieur Untel » ...). Une fois cette distinction faite, il est important de s'assurer de leur apprentissage systématique grâce à une prise de notes consciencieuse et à leur mémorisation.

- Écouter à plusieurs reprises la même nouvelle pour : prendre note des mots-clés spécialisés qui jalonnent le document sonore afin de compléter les listes de vocabulaire spécialisé que les étudiant(e)s auront commencé à établir à partir des lectures préliminaires de journaux et de magazines traitant de l'actualité nationale et internationale qu'ils/elles auront faites; émettre des hypothèses quant au contenu de la nouvelle écoutée puis confirmer ou infirmer ces hypothèses grâce à des écoutes supplémentaires.

Pour réussir à atteindre l'objectif principal de ce type d'exercice qui vise principalement l'acquisition et la maîtrise d'un lexique spécialisé dans les différents aspects de l'actualité nationale et internationale, une fois parvenus à ce stade de l'activité d'écoute, les étudiant(e)s devraient travailler en groupes de deux pour:

- Pouvoir discuter (en français) de la justesse des hypothèses qu'ils/elles auront émises sur le contenu sémantique de la nouvelle écoutée puis arriver à un consensus;

- En faire, ensemble, un compte rendu oral, en essayant d'être aussi précis que possible et en s'efforçant d'utiliser le nouveau lexique récemment appris;

- S'aider mutuellement, s'il reste encore quelques passages de l'écoute qu'ils/ elles ont du mal à comprendre, afin de s'assurer qu'ils/elles en ont retenu l'essentiel et que ce qu'ils/elles en ont compris forme un tout logique et cohérent;

- Comparer leurs listes respectives de vocabulaire spécialisé pour, si besoin est, les compléter, et ainsi mieux maîtriser ce type de lexique qui leur permettra d'accéder à une meilleure connaissance du monde et de mieux se débrouiller dans la vie de tous les jours.

Activité de post-écoute

Pour s'assurer de l'acquisition à long terme de ce lexique spécialisé, les apprenants devront écouter aussi souvent que possible les nouvelles et ré-utiliser activement ce vocabulaire en s'engageant dans des discussions sur l'actualité et en jouant, dans le cadre de la classe, le rôle de commentateurs à Radio-Canada ou celui de journalistes de la presse écrite.

Adaptation One: Current events in the classroom

	Speaking	Writing	Listening	Reading	Language & Learning Awareness
Communicative & Experiential	●	●	●	○	
Language			●		○
Culture					●

Notes

Grade levels and programs:	4 to 11 immersion and core French, ESL and other languages, adult
Grouping strategy:	Individual, pairs
Equipment required:	Access to school PA system, audiotape, videotape
Preparation required:	Reservation of necessary equipment

To reinforce speaking and listening skills, beginning and intermediate level students work in small groups to write and then audiotape or videotape a newscast of school events. Alternatively, younger students could write and then read the daily announcements in the target language over the school announcement system. If students prefer, they could prepare sportscasts, weather bulletins, or daily news items. The following CBC websites provide a range of activities to accompany a news report: www.radiocanada.ca (French-language network), www.cbc.ca/forums (English-language network, for grade 8 and older students), www.cbc4kids.ca/teachers (English-language network, for younger students).

More advanced students might prefer to produce a documentary in the target language or, for example, videotape a student panel discussion about a current news event. If possible, these presentations could be shown at a parents' night or open house.

Adaptation Two: Media literacy

	Speaking	Writing	Listening	Reading	Language & Learning Awareness
Communicative & Experiential	●		●	○	
Language					●
Culture					

Notes
Grade levels and programs: 7 to 12 immersion, 11 to12 core French, ESL, adult
Grouping strategy: Individual, pairs
Equipment required: Videotape, audiotape
Preparation required: Taping of radio/TV items, newspapers

For more advanced students, a media literacy activity encourages students to compare different styles of reporting on radio, television, or in newspapers. Teacher and students tape as many different examples of news items in the target language as possible and provide examples of news reports from newspapers. After examining various styles of reporting in each of the three media, students discuss in groups the degree of formality and level of language and style and any evidence of biases in the examples. Alternatively, students could provide written reports on their observations or indeed write and produce their own newscast.

Cross media comparisons about style of reporting, political biases, and impact on the viewer/reader/listener can also be tried. For example, what impact does the addition of images in television or newspaper accounts have on a viewer's interpretations of events?

The Dresser, the Lamp, and the Oven: An Activity for Learning and Practising House-Related Vocabulary

Diane Chaffee-Sorace and Baiba Abrams

	Speaking	Writing	Listening	Reading	Language & Learning Awareness
Communicative & Experiential					
Language	●	●	○	○	○
Culture					

Notes

Grade levels and programs: All
Grouping strategy: Pairs, small groups
Preparation required: Vocabulary sheets for Password game.

Editors' Introduction

This four-part activity helps students acquire home-related vocabulary and reinforces their Language/Listening, Speaking, Writing, Reading, and Language & Learning Awareness skills as indicated in the chart. In the first part of the activity, the students play the game of *Password* which requires players to use synonyms or antonyms in order to win. Thus the principal focus here is on speaking skills and the subsidiary focus is on listening skills. The second part of the activity takes the form of a vocabulary review as students draw the interior plan of a house and place furniture in the rooms. This vocabulary review is indicated by the subsidiary emphasis in the Language/Language & Learning Awareness cell. The third section, most likely to be relevant to post-secondary or adult classes, asks students to exercise their writing skills as they write an advertisement to rent or sell a home. Finally, students read their advertisements to the class and, in turn, the listeners question the readers about the amenities of the home/apartment in the advertisement. For this activity, the principal focus is on Language/Writing with subsidiary foci on reading and speaking.

Description of the activity

For many students enrolled in intermediate-level Spanish courses at Loyola College, there was no interesting way to learn and practise house-related vocabulary. When told to memorize nearly 45 Spanish words, students accomplished the task with varying degrees of effectiveness, forgetting or misspelling 10 percent or more of the words on their exams. To help our students with their vocabulary acquisition, we decided to develop an activity that would be both educational and enjoyable for our classes. The result of our collaboration is a four-step exercise requiring between 25 and 30 minutes for completion. Before participating in the activity, students need to review or to study for the first time the house-related terminology in their textbook. After they have done so, they begin the exercise with step 1, a game of *Password*. Next, in step 2, the students complete a floor plan of a furnished house, and then, in step 3, they write an advertisement to rent or sell the building. Finally, in step 4, the instructor asks some students to read their announcement to the class. Pretending that they are trying to find a lessee or buyer for the house, these students answer any questions that their peers may have about the dwelling.

Preparation of materials

Write 28 Spanish words or phrases relating to the house, such as 'el tocador' (the dresser), 'la lámpara' (the lamp), and 'el horno' (the oven), on two sheets of white paper – 14 per sheet in two columns of seven with ample space between entries. If the students are learning the vocabulary for the first time, write the English translation in parentheses under the Spanish. However, if they are only going to practise the vocabulary, do not write the English. Name one of the sheets 'List A' and the other 'List B,' as shown below:

LIST A			LIST B	
un horno (oven)	un abrelatas (can opener)		una cómoda (chest of drawers)	un televisor (television)
una alfombra (rug)	un estante (bookcase)		(unas) cortinas (curtains)	una ducha shower
un escritorio (desk)	(unos) cuadros (pictures)		un armario (closet)	un retrete (toilet)
una tostadora (toaster)	(unas) lámparas (lamps)		un horno de microondas (microwave oven)	(unos) gabinetes (cabinets)
(unas) camas (beds)	una bañera (bathtub)		un fregadero (kitchen sink)	una refrigeradora (refrigerator)

una computadora (computer)	un tocador (dresser)		una mesa con sillas (table with chairs)	un lavaplatos (dishwasher)
una chimenea (fireplace)	(unos) sillones (armchairs)		un sofá (couch)	un lavabo (bathroom sink)

On a separate piece of paper, draw a diagram of the interior of a house, and label the rooms and areas of the building as illustrated in Appendix A. Make enough copies of each list and of the diagram for half of the students in the class.

The activity

Step 1. Divide the class into pairs ('Student 1' and 'Student 2'), and give a copy of List A to Student 1, a copy of List B to Student 2, and a copy of the diagram of the interior of the house to each pair. To begin the activity with step 1, the game of *Password*, Student 1 looks at the first word on List A (the password) and gives Student 2 a clue for guessing it. For example, if it is 'horno' (oven), Student 1 should say a word or phrase in Spanish such as 'cocina' (kitchen), 'cocinar' (to cook), 'electrodoméstico' (electric appliance), 'quemadores' (burners), or 'microondas' (microwaves) that will suggest the term to Student 2. Student 1 may also use synonyms and antonyms, but not definitions or explanations, to elicit the password from Student 2. Typically, if Student 1 gives the clue 'cocinar' (to cook) to Student 2, Student 2 may respond with 'cocina' (kitchen). Student 1 must then think of another hint, such as 'electrodoméstico' (electric appliance) for Student 2. Probably suspecting by now that the password refers to a kitchen appliance, Student 2 will most likely respond by naming one, perhaps 'estufa' (stove). Student 1 may then ask Student 2 for a synonym, and hopefully, Student 2 will say 'horno' (oven). After the password has been guessed, Student 2 helps Student 1 ascertain the first word on List B by giving clues. Each pair of students continues to play the game until all the vocabulary on the two lists has been identified.

Step 2. After the students in a group have guessed the passwords on both lists, they are ready to begin step 2. Tell them to take the diagram of the interior of the house and to draw the furnishings represented by the passwords on List A and List B – 'la lámpara' (the lamp), 'el tocador' (the dresser), 'el lavaplatos' (the dishwasher), etc. – in the appropriate rooms or parts of the building. Since students were asked to review or to study their vocabulary before beginning this activity and since the names of the rooms and other parts of the house — 'la alcoba' (the bedroom), 'el pasillo' (the hall), 'la sala' (the living room), 'la escalera' (the staircase), 'el vestíbulo' (the vestibule), 'el cuarto de baño' (the bathroom), 'el comedor' (the dining room), 'el patio' (the patio), etc. – usually appear in textbooks along with those of home furnishings, the members of the class should be able to determine where to sketch the objects on the diagram. However, if the necessary terms do not figure in the book, prepare a list of them for the students to consult during step 2.

186

Step 3. For the third step of the activity, instruct the students to create for a newspaper an advertisement to rent or sell the dwelling that they have drawn. Tell them to describe the house in general (its rooms, its modern conveniences, its backyard, etc.), in addition to the appealing characteristics of the neighbourhood in which it is located (the availability of shopping plazas, the many playgrounds, etc.). Here is a sample advertisement:

¡PARA ALQUILAR!

UNA CASA MODERNA Y ELEGANTE CON VISTA AL PARQUE

EN LAS AFUERAS DE BALTIMORE

Descripción:

¡Esta casa amueblada es una ganga! Situada en Ruxton a sólo dos millas de todo tipo de tienda, tiene tres alcobas soleadas; una sala espaciosa con sofá, sillón, mesa, estante, lámparas, computadora y televisor; una cocina renovada con mesa, sillas y varios electrodomésticos; una piscina limpia; un césped meticulosamente cuidado y un patio con árboles y flores. La casa está cerca de un parque que es perfecto para los niños; el parque tiene columpios, un tobogán, un cajón de arena y un lago con cisnes.

Comodidades:

AIRE ACONDICIONADO

CHIMENEA

UN LAVAPLATOS SILENCIOSO, UNA REFRIGERADORA GRANDE Y UN HORNO DE MICROONDAS NUEVO

UN BAÑO MODERNO CON DOS LAVABOS

Alquiler:

¡Es muy barato! ¡Cuesta sólo 75.000 pts. el mes! Si quiere hacer una cita para ver la casa, llame a la Sra. Susana Rodríguez (582-72-94) por la mañana.

FOR RENT!

AN ELEGANT MODERN HOUSE WITH A PARK VIEW IN THE

SUBURBS OF BALTIMORE

Description:

This furnished house is a bargain! Located in Ruxton only two miles from every kind of store, it has three sunny bedrooms; a spacious living room with a sofa, an armchair, a table, a bookcase, lamps, a computer, and a television; a renovated kitchen with a table, chairs, and several electric appliances; a clean swimming pool; a meticulously manicured lawn; and a patio with trees and flowers. The house is close to a park that is perfect for children; the park has swings, a slide, a sandbox, and a lake with swans.

Elements of Comfort:

AIR CONDITIONING

FIREPLACE

A QUIET DISHWASHER, A BIG REFRIGERATOR, AND A NEW MICROWAVE OVEN

A MODERN BATHROOM WITH TWO SINKS

Rental Rate:

It is very inexpensive! It costs only 75,000 pesetas a month! If you wish to make an appointment to see the house, call Mrs. Susana Rodríguez (582-7194) in the morning.

Step 4. After the students have written their announcements, choose two or three groups to take turns reading their work to the class. Request that the class, while listening to an advertisement, pretend to be interested in renting or buying the house described. Instruct the students who have heard the advertisement to ask questions about the house. The readers should answer the class's inquiries.

Conclusion

Our four-step activity affords students the opportunity to learn and practise vocabulary by reading, pronouncing, writing, and hearing it, thus simultaneously reinforcing the four basic skills of language acquisition. Our activity functions very well in intermediate-level Spanish courses. After employing it for three years, we have found that students score higher on the house-related vocabulary sections of their exams, remember more of their newly acquired words, make fewer spelling errors when writing these words, and recognize them in written and spoken form more often. Most importantly, the students not only enjoy participating in our activity, but they also believe that it is a beneficial way to learn and practise vocabulary.

Appendix A

La Planta Baja

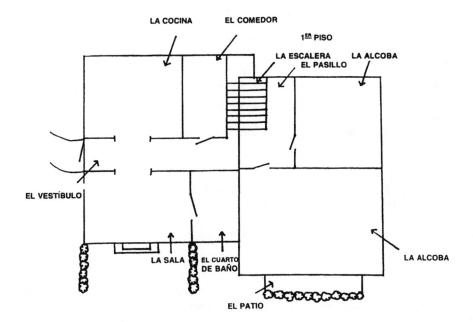

Adaptation One: Target language catalogues

	Speaking	Writing	Listening	Reading	Language & Learning Awareness
Communicative & Experiential	●	●			
Language					○
Culture					

Notes

Grade levels and programs:	4 to 8 immersion, 5 to 8 core French, ESL
Grouping strategy:	Individual
Equipment:	Art supplies
Preparation required:	Target language catalogues

To begin this activity, the teacher tells students about their class project that involves a competition to see which student can design the most radical make-over of either their bedroom or family recreation room. First, students work individually to prepare a drawing and a short text to describe the current state of their bedrooms or recreation rooms. The teacher assigns a budget (to provide practice with numbers) and tells the students to let their imaginations run wild. Students create a poster showing a detailed plan of the remodelled room. Students are encouraged to cut out pictures from target language catalogues (e.g., Sears, Ikea) to decorate their posters. The features of the room and its furnishings would be labelled in the target language and described in a 'before-and-after' article students write in the target language to be 'published' in a fictional design magazine. This article would also include a rationale for the students' remodelling decisions and a report on the money spent on remodelling the rooms. Students would also prepare an oral presentation featuring their before-and-after story and their artistic work. Everyone would then vote on the most creative make over to culminate the competition.

The discussion among students as they prepare, label, and then write descriptions of their rooms provide the principal foci as shown in the chart above, Communicative & Experiential/Writing and Speaking. The vocabulary learning is indicated by the subsidiary focus in the Language/Language & Learning Awareness cell.

Adaptation Two: Second-hand furniture

	Speaking	Writing	Listening	Reading	Language & Learning Awareness
Communicative & Experiential	●			●	
Language					
Culture					○

Notes

Grade levels and programs:	Post-secondary, adult
Grouping strategy:	Small groups
Equipment required:	Newspapers, photos (optional)
Preparation required:	Selection of classified ads in the target language and special photos (optional).

This activity would be most relevant for older students who engage in a group activity to furnish an apartment or house as economically as possible with second-hand furniture advertised in the classified section of a target language newspaper (on-line or in paper format).

Before beginning the activity, students and the teacher might talk about their experiences in second-hand stores and with garage sales. This pre-activity phase could also include discussing the differences between new and used furniture and students' opinions on buying used items. Students work in groups of four to decide on their purchases and are given a time limit. The teacher then assigns a budget for students to work within. Teachers could also add an exciting component to this activity by simulating a silent auction in the class using photos of 'special' used items (e.g., beautiful antique items, funky retro accessories etc) the students might like to feature in their homes. In this case, students would shop from the auction as well as classified ads.

They report orally, in the target language, about their priorities, what they were or were not able to acquire, and at what prices. Following these presentations, the nature of articles for sale in the classified ads and the importance the students attach to various furnishings could lead to interesting discussions about cultural practices.

Author Biographies

Jill Bell is a Professor in the Faculty of Education of York University, where she teaches courses on language and literacy. She has worked in the field of education for many years as an ESL classroom teacher, teacher educator and researcher and has published a wide range of materials for ESL teachers and learners. Her research focusses on second language literacy in non-academic settings.

Sharon Lapkin is a Professor in the Modern Language Centre and Second Language Education program of the Ontario Institute for Studies in Education of the University of Toronto. Her research projects center on French second language education in Canada and range from program evaluations of core French and immersion to qualitative studies of language learning in progress through detailed analysis of transcribed learner dialogues. Since 1995 she has been co-Editor of the *Canadian Modern Language Review.*

Miles Turnbull is an Associate Professor in the Faculty of Education at the University of Prince Edward Island. He works in the pre-service program in French second language teaching and also in the graduate program in leadership and learning. Before joining the faculty at UPEI, Miles was an Assistant Professor in the Modern Language Centre at OISE-UT and he worked in core and immersion French programs in three Canadian provinces. His research interests include French as a second language (core and immersion), teacher development, teacher belief systems, project-based and experiential learning, educational technology.

Baiba Abrams (MA, San Francisco State University) is an Administrator and an Instructor of Spanish in the Department of Modern Languages and Literatures at Loyola College in Maryland. She has taught Spanish literature, culture, and language courses at four colleges and universities throughout the United States. Her main teaching and research interest is pedagogy.

Christine Besnard est docteure ès lettres (CRAPEL, Nancy, France) en linguistique appliquée à la didactique du français L2. Elle a publié plusieurs articles et livres en didactique du FLS et est co-auteure de : Pratique des affaires et correspondance commerciale en français, L'université de demain : courants actuels et apports de la didactique des langues à l'enseignement du FLS, Apprivoiser l'écrit-techniques de l'écrit et stratégies d'auto-perfectionnement. Ses recherches actuelles portent sur l'apport de la psychologie cognitive au domaine de l'apprentissage des L2.

Catherine A. Black, (BA, (English), Grenoble; MA (French) Waterloo; PhD (Linguistics), Laval), is an applied linguist. Her research interests include drama techniques in the teaching of FSL, non-verbal and cultural behaviours, and computer assisted language learning.

Robert Campbell est enseignant en immersion au niveau secondaire à Winnipeg.

Annick Carstens est enseignante en immersion au niveau secondaire à Winnipeg.

Diane Chaffee-Sorace (PhD, Duke University) is the Chair of the Department of Modern Languages and Literatures and a Professor of Spanish at Loyola College in Maryland. She has taught language, literature, and culture courses at five colleges and universities. Her publications have reported on Spanish Golden Age poetry and pedagogy.

Helen Christiansen est professeure agrégée au Baccalauréat en éducation française à l'Université de Regina. Elle se spécialise dans l'acquisition de la langue seconde et la formation des enseignants de français de base et d'anglais langue seconde.

Beatrice Dupuy is an Associate Professor in the Department of French & Italian at the University of Arizona where she teaches courses in the areas of language acquisition and pedagogy. Her research interests include listening and reading as it pertains to second language development.

Elizabeth M. Knutson (PhD, University of Pennsylvania) is an Associate Professor in the Language Studies Department of the US Naval Academy in Annapolis, MD, where she teaches French and Spanish. She was formerly a language training supervisor and head of French and Italian training at the Foreign Service Institute, US Department of State (1984–1990), and is co-author of an elementary and intermediate level textbook, *Contextes: French for communication*. Her research interests include both literature and foreign language pedagogy.

Bernard Laplante est professeur agrégé à l'université de Regina. Il enseigne en didactique des sciences et des mathématiques. Il poursuit des recherches sur l'intégration de la langue dans l'enseignement des sciences en immersion, les portfolios langagiers et l'identité des enseignants.

Geoff Lawrence is an experienced second language teacher with an M.A. in second language education from the Ontario Institute for Studies in Education of the University of Toronto (OISE/UT), specializing in technology-enhanced instruction. Geoff currently teaches in the Professional Writing and Communications Department of the University of Toronto and designs technology-enhanced educational programs.

J. Clarence LeBlanc is a teacher at Tantramar Regional High School, New Brunswick, author of numerous papers on the field of second language education, and recipient of a National Special Recognition Award from the Canadian Teachers Federation.

Icy Lee is an Assistant Professor in the Department of Education Studies at Hong Kong Baptist University. Her research interests are in the areas of ESL writing, learner autonomy, and teacher development. She has published in a number of international journals such as *ELT Journal, System, Canadian Modern Language Review,* and *TESL Canada Journal.*

François Lentz est conseiller pédagogique en français (immersion) au Bureau de l'éducation française, Éducation et Formation professionnelle Manitoba, et chargé de cours en didactique du français au Faculté d'Éducation du Collège universitaire de Saint-Boniface à Winnipeg.

Yasuko Makita-Discekici received her PhD in Curriculum and Instruction (specializing in reading and language studies) at Southern Illinois University. She is an Associate Professor of Japanese at the University of Guam, USA. Her professional interests include foreign language education, curriculum design, Japanese language for special purposes, and second language acquisition.

Maria Mantello After several years teaching Extended French and French Immersion, Maria Mantello has turned her attention to ESL and library partnerships with teachers. Her experience as teacher-researcher has generated a full- length study, as well as conference papers and articles.

Jeff McQuillan (PhD, University of Southern California) is a writer and lecturer living in Los Angeles, California. He is author of *The Literacy Crisis: False Claims, Real Solutions* (Heinemann, 1998) and co-editor of *Heritage Language Development* (Language Education Associates, 1998). He was formerly an Associate Professor of Education at California State University, Fullerton.

Christine Pelletier enseigne à Prince George en Colombie-Britannique depuis 1991. Elle s'intéresse particulièrement à améliorer les compétences langagières des élèves d'immersion et du programme francophone.

Henri Péloquin est enseignant en immersion au niveau secondaire à Winnipeg.

Hélène Roy est enseignante en immersion au niveau secondaire à Winnipeg.

David J. Shook is Assistant Professor of Spanish and Coordinator of first year Spanish classes at the Georgia Institute of Technology; current interests include foreign language reading, input processing, methodology, and teacher education.